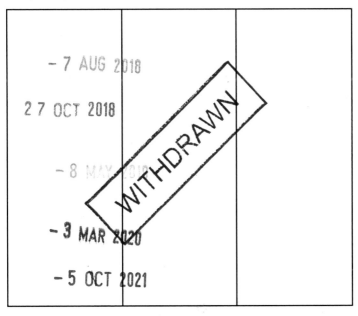

The
Life
of
Stuff

www.**penguin**.co.uk

The
Life
of
Stuff

A memoir
about the mess
we leave behind

Susannah
Walker

Doubleday

LONDON · TORONTO · SYDNEY · AUCKLAND · JOHANNESBURG

TRANSWORLD PUBLISHERS
61–63 Uxbridge Road, London W5 5SA
www.penguin.co.uk

Transworld is part of the Penguin Random House group of companies
whose addresses can be found at global.penguinrandomhouse.com

Penguin
Random House
UK

First published in Great Britain in 2018 by Doubleday
an imprint of Transworld Publishers

All photographs courtesy the author except for Eaglesham House
(page 283), which is reproduced courtesy of Historic Scotland.
Line illustrations © Viv Mullett, the Flying Fish Studios

A CIP catalogue record for this book
is available from the British Library.

ISBN 9780857525406

Typeset in Sabon 11/15¼ pt by Falcon Oast Graphic Art Ltd.
Printed and bound by Clays Ltd, Bungay, Suffolk.

Penguin Random House is committed to a sustainable
future for our business, our readers and our planet. This book
is made from Forest Stewardship Council® certified paper.

MIX
Paper from
responsible sources
FSC® C018179

1 3 5 7 9 10 8 6 4 2

For Tim

contents

contents

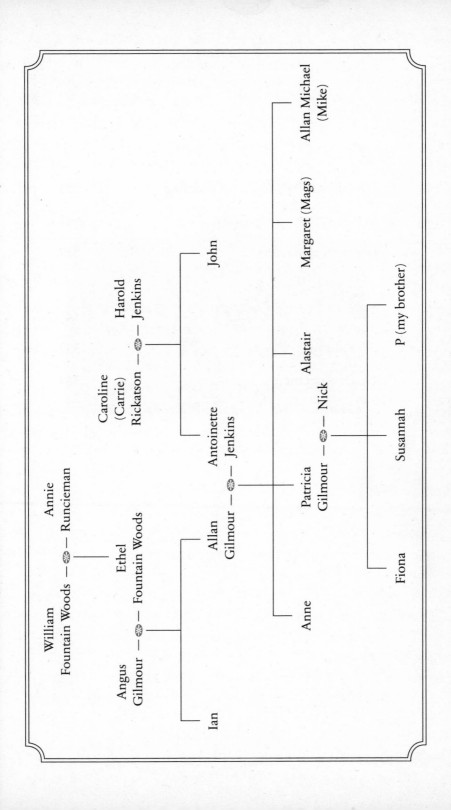

*B*Y THE TIME *my mother died, her unhappiness had taken on solid form in the state of her home. The once-pristine Georgian cottage, as neat and regular as a doll's house, was now swamped in papers and rubbish. Pipes had burst and the roof had leaked, but the holes where the water had poured through were never fixed. Rot and mould were spreading across carpets and walls; spiders' webs draped down from the ceiling; the furniture had been ruined by damp and mice. Regardless of what she had – or had not – done for us when she was alive, it still fell to me and my brother to sort the mess out.*

I took this on as the necessary duty of a daughter, but at the same time raged at her selfishness. Above all, I felt devastated that the intelligent and acute woman that I'd known, and sometimes loved, could have tolerated living in such wretched misery. As I cleared her house, the questions kept rising. How had this happened? Why couldn't I have helped her? One thought haunted me above all others. Who had my mother really been? I had no idea, in part because of her depression but also because she was my mother and so I was always standing too close to see. I was never going to turn her into an ideal mother, that I knew for sure. But nor did I want to tear her apart for failing me. I wanted to find out what kind of person she had been, and what parts of herself she had passed on in turn, but I was afraid that I had left this far too late.

Slowly, as I sifted through the heaps of rubbish and treasures, I began to realize that she might have left me the answer after all. I could find my mother at last in the things she had left behind.

prologue: red glass bird

ORNAMENTAL BIRD, FORMED FROM
OPAQUE RED GLASS WITH AN OUTER
CLEAR LAYER SURROUNDING

Murano, early 1960s (?)

Hand-blown glass

Provenance unknown

THE RED GLASS bird sits on the bookshelves behind me, where it lives as a reminder of my mother. For many years it sat on the side table in her sitting room, and now she is dead it has passed to me. It's not a sentimental heirloom, as I don't know how she came to own it in the first place. A decorative paperweight, the kind that was produced in tens of thousands during the fifties and sixties when she was setting up home with my father, it might have been a Christmas present or a souvenir from someone's Italian trip. It might even have been a gift from my father himself.

Pieces like this turn up at car-boot sales and in kitschy antique shops all the time; it's nothing special. The ruby-red core is enclosed in a thick layer of clear glass, which has been stretched out in points to form the bird's wingtips and tail, each as sharp as the day it was made. It's heavy too, and when I hold it in my hand I can't help thinking that it would make an excellent weapon if I ever find myself cornered. The elongated wings remind me of a swallow, except being a paperweight isn't much of a job for such a flighty species. Perhaps it's just a bird in general: an ornament, nothing more.

I have no other associations or memories that go with the bird. All I can tell you is that it used to belong to my mother, and now it's mine. But that's why I like it so much. Most of the things my mother left behind were far more complicated.

*

For most of my life I've been worried about what I might inherit from my mother. A complex and unhappy woman, she'd had a childhood of losses and sadness. She married hoping for a new start but her first child, a daughter, died at a day old. After my birth, two years later, she had deep postnatal depression, then again when my brother was born, followed by several years during which I refused to sleep and my brother was repeatedly and seriously ill. My parents split up and my mother had a breakdown, although I don't know what order this happened in, which cause and which effect. The unhappiness was the same regardless. I was eight years old and never lived with my mother again.

Instead, I was looked after by my father and his second, Belgian, wife, a reconstituted household which included not

My mother and me in 1969.

only my brother but also a new stepbrother. My father had decided that this was all for the best, and under this new regime any mention of unhappiness or the past was taboo. I was left to draw my own conclusions about what I had seen.

This wasn't too difficult to do, because my mother and I were mostly apart. For a few years after the divorce, my brother and I did see her every second weekend and in the holidays, but this was disrupted when she moved across the country to East Anglia for a while, and then even more when I was eleven and my father got a job in Denmark. Then we flew over to see her at Easter, in the summer holidays and at one half-term. By the time we returned three years later, the pattern had been set. I was a teenager, more interested in friends and parties than either of my parents, so I got the train to see her once or twice a term.

Instead, much of our relationship took place by letter. I still have a big bundle, but they don't tell me very much about what my mother thought and felt. They mostly date from my teenage years and she's busy at this time, teaching English to Vietnamese refugee women and helping out in local politics, while I am writing home about school productions and my mock exams.

This back and forth seems painfully remote, but to my mother it probably felt normal. Much of her childhood from the age of seven had been spent at boarding school, seeing her mother only in the holidays, and even then not always, any communication otherwise in the shape of a formal letter. To her, this was what mothering looked like, and she passed this distance on to me.

My mother was an enigma or an idea rather than a real person. To fill in the gaps, I told myself many different stories about her as I grew up. When I was unhappy, I knew that I would have been better off with her; when I was sad, she would have comforted me; but these were fantasies, not the truth. Looking back at the letters now, what leaps out at me is how often she apologizes for missing my birthday. Her card had been written but got lost in the mess on the hall table, she forgot, she is so very sorry. Sometimes she is writing this six weeks later. My eleventh, thirteenth and fourteenth birthdays went entirely unmarked by her on the day. Other people might have found her omissions shocking, but I don't remember being upset; by then I was used to the kind of mother I had.

I comprehended some of her troubles, even as a child. The most important lesson I understood was that ending up like my mother was a fate to be avoided. Long-legged and elegant, with big eyes and a slightly wary manner, my mother had the air of a deer watching you from afar. She was not just beautiful; being fragile and in need of a rescuer made her even more attractive to men. I learned from her life that this appeal led to marriage and children, which inevitably resulted in catastrophe. Much more sensible, I concluded, not to take the risk. Instead, I tried to become tough and independent, as little like her as I could manage.

I couldn't entirely separate myself from my mother, however hard I tried. Some likenesses were impossible to ignore. Given my father's complete lack of interest in how anything except a car looked, my love of art must have been her gift. My handwriting, when I wasn't paying attention, was an exact facsimile of hers. Above all, we shared the same fascination for stuff. Visiting her as an adult, I discovered that we liked museums, car-boot sales and collections; we both arranged interesting objects on our shelves, bought quirky ornaments from junk shops and auctions. Most of all, our eyes remembered every single thing we saw and where it had come from.

Once when I came to stay, we visited a 1940s prefab house that had been restored and refurnished nearby. I was the one studying design history, but it was she who could name and date every object in the place. We were clearly kin.

This particular visit took place during one of her good patches, a time when it felt safe for me to acknowledge our likenesses. During these times, she held down jobs, volunteered, became a councillor in her home city of Worcester. She laughed and was interested in what was happening in my life. I wasn't so scared of becoming her.

As my mother got older, the good times became less frequent, and I acquired a new list of things I didn't want to inherit. The first was a dependence on alcohol. Both this and possibly the love for whisky in particular had been passed down in turn from her Scottish father, whose drinking, she told me, had caused her own parents to divorce back in the 1940s. I also didn't want to share her intense depressions. And in the last years of her life I definitely didn't want to acquire her messiness, hoarding and squalor.

For the last twenty years of her life, my mother battled against the chaos which threatened to take over her home. She didn't succeed, and over time the untidiness turned into hoarding. I would come to see her and find the remnants of my last visit still on the kitchen worktops, uncleaned and unmoved; her life slowly sinking into inertia.

My brother and I tried every technique we could think of to help with both the house and the drinking. I took her on holiday; my brother invited her over to stay in China, where he was working. We found her therapists, encouraged her to go to the doctor, then we played hardball and refused to speak to her when she was drunk. Time and again we came up to visit and tidied her house. Nothing we did made a difference. The mess crept back, and my mother bought more whisky, determined to live her life drinking, in a heap of papers, books and junk. We could not make her believe that she deserved better.

In the end I had a baby and refused to bring her into the house. My mother and I spoke on the phone and, sometimes, she would drive down to visit me. After a while, she stopped letting my brother through the door. Both of us knew why, and what state the house was probably in, but by that point we also knew my mother wasn't going to change.

After she died, I wanted nothing more than to get rid of the whole despairing mess for good, but I also needed to find out how it had come to be in the first place, and that meant understanding my mother. The obvious way to do this was through her things.

This wasn't the most surprising idea I've ever had. My whole life has been spent in the company of physical objects. I observe them, collect them in my home and consider them. I've worked with collections in museums and made television programmes about buildings, homes and things, and now I write about the history and hidden meanings that can be found in them. I don't only think about stuff but also with it, unable to settle unless I have arranged it properly around me. In short, objects occupy far too much of my mental space. I can stand in any room of my house and tell you the biography of every item there – where it came from, who it has belonged to before, where it has stood in other houses and quite often what I have thought and felt about it at other times in my life. Often they have become carriers for intense emotions as well.

prologue: red glass bird

I don't feel bad about my relationship with stuff in the slightest. To me, it's like having an incidental extra form of perception, like synaesthesia or perfect pitch. Objects can speak to me, and I like hearing what they have to say. By the end of my mother's life, her world had been taken over by things. They occupied her home, stacking and piling and strewing until she could hardly live in a place that had up to then been her sanctuary; they formed barricades and blockages that separated her from other people, including her children. But things were what bound us together as well as what pushed us apart. If a trace of my mother remained anywhere after she died, it would naturally be in the great unsorted heap of stuff she'd left behind.

We all believe that some part of a person resides in their possessions and can remain there after death. Why have family heirlooms otherwise? In my mother's case it's particularly appropriate, since this obsession came from her in the first place. She knew very well that objects have biographies and personalities and presence. Some of her most unhappy emotions and experiences had ended up embodied in things she owned. Above all, the terrible dereliction of her house was a way of expressing herself through stuff. The undifferentiated stacks of rubbish represented the deep despair which haunted my mother for her entire life. One of the ironies of hoarding is that people only make such a mess with things because they care about them very deeply indeed.

Hoarders are not alone in this. Barring a few ascetics, almost every single person alive today lives with, amongst and through stuff. In countries like Britain where consumerism prevails, we own more than ever before and our possessions form an inescapable part of not only our outer lives but our inner landscapes as well. Many people have collections;

far more of us have family photographs and childhood mementos. We hide things in cupboards and never use them, rent increasing amounts of storage space for the stuff we can't fit into our houses, and we almost all believe that it is not only right but important for the government to keep vast stores of unused objects on our behalf in museums where they will never be thrown away.

Most of all we see our possessions as anything but inert. They are capable of magic – able to lend us powers or change our lives. We believe that objects can contain the essence of human personalities or freeze time. From earliest childhood, our belongings can help us feel safe, or act as repositories for emotions that we can't deal with any other way. We live so intertwined with our possessions that they end up incorporated into our selves. Deep down we all think like hoarders.

Even so, when I dare to describe how my mother's house ended up, I imagine most people would react as they would to seeing a television documentary about hoarders and their homes: a guilty voyeurism combined with deep relief that, in comparison, their house is clean and tidy, so this could not happen to them nor anyone they know. I'm not immune to this feeling either; one of the things I wanted to understand was what made my mother flout the normal rules of society so completely by the end of her life. Yet the more I look at who she was and what she did, the more I realize that my mother wasn't so different to the rest of us. The only distinction was the intensity with which she operated. We are all in the same boat, every single one of us, and this vessel is loaded to the brim with things. My mother's house can act as a mirror for how each one of us lives, as long as we choose to look closely at the objects that surround us rather than turning away.

the house: *first arrival*

END HOUSE OF TERRACE, THREE STOREYS

Worcester, *c.* 1800–1820 with later additions

Reddish-brown brick in Flemish bond with plain tile roof

Purchased in 1981

F OR ONCE I'VE managed to get a parking space right outside my mother's house. Except I don't want to go in. Now that I've drained the last flavourless drops of a takeaway coffee, I'm texting my husband, T, staring at the flat grey January sky and looking for any excuse to prolong these last few minutes. Anything but walk across the pavement and open her front door. Even that isn't going to be straightforward. My eye keeps being caught by the rough metal hasp that's been screwed into the door and frame, held shut by a big silver padlock. Not everything about my mother's house is as regular as it appears at first sight.

The reason I am here, instead of at my desk ninety miles away, is that my mother was taken to hospital yesterday after a fall in her bedroom. In itself, this is not as shocking as it might be: my mother is seventy-seven and getting frail, with lungs that scarcely work after an adult life dedicated to smoking forty or more a day. A part of me has been expecting this crisis for a while, so there's been a certain inevitability about my two-hour journey up the motorway this morning. It's only what any good daughter would do.

The problem is, I'm not sure I am a good daughter, or have ever been. This is my big chance. I can inhabit the role with a bit of conviction for a change. The situation does at least play to my strengths. Much of my working life has been spent being calm and organized in the face of high stress, so I spent yesterday afternoon on the internet researching respite care and home helps, while working out how many times I might be able to make the journey in a week. Underneath all the practicalities, though, I could trace a fine thread of resentment. Why should I be looking after my mother now, was the thought I kept coming back to, when she'd never been any good at caring for me?

My mother has many qualities, being an interesting, intelligent and often funny woman. In her youth she was elegant and attractive, her high cheekbones and slim waist suiting the 1950s fashions. In later life she read widely, had a range of jobs and volunteered for many causes, but the one thing she was never any good at was being a mother. All of which explains why I am here now, hiding in the car rather than heading for her front door. I know what's waiting for me in there, and I've had quite enough to deal with this morning as it is.

By yesterday evening, I'd finally managed to speak to the nurses on the ward, who reassured me that there was nothing seriously wrong and that my mother seemed positive and entirely lucid. Nonetheless, I hadn't slept well and drove up the M5 wired on coffee, hands tight on the wheel, trying to concentrate on the radio without success as my brain worked through logistics while at the same time filling with a mix of rising panic and extreme focus. By the time I reached Worcester, panic had won the battle.

Given its name, I expected the Royal Infirmary to have been housed in Victorian red brick somewhere near the city centre, but no longer. Now it had been relocated somewhere off the ring road, and I couldn't find the right roundabout. After getting lost for the third time, I pulled up by a field gate and almost cried. But this was all the fault of the road signs, which weren't doing their job properly. Nothing to do with my mother at all.

When I finally arrived, I found a university-like sprawl of modern buildings in brown brick and glass, interspersed with footpaths and acres of car park. I walked for what felt like hours past new cancer units, bike sheds, a building site, two atriums and a woodland area before I came to the right place.

My mother was in the Medical Assessment Unit, an after-thought squeezed in next to A&E. This arrangement reflected the ward's rather provisional nature. The MAU had been created as a kind of holding bay for patients who had come into Casualty and needed to be in hospital, yet didn't have an obvious place in their hierarchy of wards and diseases. My mother clearly was not well, possibly in several different ways, but nobody seemed able to pinpoint exactly what these might be. Until someone decided what the problem was, the assessment unit was the only place for her.

Not that the staff were at all worried. Yes, my mother had had a fall, but she didn't seem to have injured herself beyond a few bruises. She was a bit dehydrated and still on oxygen, but there was no reason at all why she shouldn't be going home in a few days' time. Really, she was doing very well. There did seem to be a bit of a problem with her dentures, but the dentist would come down, perhaps tomorrow, to see if this could be sorted out. This last was said as I trailed behind the nurse, who was leading me through the close-packed ward in search of my mother's bed. If the nurses said so, of course everything was fine.

Except when I got there, it wasn't. For a split second I wasn't even sure this was my mother, because the old woman sitting in the armchair, clad only in a hospital gown, didn't look anything like the person I knew, the one who'd driven up to my house just a few weeks ago, smartly dressed and precise as ever; the one whom I recognized as my mother, if a bit older each time. This woman's skin was deeply creased and hanging loose on her face, her eyes were shrunk and sunken, and one was surrounded with a lilac bruise that spread on to her cheekbone as well. Her gown had ridden up, showing more bruises, yellow, brown and blue, across her legs. Those few seconds of falling had aged her by twenty years. More than that, she had been tumbled over and beaten by life. This was my mother, but looking like a photograph from *Crimewatch*, the record of a brutal mugging on a frail, elderly victim.

In that brief second, I caught a glimpse of panic in her eyes too, as though she'd seen her own image reflected in my gaze and was as horrified as me. Then she collected herself, disappearing behind the facade I recognized as her.

'Hello, dear,' she said, waving one hand. The voice was hers, but the words only just recognizable. The nurses had rather understated the problems with her dentures, which were flapping loosely in her mouth, making it hard for her to speak. She put her hand up to stop them falling out.

I tried to look elsewhere, but the nurse had disappeared, leaving just me and my mother. I needed to seem normal and jolly for her benefit, and in the presence of the many other visitors in the ward, but I wasn't sure I was going to manage the performance.

'Sorry about the dentures.' At least I thought that's what she was saying. My mother was waving her hand around again, as though this would make up for the loss of her normal articulacy, while trying to tell me something about the air in the ward drying her mouth out.

My brain was so flooded with thoughts that I couldn't find any words either. How had this happened? If this was fine, what did not fine look like? Since when had my mother worn full dentures, and why the fuck didn't they fit? It looked as though she had borrowed someone else's, but I didn't think even my mother would do that.

Driving up, I'd been convinced that I would sit with her and be kind; I would listen to her talk and exchange confidences, have the kind of open conversation that we'd not managed for years, if ever. Even in the best of circumstances, this would have been a delusion; the ward was hot and noisy, the beds packed too close. There was no place here for any sort of intimacy.

Worse, though, the horror of the situation was eating me up. I didn't want to stay in this arid, claustrophobic room for a second longer than I had to, unable to bear sitting with this strange bruised old lady who had taken the place of my mother. Especially when every battered word reminded me of the state she was in. I'd entered the hospital wanting to be compassionate, but instead I was desperate to run out, gulp fresh air, drive straight back down the motorway and pretend that none of this had ever happened.

So I did what I always do in the face of stress and upset, and took refuge in organization. My mother needed fresh night-clothes instead of the papery hospital gown, some toiletries and a pocket radio, so that Radio 4 could continue to be the accompaniment to her every waking hour, just as it was at home. She also wanted some treats, because the hospital food was awful. I made a list to her instructions. Of course I would sort this out.

'Right, I'll head off to the supermarket and get all of that.'

I heard my own voice, too loud and harsh, hoping that my mother couldn't sense the stress in it.

'And denture fixative.' She said something else, but I couldn't make it out. I hoped it wasn't important.

'Then I'll come back for a bit before I have to go home.' My brain was already making the calculations. Soon after that I'd have the excuse of needing to pick my daughter up from school. I wouldn't have to stay here for very long at all.

The list was why I was now sitting outside her house. I'd got lost, again, on the way to Tesco, which had been concealed at the heart of a housing estate whose streets and cul-de-sacs spiralled around it as though the supermarket was a secret temple of the suburbs. There I'd bought new nightgowns, a small radio and expensive biscuits, sweet and savoury. Nothing refrigerated would survive the heat of the ward. My mother had given me her key, so all I needed to do was pop into the house and pick up her sponge bag.

This simple task was the reason I was still sitting in the car, because it was the one thing in the world that I didn't want to do. I knew what was waiting for me behind that door, because the policeman had told me.

He'd rung yesterday, a blank January morning where nothing much was happening except that I was drinking a cup of coffee at my desk instead of working. I picked up the phone to find PC Harford, calling from Worcester and asking for me by name. He had apologized for interrupting my day.

The events were outlined with a brief but precise description, as was his professional duty. My mother had fallen and rung 999 for an ambulance. He'd been called to break down the door so the paramedics could get in. My mother was in hospital, but not seeming to have any serious health problems.

On one level the phone call was shocking, but at the same time it wasn't unexpected. My aunt Maggie – my mother's efficient and energetic youngest sister – and I had been talking on the phone just a few weeks beforehand, wondering what on earth we were going to do about my mother. Mags thought that she was looking thin and was worried about her health, while I was pretty sure she might have started drinking more seriously again. Ours wasn't a difficult conversation, nor even the first. We found solace in sharing our fears with each other because we both knew that nothing could be done. Each of us had tried to confront my mother in the past, to offer help, suggest she needed to see the doctor. Each time, she pushed us away. In our last call we'd agreed that the situation was only ever going to change when a crisis came. And now here it was, much sooner than expected.

'Did you know what kind of state the house was in?' the policeman asked me.

He took my uncertain silence as an opportunity to explain. The back door was broken down, didn't close. There were brambles growing through the gap. Electric radiators were standing in puddles; lumps of plaster were hanging from the ceiling in the hall. The roof had been leaking for he didn't know how long and the entire top floor was sodden. 'And when I went up there to look, my foot went right through one of the floorboards.'

The indignity clearly hadn't helped his mood. 'My mother told me that she'd had the roof fixed,' I said.

'But did you know how she was living?'

'No,' I said. Clearly not. In my head the house was messy, and there was a lot of unopened post, and maybe some damp furniture – my mother had mentioned the leak in the roof and that she'd had to get it mended. I had not known how much else she had left out, how badly things had deteriorated.

PC Harford took this as a sign that he should reiterate the details all over again. The back door, the damp, the chaos. And the hole in the floor upstairs. His foot. What's more, he'd put a flag on the file for social services, to make sure that she wasn't allowed to go back there while it was in this state. He'd be referring her to the Vulnerable Adults Unit.

'She wouldn't let me in,' I said. Not that I'd tried for a long time. Perhaps the Vulnerable Adults Unit would be phoning up to tell me how neglectful I had been as well.

'But did you know what it was like?'

I was starting to hate this man. He obviously came from the normal world, a place where families cared about each other and showed it. Where mothers had looked after their daughters, and daughters then took care of their mothers in turn. In his eyes I had failed entirely in the most basic duties of a person. He was a policeman, so he must know right from wrong.

'I'd better call the hospital and see how she is doing,' I said, wanting to bring the interrogation to a close.

He gave me the ward name, as well as his own contact details in case I wanted to follow anything up. I couldn't think that I would.

After putting the phone down, I could only sit there. PC Harford had left me feeling guilty and ashamed but also furious almost to the point of tears. Of course I'd been aware that the house was in a state, even if I hadn't known all the details that he had very insistently and repeatedly wanted to impress on me. For the last fifteen years at least, I'd been trying to clear up, to make her happier, stop her drinking. I'd used any means I could to persuade my mother to lead a straight-forward life, but not one of them had worked. Whatever I did, my mother refused to be reformed. Even if I had already known every single detail PC Harford had spelt out to me on the phone, had been aware of all of my deficiencies as a daughter, I still wouldn't have had the slightest ability to do anything about what had happened to my mother, to the house and to his foot as it went through the floor. Nothing and no one could have altered what he found in there.

Had I known then what I've subsequently learned, I would have had a thing or three to tell him in return, but at the time all I could do was sit and stare at my darkened computer screen in acquiescent shock.

Having finally got the padlock off the hasp, I push at the door slowly. On the striped wallpaper, my mother's framed en-gravings of Worcester are hanging just as they always have done, and for one long second I almost believe that I will be able to deal with this. I can see heaps of papers, but they're not blocking the entrance. My mother's house is still here. But as the door opens, a heavy smell of must and damp paper and unstirred dust rises up to meet me. And her hallway is dark, so dark, as though every window has been boarded up. I look through to the kitchen, where a thick tangle of dark-green branches and brambles are pressed against the glass. This is not so much a home now as a bunker.

I need to lean my shoulder against the wood of the door to open it wider, as something has wedged behind, resisting. Right in front of me, the ceiling has caved in, great scrolls of lining paper and plaster dangling down around a dark hole where water has burst through; a matching dark stain on the carpet below. I need to get past the accident quickly in case something falls on my head, but that means going in further, which I don't want to do.

Every flat surface and the floor is stacked with paper and bags and boxes, and I can't see and don't want to imagine what else as well, but underneath I can still see the lines of the place I knew, the house that my mother used to live in. In the corner by the door, under plastic bin liners, old fixings and a broken mixer, stands my grandmother's old freezer, which my mother has been going to get sorted out for the last sixteen years, while in the middle of the floor is her own fridge, bought when the one in the kitchen broke down. She never quite got round to installing the new one, so the faulty one sat useless in the kitchen, while her milk and yoghurt and ready meals lived in the new fridge in the hall. As her hallway was as wide as a normal room, this wasn't in her way, so the set-up never seemed to bother her, however much my brother and I tried to persuade her to get the two fridges swapped over.

With one last shove I am in, but I leave the front door ajar behind me as I step inside. I need to keep an easy escape route; this seething mass of rubbish could so easily rise up and imprison me as well. Two more paces in and now I can see the dining room. This is worse. Her lovely mahogany dining table is on the floor in pieces, all the matching chairs invisible under more and more paper. In fact the far end of the room has disappeared into what looks like a midden or a tip, the accumulated stuff rising up against the wall until it almost reaches my full height. I can see food packets and rubbish amongst the post and *Telegraph*s too. God alone knows what is nesting in there.

Ahead of me, at the back of the house, is the kitchen. Here I can see that the policeman was right. The plywood panel of the back door has rotted, or been stoved in, and it's been like that for some time, because brambles are snaking their way inside. What he said about the rest of the room was true as well. The whole floor is awash with a thick black silt, and in the deepest part of the puddle sits an electric radiator, only buffered from the muck and water by a small stack of newspapers. I can't see much more in the darkness, and I don't want to either. No one should be living like this, he had said, and he was right. Except I have no idea how to tell my mother this. She wants to come home. This chaos is what home looks like for her, however much I hate what I see, however much PC Harford can't believe it.

Her toilet bag is in the bathroom, which means stepping gingerly upstairs past the stacks of books that almost cover every single tread. The twisty irregular staircase must have been difficult enough on its own for an old woman with broken lungs, but like this I can only think that it's a miracle she hasn't fallen before now.

At the top of the stairs, I can see the whole first floor. While there's no muck or water up here, no rotting food or damp newspaper, somehow it feels sadder, because there is light and so every detail of what has not been done is visible. The window is filthy, its sill stacked with useless bits of plastic, old lightbulbs, a broken blind fitting. Her study is a sea of paper, while in the bedroom I can see clothes and tights and pants, newspapers and packaging spilling right out of the door. The bed is unmade, and even from here I know that the sheets haven't been changed for months, if not longer.

Worst of all is the landing in front of me: a dumping ground for things she didn't want or like but couldn't be bothered to move. Faded towels, a laundry bin that's full but covered in more junk. I think again of the kitchen and realize that I have no idea how she's even been washing her clothes. There are single pop socks, stained tops, more books. Most upsetting of all is the old cat bed, still against the radiator, brown fur rubbed into its fleece. My mother's old Burmese cat died ten, maybe twelve years ago, and this relic hasn't moved since then.

Unable to bear this any longer, I step into the bathroom to grab her sponge bag, refusing to look at the dirty bath, the peeling wallpaper, the ivy creeping in through the window. Then I flee the house as quickly as I can manage. Overloaded with squalor and sadness, I want to forget as soon as possible.

Except the house doesn't want me to leave. The temporary lock has been screwed on askew, and when I close the door, it's almost impossible to fix the padlock back into the hasp. I struggle on the doorstep for what feels like ages but is probably only a few minutes, breaking my fingernail, swearing, wondering if I can just leave the door wedged shut but not locked, because surely no one will steal anything from a place that already looks like a dump. Eventually, I secure it and can step back into the safety of my car. I've left the house behind, but the smell of damp and mould stays in my nostrils for the rest of the day.

black teapot: *better times*

BLACK TEAPOT AND COVER

England, *c.* 1840 (?)

Black Basalt with applied relief, no factory mark

Bought from auction in late 1980s

M Y MOTHER'S HOUSE hadn't always been in a bad way, far from it. When she first moved into Rose Terrace, more than thirty years ago, the building had been a wreck, and it had been her who'd rescued it from dinginess and neglect. Not only had she sorted out subsidence and installed central heating and a new kitchen, my mother had tackled the painting and wallpapering in every room herself. She was most proud of the dining room with Harrods-green striped paper on the walls, smoked-glass shelves in the alcove and dark Georgian table and chairs. This became her favourite room, where she not only ate but sat and read the newspaper, a cigarette burning away to ash alongside her. Rose Terrace was her sanctuary after a dark part of her life, and she was very happy to have arrived there.

When my parents divorced in 1975, my mother lost not only her husband but her children too. This was my father's decision, and he pretty much always got his own way. The fierceness of my father's personality and determination can be measured by the fact that my brother and I lived with him and his new wife after the divorce, a situation unheard of in the early 1970s. My mother's resistance had been worn down by eight years of child-rearing, lack of sleep and living with his intense will and opinions, so he even persuaded her that this was the right thing to do.

My father's dominance was never accomplished by force

or shouting, nor even cunning. If he were in a room, people would gravitate to him; if he were in a meeting, people would end up agreeing that his plan was the best. The result was delivered through charm underpinned by will, but it never failed. My father was always right. He liked it that way too.

After the divorce, he had a very definite view of events: the separation and this new family was the best thing that could ever have happened to us, and we were all very happy now. He would have written my mother out of history entirely if he could, but had to settle for refusing ever to discuss her or the first eight years of my life. Why remember a mistake?

The only obstacle lived in his own home. Me. I was his child, in his likeness, with his own iron will, and I chose to hold on to my opinions, memories of the past and my own version of events very tightly indeed.

Not having inherited this core of steel, my mother had little option but to be steamrollered into letting go of me and my brother. She'd learned to defer from birth, having spent an entire childhood a few paces behind her forceful sister Anne, eighteen months her senior. This could explain why she chose my father: being so used to living in the shade of someone else's certainty, he must have felt safely familiar. That's the only reason I can find for their marriage. Other than that, it's not so much a surprise that my parents divorced; I find it harder to understand how they came to be with each other in the first place.

Having decided that he would keep the children, my father held on to the house too. This meant that my mother was left at the age of thirty-eight alone and with nowhere to go. At first she moved in with her own mother, Antoinette, back into her old childhood home in Worcester and the room last occupied by her youngest brother years before, the dramatic red and black textured wallpaper still unchanged from the 1960s. When we visited each fortnight, I would lie on her bed and stick my finger into the squared cells of the paper, examining their dark edges and red centres, feeling the roughness of its finish against my skin. The room smelt of cigarette smoke and Lentheric Tweed, her favourite perfume then, although at some point she moved on to Fiji, which I liked better because I'd seen the adverts in the *Sunday Times Magazine*. Perhaps she wanted a new scent for this new chapter in her life, as a kind of rebirth, even though at the time it must have seemed much more like a dead end, a disaster in which she had lost almost everything that mattered.

My brother and I would stay the night, sleeping next door in my grandmother's guest room, with its high beds with veneered headboards and a matching tall brown wardrobe which held old suits and our board games on the top shelf.

This routine meant that we saw a lot more of my grandmother as well. By this point, she'd evolved into the very model of a 1970s granny: grey hair in tight curls on her head, knee-length Crimplene dresses with no discernible waist, tan stockings and sensible shoes, usually brogues. To me, she was a benevolent enigma, giving the sense that she perceived the world through a cloud. 'That's nice, dear,' was her response to almost everything, leaving me never entirely sure that she'd been listening.

This vagueness didn't arrive with deafness or age. I found the same expression in almost every photo of her I saw: present when she posed for the camera after her wedding, looking resigned to her fate; even when she was a student

*Antoinette camping with her brother
John in the early 1920s.*

with her friends. Only as a very small child, tumbling through
the grass and playing cricket on a camping holiday, did
Antoinette seem to have been fully alive.

I can believe that some part of my grandmother was stuck
for ever as an eight-year-old girl. My mother once told me
that her favourite song had been 'The Teddy Bears' Picnic',
while her greatest enthusiasm was soft toys. Unlike a child, she
didn't just collect them but manufactured them from scratch,
becoming WI national champion at least once. The Womble
she made me from just a picture my mother gave her was
better than any that could be found in the shops.

Only through sewing did we make contact. On our fort-
nightly visits, my grandmother spent the long Saturday

afternoons teaching me to make the most basic of creatures from fun fur stretched over yoghurt pots, a pastime I never tired of. That was the way things were for what seemed then to be quite a long time but was actually less than a year.

I am hazy about timing and details, partly because I was still only nine and was never told the half of it, but also because I was desperate to forget how unhappy the divorce made me. At some point my mother moved to the farthest Cambridgeshire Fens for a job as an estate agent, and I can remember going to the windy Norfolk coast when we visited her, walking miles to the sea which receded across the flat grey sands almost to the point of invisibility. We ate chips and played on the slot machines, just as we did when we visited our cousins and went to the beach with them.

Like many of my mother's jobs, this didn't last for long. The new man in her life swindled her out of a large sum of money, and so she slunk back to her mother's house in Worcester, back to the spare room, another job as an estate agent, us visiting every fortnight and what must have been an overwhelming sense that, despite all her efforts, she would remain stuck there for ever.

The other person who was sometimes also present when we came to see her was my mother's sister Anne, who had a personality so strong that she was the only person in the world who could strike fear into my father. 'She could charm the birds off the trees,' he would say, but this wasn't said approvingly. My mother felt that Anne had been a blight on her life, domineering and overshadowing her childhood, although she never explained to me how this had manifested itself.

She didn't need to. I understood anyway, because almost all the memories I have of Anne are marked by intense fear.

Anne at her wedding to Christopher Olford, my mother and grandmother in the background.

Fortunately she only made rare appearances. By the time I was nine or ten and could remember her properly, she had left the country after roaring through a difficult divorce in which she too had left her children with their father followed by a nursing career in London, when she lived in Fulham and used Harrods as her corner shop.

The problems really started when Anne decided she could talk to me as an adult. By then she lived in the West Indies, on the small island of Bequia, where she was proud to be the only white woman who danced in the carnival, returning every year or two to see her mother and any other of her relatives who might come into view.

A snapshot of one of these visits has been seared on to my brain by embarrassment. I am sitting in one of my grandmother's armchairs, dark brown and built in the 1930s with high arms and a seat sunk down by the failure of its ancient springs. A tall woman, Anne is standing over me so that I am unable to escape its depths.

'Well,' she booms at an impossibly un-private volume, 'I hope you are getting out and having lots of fun.'

She puts great emphasis on the word 'lots', and I know exactly what she is implying. She hopes I am having a great deal of sex. But I am not. I am an unhappy and overweight teenager, so terrified of any kind of intimacy that my hair is stiffened with half a can of hairspray each day and I drape myself with belts covered in metal studs. Of course I have no answer for her. All I want is for the chair to finally give in and swallow me into its depths. At the other end of the room, I can see through the French windows to where spring sunshine is beginning to fall on the lawn and the peonies. Stuck in the chair, all I can do is nod, hoping that this will satisfy her.

'Excellent.' In my memory she looms exaggeratedly huge, and I am afraid she is going to trap me here for ever. Finally, however, she moved off to interrogate someone else and I was able to haul myself out of the chair and disappear down to the far end of the garden, where I could pretend to be interested in the vegetables and contemplate how useless I was.

In 1980 my mother's life got a lot better when my great-grandmother, Carrie Jenkins, died. From my mother's account, she was the kind of person who improved things by dying, and this wasn't only true for my mother. Carrie's daughter, my grandmother Antoinette, achieved a far greater eman-cipation. Carrie had been rich, but also cantankerous and controlling, and my grandmother had been almost entirely dependent on her for money. Now, at the age of sixty-six, my grandmother was not only free for the first time in her life, she also had the means to do whatever she wanted. The solid and sensible red-brick suburban villa in the Worcester suburbs was exchanged for her heart's real desire: a picture-postcard half-timbered cottage in the countryside out towards the Malvern Hills. Here she installed the three things she'd always wanted: a four-poster bed, a Jacuzzi bath and a ride-on mower. Her ambitions fulfilled, my grandmother settled down to tend her garden and stitch industrial quantities of patchwork.

The money she'd inherited from Carrie Jenkins gave Antoinette not simply the funds to pay for her own dreams but plenty to spare, so she divided the remainder out between her four surviving children: Anne, Mags and my mother, along with her last-born son, Mike (baptized Allan Michael). My mother was able to buy Rose Terrace with her portion. She never moved again.

At the time when my mother bought the house, its charms weren't immediately obvious. Perched on top of a steep hill at the edge of Worcester, the views over rooftops and, if you craned a bit, the cathedral gave it pretensions to a good setting. The quirkiness of the area appealed to her, from the multi-generational Indian families settled into the red-brick villas to the ancient Italian deli which had been serving workers as they rushed to and from the engineering works since the 1940s. The factories had closed, but Ceci's carried on, serving then rare gourmet treats like artichokes in oil and risotto rice to my mother and any other brave soul who ventured past.

The Victorian terraces that stretched in chains down the slope to the city were not gentrified or even up and coming. At one point, my mother had daily company in the house for several weeks as a pair of police officers made use of the fine view from her top-floor windows. They were keeping watch on the video shop at the bottom of the hill, because it was under suspicion of being a brothel, a situation which greatly entertained my mother. The prospect of dodgy neighbours didn't concern her, because above all she adored her house.

I've known Rose Terrace for so long that I can still picture it in my mind as it was when my mother looked after it. One end of a miniature Regency terrace, its proportions were neat and regular: the door and one sash window on the ground floor, then another symmetrical pair of windows on the floor above, and another two on top of that. The porch was supported by small scrolls of plaster leaves, and a red-brick chimney marked each end of its roof. The house had been extended, piecemeal, at the back, so that by the time my mother bought it, there were four bedrooms as well as a bathroom upstairs. She'd wanted room enough that my brother and I would always feel welcome. From the outside, though, the house still looked neatly unaltered, with its matched windows and the front door painted a deep gloss red. Despite its location, the house was in many ways a very suitable one for a woman of my mother's age, situation and class. The building had enough history to be respectable, even admired, and with its small proportions but many bedrooms it was perfect for the divorced woman who might have family visitors. Rose Terrace and my mother were perfectly matched, and by the time she had finished the restoration, it had become even more suitable than before.

Along with the money from Carrie Jenkins, there also came furniture. My mother loved to repeat the story of how she had gone to help clear out Carrie's house only to find her own very practical mother, Antoinette, about to tackle a lovely satinwood chest of drawers with an axe, intending to render it into kindling. She told this simply as an illustration of how tastes change, but given the way that my grandmother had been treated for the last sixty years, I suspect there may have been an element of catharsis in the attack too. My mother stepped in to rescue the drawers from their fate, along with a pair of side tables and a dark Victorian chiffonier: perfect accessories for her brand-new home.

For several years the house marked a good patch for my mother, and that's what the great black teapot represents. A hulking piece of high-Victorian style, every part of its squat shape is covered with a relief of swarming foliage set on a textured ground. Nothing remains undecorated – even the bottom doesn't escape. The black matte glaze makes it seem from a distance that the pot has been cast out of iron rather than clay, an effect that I suspect its makers wanted, if only subconsciously. The result must have seemed dashingly modern to Victorian eyes, even if to us it has become an over-cluttered monstrosity.

It lived in the dining room, on the glass shelves in the alcove, next to some porcelain coffee cups that my mother believed to be late eighteenth century and therefore rare, along with seven mismatched eighteenth-century glasses she'd been given in repayment of a loan. Stories like this attached themselves to almost every object she owned, and the teapot was no exception.

I like stories as much as my mother ever did. For me the teapot matters not only because it's a magnificent thing but also because it triggers a very specific memory, one that tells me not just about my mother but also the ties that bind us together.

At the tail end of the 1980s, when I'd left college and begun to work, I'd driven up to Worcester bringing two friends with me. These were very good times indeed, a moment when we both felt able to sustain the kind of relationship that a mother would have with her twenty-something daughter and I wasn't yet scared of what my friends would find in the house.

Oddly I see this picture from above, as though I had died and was looking down on myself and my friends and my mother from the level of the curtain pole, the sunlight streaming in through the window below me. The moment takes place early on in our visit, so we are all standing around awkwardly in her dining room because no one yet feels relaxed enough to sit on a chair. My mother proudly lifts up the teapot from the shelves for the three of us to look at. She has only just bought it from an auction, for not very much money at all, because no one else wanted it.

'It was so awful,' she says with a smile, 'so I had to have it.'

My friends collapse with laughter, to my mother's surprise, so they have to explain. This phrase is exactly what I say about every single piece of Technicolor 1950s china I bring home from the junk shops and flea markets of North London. My most recent prize had been a salt and pepper set, thick earthenware shaped into the form of two red and white lamb chops. I'd had to buy them, otherwise I knew I'd spend the rest of my life describing what I'd seen but not bought because they were so bizarre. Exactly like my mother.

She was good at talking back then, not only to my friends but to me. Whenever I visited, she would tell me stories over supper and a glass of wine about the aunts who would no longer speak to my father, or how great-grandmother Carrie had been known to the rest of the family as 'the old battleaxe', gleefully imagining her horror had she lived to see Anne living with a black man in the West Indies.

Occasionally, after the second glass of wine she would touch on more serious subjects as well. More than once she explained how she had thought that leaving me with my father was the best thing to do. She looked at me across the dining-room table, the plates cleared away to reveal the green mats with their cathedral scenes underneath. The first cigarette after dinner was in her hand, the ash slowly drooping into a curve. Had she done the right thing?

I took another sip of wine. Every possible answer was wrong. Either I agreed that I'd been better off without her, or I told her she should have fought harder to keep me and my brother. Whatever I said could make her miserable, which was all too easy to do.

'It's impossible to tell.' I tried to smile at her. 'We'll never know what would have happened the other way round.'

She simply nodded back. I had managed to give her a re-assuring answer.

The moment passed, and she went back to talking about parents and aunts and my brother. The evening settled in around us; books stacked behind the chairs, the teapot in its place on the shelf. Our relationship was at its best then, and if I tried to call up a picture of her in my head, I would see her sitting at that dining table, still sat straight in her chair, squaring up to the world, amused but thoughtful. She would pause during conversations as though she were thinking about the matter, and when she did this there was always a sense of a presence beneath the surface, something which was watching you and quite possibly judging as well. I can see now that this would have been uncomfortable for someone who wasn't used to her or didn't trust her, like sharing a sofa with an unpredictable Oriental cat. The claws were sheathed for now, but it would be impossible to forget that they were there.

She did judge other people. Although she always made

fun of her grandmother Carrie Jenkins for being a snob without having any reason to be, she was more than able to look
down on people herself. If, when I was in the car with her, we
saw a modern housing estate, she would almost always sing
'Ticky-tacky little boxes' as we passed. Why, she would ask me,
did anyone choose a house like that?

I was safe; she never judged me. She might have been
frightened of my energy, unsure of whether she'd done the
right thing in leaving me with my father, or simply capable of
sometimes forgetting that I was a person with feelings, but I
had come from her and so, whatever choices I made, they were
of course the right ones. In any case, in matters of taste, we
mostly agreed. We knew what was funny and what was dull,
where a pot needed to be placed to sit right on a set of shelves,
how to lay the table so that it looked well.

This is the mother I prefer to remember: bright, happy and
engaged with the world. A mother who paid attention to me.
My greatest sadness was that this person didn't stay around
for long enough. Drinking and depression sat on her like
stone, making her selfish and sullen, and, in the end, submerg-
ing her in rubbish.

I can't pinpoint exactly when the problems began for my
mother, but I do know what caused them. One of the reasons
that my mother was happy when I visited her with my friends
was that she had a new man in her life. We'll call him Patrick. I
can't describe him as her boyfriend, because they were in their
fifties, but he wasn't her partner either. That's because Patrick's
big disadvantage was that he was married. He still managed
to spend a lot of time with my mother but had decided he
would only separate from his wife when their children had

all left home at eighteen. I know that's what all married men say to their mistresses, but we never got the chance to find out whether he meant it or not because he died, suddenly, of a massive heart attack in 1988. My mother was distraught, but had to sit at the back of the church pretending that she was no more than an acquaintance. By then she was fifty and probably believed that she'd never have a relationship again. This was when her drinking began.

I was an adult myself, living three hours away in London with a job that took up all my weekday hours and sometimes weekends too, so she could easily keep this from me. Once or twice I found whisky bottles under the sink, but after this shaming she hid her drinking from me, only ever ringing when she was sober, and getting through no more than one or two glasses of wine each evening when I came up to stay. She persuaded me that the problem had gone away, and over the next year my mother did eventually cut down. At the time, she told me that it was through plain willpower, but she later admitted to asking her doctor for help, even though she was never very good at accepting it.

Part of the reason for her recovery, I am sure, was that she needed to look after her own mother, Antoinette, who was, after a bout of bowel cancer and a serious car crash, more frail and less able to shop for herself, although still living in her half-timbered dream cottage out in the countryside, with my mother popping round two or three times a week to deliver Marks & Spencer ready meals and run errands.

There was a certain irony in my mother ending up with this responsibility, because she, of all her siblings, felt that she had not been loved as a child. When I described this situation to my therapist, the motherly lady I was seeing replied,

42

'Well, you don't keep coming back to the table if you've had enough to eat in the first place.' I understood what she meant completely.

My grandmother never became entirely dependent. Instead, twelve years after Patrick, she too died of a sudden heart attack, on a visit to Anne in the West Indies.

That had to be the best way to go, said my mother when she phoned me up to talk, dying suddenly, without really knowing what was happening, and before you lost your marbles – and on a tropical island to boot. Not bad going when you're eighty-six. My mother was trying to be cheerful, but this was the final and most terrible calamity. For her whole life, the hope had always been there that, if she went back to the table often enough, one day she would finally get served. Now that was never going to happen.

Antoinette, unsentimentally, had left a will stating she should be buried wherever she died, which didn't even give my mother a funeral with which to lance her pain. She knew that this mattered immensely, but understanding the source of her upset didn't stop the arguments. The reason she'd rung me in the first place was to complain about Mags, who'd bagsied for her own daughter the good stainless-steel saucepans that my mother had hoped would go to me.

I didn't mind at all, but to make up for it my mother took me round my grandmother's cottage to choose some other heirlooms as compensation. Anne hadn't yet organized a flight out of the West Indies, and Mags was waiting for her to arrive, while Mike now lived in Scotland and preferred to steer clear of his sisters, particularly en masse, so for the moment my mother was entirely in charge. I was given a silver vase, some loose black and white pictures and Carrie Jenkins' old secateurs.

'And I want you to have these as well.' My mother pulled out two big carrier bags from the bottom of an oak cupboard.

I recognized the contents as soon as she opened one up: white linen and purple pleats, shiny blue silk covered in embroidery. When my great-grandfather Harold Jenkins, Carrie's husband, had travelled all across Asia and Arabia in the 1930s to sell mining machinery, he'd brought back not the usual souvenirs of carved ornaments or dolls but the clothes he'd seen worn around him: a full set of men's Arabic robes, a woman's burka, a kimono of deep-blue silk. As a special treat, they were brought out for us to admire when we visited as children, but I hadn't seen them for years.

'Well, I don't want Anne to take them. They'll only rot over there in Bequia. It's too humid.'

'Are you sure?' I didn't want to get drawn into their arguments.

'You've worked in a museum and you like clothes, so I know you'll look after them.'

My mother, unusually determined, folded up the bags again and marched them over to a spot by the front door. Clearly she wanted them out of the house before Anne got anywhere near Worcester.

At that point in her life, my mother was more concerned to give things away than hold on to them herself. Given that hoarding is so often precipitated by sentiment and loss, and my grandmother's death had been such a blow, it's surprising now to realize how few of the family possessions stayed with her. All she kept was what the rooms in Rose Terrace could hold – a selection of ornaments and some glasses, the photo albums and a couple of pieces of silver. The only big items were the two solid brown 1930s armchairs that had sat in my grandmother's front rooms for my entire life. Even these weren't excessive; my mother put them in her own sitting room but took the old chairs to the tip when she did.

What's particularly strange about this is that Rose Terrace was already in the first stages of disorder. I wouldn't class my mother as hoarding back then, but when I came up after my grandmother died, I discovered newspapers stacked on the dining-room chairs and in the hall, while dirty dishes and old ashtrays and Tupperware almost covered the cluttered kitchen worktops. I'd asked her if I could at very least cut back the vine that was threatening to overwhelm her newly redesigned garden, but, possibly because she was still disorientated by bereavement, she let me do far more. I ended up cleaning the kitchen, stacking up unread post in the hall and wiping dust and cigarette smoke from the window frames, achieving as much as I could manage in a weekend. At first my mother sat in the dining room drinking vodka and orange so strong that the juice in the glass seemed translucent and doing the crossword while I worked around her. On the second day, though, she began to join in, sorting through her study until by the time we both finished, it had almost been restored to order.

None of this is the most vivid memory of my grandmother's dying. A month or so later, I was back in Rose Terrace, but this time not on my own. Anne had flown over from the West Indies and Mags had driven across England so that they could sort through my grandmother's house and fight. The two sisters sat on the sofa in the sitting room while my mother and I ran back and forth fetching cups of coffee, biscuits and glasses of water.

Exasperated, I'd given up on being a servant and was out in the hallway, packing Antoinette's possessions into boxes. I

My mother in her sitting room at Rose Terrace in about 2001.

heard Anne's usually booming voice lower to a whisper, then Mags put her head around the door and beckoned me into the sitting room. Anne, tall as well as overbearing, had taken most of the sofa. Sitting back, she spread her legs out while Mags perched at the other end, leaning forward as though her restlessness would drive her into action at any moment.

Mags gestured me to the armchair, but I didn't sit down. I'd already been on the receiving end of two long diatribes from Anne, including one about how I had to bring the robes and kimono back from London because they were rightfully hers as the eldest, so I wanted to be able to make a quick escape should another begin. It did, only this one was far worse. Things weren't the problem this time; it was my mother. Her house was a state, did I know how many whisky bottles were under the sink, how much had I done to sort this out and it wasn't enough, why hadn't I done more?

It had only been a month or so since I'd cleaned the entire house and taken the last batch of bottles to the tip. I'd talked to my mother over and over, but none of this had changed a thing; if anything, I had made her worse. But I never got the chance to say a single word of this. Anne carried on and on, with Mags only adding as an occasional descant that the penny had to drop inside. This made no sense to me, but what I did understand was that neither of them was offering me any help. Instead, they wanted to lumber me with their own worries and fears, to make sure that my mother was my responsibility instead of theirs.

I drove back down the motorway under a grey scudding sky, trapped in the car with my despair, fighting the urge to put my head between my legs and weep as the slow traffic jams crawled back into London. Mags and Anne had driven home to me what I'd always known. My mother's unhappiness was entirely my fault, and there was no way of remedying it. Instead, I could only endure it for ever without respite and certainly with no support from either of them.

Over the next year or two, my brother, P, and I both tried every way we could to make my mother happier: visiting, tidying, listening, buying new shelves to help sort out her study. We offered to send her to a clinic to detox, but she refused; together we bought her a computer which would give her more contact not just with us but with her sisters as well. Anne embraced email, using it to bombard my mother with jokes and memes, allowing her to be infuriating even over a distance of thousands of miles.

I also encouraged her to write her life story down, convinced that this would allow her to be free of her past. With hindsight, this was probably not the kindest nor most helpful suggestion, as it would have meant unearthing a whole nest of agonies which she was too fragile to contemplate. My mother prevaricated and researched, found out a bit about some ancestors and then gave up. I sighed and despaired once again.

During this time, I tried all sorts of strategies: going to visit and leaving her with lists of positive things to do, making sure we were in regular contact so that she never felt alone. I helped her to find a therapist, and she stuck at seeing Eva for nearly a year. She tried too: detoxing from alcohol using Valium with the help of her doctor, joining a creative-writing class and an industrial archaeology group. But nothing worked for long enough; the misery ran too deep.

One of my approaches was to get her to email me two or three times a week so that she could tell me how she'd been doing and, I hoped, feel as though she was not alone with her cares. When I reread our correspondence now, full of the back and forth of daily life, I can see that the house was drifting towards disorder enough to worry me, but also that my mother sometimes felt able to tackle it. Once she mentions in passing that she'd unearthed a letter from my father, explaining why I was being sent to a new school. Despite my mother's sporadic attempts to impose order, Rose Terrace never did get tidy. After her death, I found that same letter in the stacks of her study, unfiled and unsorted, fifteen years later.

The house slipped further and further into chaos, and nothing my brother and I did could stop this. Increasingly it became clear that my mother didn't want things to change. If either of us dared to suggest there was a problem, she would withdraw and not call us for weeks at a time. Her sisters got the same treatment if they tried to raise the subject of her drinking.

When my mother was sober, in the mornings, she blotted out reality with books instead. As a twice-weekly volunteer at the local Oxfam bookshop, she had a ready supply. Once I came to visit and discovered her bed had almost disappeared under paperbacks. Spreading out from the space where she lay, they flowed like a tidal wave over the edge of the bed and on to the floor in a great wash of words and avoidance. It looked almost like an art installation, or at least it would have done had it not spoken of such despair. Books are clean and stackable, so that was a quick mess to sort out. I had no idea what was to come.

Somehow, my mother managed to stop the computer working, so the emails petered out. She had given up on getting better. Her mood ebbed and flowed: some weeks she would speak to me regularly, sometimes she wouldn't. She'd phone up and slur her words, then remember nothing of the conversation when I next called. Sometimes she wouldn't answer the phone for a week, maybe more. I was worried and upset but also powerless; I'd run out of ways to help, and the distance between us yawned wider than ever. She no longer saw the point in trying, not even for the sake of her own children. So began her long, slow letting go.

The only thing left to do was give up. This wasn't only an acceptance that I couldn't expect kindness and affection when she was so mired in her depression and drinking that sometimes she couldn't see me at all. It wasn't even the realization that I was never going to be able to fix her. What I finally understood was that the more I ran around, wrote lists, cleaned and tidied, exhorted and organized, the worse I made her feel.

The more energy I put in, the less capable and competent she felt herself.

Instead, I tried to step back, not demand anything from her at all, letting her talk to me, or not, as she wanted. She seemed happier now I was no longer hounding her for change in every phone call, and rang me up each Thursday.

Finally, when my own daughter was born and I refused to come to the house any more, it wasn't because of the mess. The house was unkempt but still inhabitable. The only real issues were the fridge, which worked, but did so in the middle of the hall, along with a rather saggy floorboard in the bathroom where the toilet cistern had been gently seeping for a year or two. 'She'll go through that ceiling one day,' said my brother. 'If the toilet doesn't get there first.' He was only admitting what we both thought, but in the end that floor outlasted her, even when a couple of others had failed and broken.

All of this I could live with. What really kept me away was the smoking. Ever since I could remember, my mother had smoked as though it were her job, getting through forty or more cigarettes every day. And because she didn't have a job, most of these were smoked in the house. If I wanted to call up one defining picture of her, she would be sitting at the dining table after breakfast, cup of coffee next to her, making her first attempt at the *Telegraph* crossword, one elbow on the table with a pen in her hand. Her cigarette would be balanced on the bone-china ashtray next to the cup. Every cup of coffee, every meal needed its own cigarette; the crossword deserved at least two. The whole house was saturated in nicotine and tar; I didn't want to bring a newborn baby into this atmosphere. She drove down to visit us instead, although not very often.

A year or two after this, she started making excuses when

my brother went to see her in Worcester, suggesting that they lunched in a pub instead. He didn't argue. We'd both stopped fighting her by then. If we tried, she'd only retreat into her shell and drink even more, so there was no point.

Mags would ring me up sometimes to talk, particularly in the last couple of years of my mother's life. She too knew that if she tried to raise the subject of drinking, or looking after herself, the only result would be that my mother would cut contact. Once, when she couldn't get through to my mother, she phoned up the Oxfam shop to check she was all right. Anne had only recently died, and Mags was unsurprisingly concerned about her one remaining sister. But the interference wasn't at all welcome and my mother didn't speak to her for weeks. Both Mags and I knew that nothing could be done; my mother could not be made to change. We kept each other company, waiting for the disaster to happen, as we knew it would.

Which is how her once-beloved house came to be in the state it was when the policeman broke down the door.

❅ *3* ❅

embroidered cushion cover: *gone*

HAND-STITCHED CUSHION COVER

England, *c.* 1975

Canvas embroidered with wool, backed
with woven cotton

Current location unknown

Back at home, I found it almost impossible to admit what I had discovered in my mother's house. Every time I was asked how she was doing, I flinched in anticipation of people's judgement. Just as the policeman had disapproved of me – and he of all people knew what was the right thing to do – so would everyone else if they knew the truth. The shame was acute: I had failed my mother entirely, because no person should end up in this state.

I dealt with my guilt by not saying a word about the dereliction, or minimizing the situation with English understatement down to 'a bit of a mess' when I spoke to my friends. For a week or so I didn't even dare explain the full state of the house to my husband, for fear that he too would judge me. Either that or he would turn away from me, knowing that I would inevitably turn into the same disordered person as my mother.

I knew I wasn't alone, but this didn't help me to say anything. There had to be thousands of daughters like me who didn't have a proper relationship with their mothers, but we would never be able to speak up and find each other, because the world was our policeman, always judging us. The assumptions are too overpowering. Everyone loves their mother, don't they, and their mother loves them back. That's how the world runs. Mother's Day cards are always a pleasure for both sender and receiver, not the source of two weeks of intense soul-searching and grief as they were each year for me.

Not having a proper relationship with your mother is one of the last taboos.

Sometimes the pressures emerged into plain sight. In my twenties I had a close friend who had been brought up by her mother alone. The two of them were a tight-knit unit, and she simply could not believe that anyone else might not love their mother in the same way. Over a few years, her incredulity wore me down until I began to doubt myself; I simply wasn't trying hard enough to be close. So a couple of years after my grandmother died, I took my mother away for a long weekend in Italy. This wasn't a terrible holiday – we went to Naples and ate pizza – but the only picture that comes up in my mind when I think about it is the ugly concrete hotel that we stayed in by the ring road. The experience wasn't fun, and it certainly didn't bring us any closer together. My mother said sorry a lot, and I was furious with her inertia. Now, I wish I had been kinder, because she was clearly still very depressed about her mother's death. The drinking had made her put on weight, so she was wearing Antoinette's clothes, making her look old and dowdy as well as sad. I had thought that bringing her to a different place would not only cheer her up but make her more present for me, her daughter. Instead, she dragged the past along with her in her suitcase and, instead of being sympathetic, I hated this. Neither of us suggested anything similar again.

Yet I couldn't help trying. No one ever wants to admit that their own mother didn't love them, not even to themselves, never mind other people. At heart, I still believed that I was not good enough, not loveable enough, and so what had happened was all my fault.

These kind of beliefs are a truism of psychology. Almost

*Three months old, I am being held by
my paternal grandmother while my
mother looks on.*

every small child, faced with an impossible or threatening
situation, will end up believing that they are responsible. Had
they been better behaved, their parents would not have split;
had they not wished them gone, their small sibling would not
have died. In my case I believed that if only I had been a different child, my mother would have loved me like other people's
mothers did.

My mother certainly did find me hard work. As an adult,
she often told me how hard bringing up children had been.
My father had never helped, because that wasn't what men
did then, but she was so exhausted that it was no wonder their
marriage fell apart. The eight and a half years of my life that I
spent with her warranted only one other recollection, which

was of how she had taken me to playgroup at the village hall for the very first time when I was three. She'd been worried that I would be shy and nervous, but I ran in through the unfamiliar door without looking back. My mother had sighed with relief, happy that someone else would finally have to cope with me, even if just for an hour. Constantly on the go, always asking unanswerable questions, only sleeping for six hours a night, I was the child she'd always wanted, but with the volume turned up too high. That was the message of both these stories: that I was too much for her to cope with and I frightened her. I suspect that I understood this from an early age. I certainly grew up never wanting children of my own.

My brother was more laid-back, an easier child, but crucially he was also ill. Asthmatic, with a weak chest, he had double pneumonia twice before he was two, and was regularly being rushed to hospital in his early years.

When this happened, I would be dumped on the neighbours, often at short notice, and in later life, one of the questions my mother often asked me was whether I felt as though I'd been neglected when my brother was so unwell. This was more than a question about emergencies. She knew that on some level she hadn't been able to love me as she had done him and wanted reassurance from me. I always gave it to her as well, by saying that I couldn't remember anything about it, which was pretty much true. The only memory I have from that time is of a crushingly dull outpatients' ward, with cold floors and metal beds. Outside was blistering sunshine and a bright blue sky, which I could only look at through an open door while my brother had his weekly sunray treatment to help his weak lungs and pigeon chest. I was bored but also furious, understanding that his frailty meant that my mother loved him more. At night, when I was meant to be sleeping, I would lie in the dark and dream of being taken ill, so that I, at last, would get some of the attention. I never told her that part.

As an adult, I grew to understand that she found it very hard to love anyone at all. With my head, I knew that my childhood could not have unfurled any other way. But I couldn't believe it with my heart. All I knew was that my own mother could not love me, and this was caused by my own flawed and excessive nature. The hoard, her life and her unhappiness were all my fault. This was why, when the crisis came, I was unable to say a word about what I had found.

In Worcester, where my mother remained in hospital with the ripples of chaos still spiralling out around her, I could not hide behind silence. Words had to be spoken, the state of the house had to be described with as much particularity of mould spores and splintered wood as I could muster. Otherwise my mother would send herself, quite cheerily, back to living in her house exactly as I had found it. Back to the holes in the floor, the vermin, the missing door panel and the central heating that didn't work. Back to no cooker, no working bath, no washing machine. I was the only person who could stop this happening, the only one who had seen the reality of my mother's daily existence. If I didn't stop this, I really would be guilty of neglect.

To my relief, what I received from almost every single person I spoke to at the hospital was gentleness and sympathy. The nurses were kindest of all, reassuring me that I should not feel guilty, because I could not have known. Their ward regularly admitted old ladies who had seemed to be holding it all together when they were out and about in the world

– my mother too had been arriving for her volunteer shifts at the Oxfam bookshop every week, neatly dressed and apparently normal – but who returned to conditions of Dickensian misery when they got home. Only a crisis ever caused this to be discovered. My mother wasn't exceptional at all, it seemed.

The problem was that she couldn't stay in the safe, understanding ward for ever. Her wrecked lungs meant that she wasn't well, but at the same time she had no treatable disease that would give her a place in the hospital. So my mother sat in the Medical Assessment Unit, frail but defiant, more than alert enough to be rude about the pallid sandwiches and reconstituted soup, and sometimes argumentative to boot, while the nurses and social workers talked about discharge. Because if you couldn't be healed by the hospital, you needed to be somewhere else, and quickly. My mother was very happy to agree with this. She wanted out as well, and that meant her own home.

'I might need a bit of help for a few weeks until I get my strength back,' she had announced when I'd returned to deliver her nightclothes, radio and biscuits. 'But after that I'll be fine.'

There was nothing at all I could say in reply. If she thought of the house as 'fine', no words of mine would be able to reach over that gulf of understanding. I was going to have to solve the problem some other way. The policeman had described her house as 'uninhabitable'. Surely this had to count for something.

The weekend consisted of wandering around my own house in a blank daze, interspersed with long telephone calls with the hospital. The duty social workers were as understanding as the nurses. They too had seen this all before, and plenty more besides that I could not even imagine, so in those first few days they offered me the reassurance that she might be discharged to a care home for a month or so, something that could be funded by the NHS. This would give me and my brother time to work out some tactics.

There was only one person who didn't seem to understand, and unfortunately this turned out to be the regular Monday-to-Friday social worker assigned to my mother's ward, whom I'll call Helen. At first she existed only as a disembodied but sharp voice at the end of the phone line. Over the next few days, before I could come up again in person, a routine developed. I would ring the office and explain the state of Rose Terrace in as much detail as I could bear. My comments would be duly noted, as I desperately tried to make my point across 90 miles of distance and Helen's professional cynicism. I'm sure her job included budgets she had to squeeze the most out of and targets she had to meet about how many frail but not properly ill old women she had to get back out of the door every week. None of these obstacles was insuperable. The real problem was my mother.

Each time I thought I had won the argument, Helen would then go on to the ward and talk to my mother, who would be entirely lucid: back to reading books, listening to Radio 4 and doing the day's *Telegraph* crossword. So when my mother said that she would be fine at home, of course Helen believed her.

She had to. My mother had what is called in the jargon 'capacity', the ability to make a rational decision about her own treatment and circumstances. The social workers could only follow her wishes. Except that her wish was to go home, a place where the kitchen did not work, the smell of damp permeated every curtain, cushion and chair, and the back door was permanently open to the January cold. Every part of her was sane, the one exception being the way in which she was living. My mother seemed to think she occupied an entirely normal house, an image which bore no relationship to the disorder which lay behind the front door.

After Helen and I had been back and forth like this a couple of times, I realized that I needed a different tack. My first attempt was to try and get the house condemned as unfit for human habitation. This turns out to be surprisingly difficult to do, at least it is for a homeowner. Had my mother been renting, a single phone call to the environmental health department would have been enough. One website warned me that 'the fitness standard is quite low: only homes in serious disrepair will fail'. I found a checklist, and Rose Terrace would easily have been condemned, at very least on the grounds of extreme damp and not having a working kitchen, never mind the structural issues like the failing floors. But because my mother was the owner and the occupant, and an Englishwoman's home is her castle, regardless of how many rats she is sharing it with, no one wanted to know, never mind take responsibility either for her welfare or that of the building.

My next move – as suggested by a group of kindly strangers on the internet who had been in similar situations themselves – was to take photographs of the state of the house to show Helen. This I did not want to do in the slightest. It not only meant returning to the house but, worse, required me to confront the truth of what was there, in order that other people might see it. More than that, in recording what I saw, I would ensure that this terrible mess – and my shame – would be indelible.

I prevaricated for a couple of days, trying to imagine any other way there might be of making my point, but there was no getting around what needed to be done. On my next visit, I steeled my nerve and went back to the house with my camera.

When I look back at the photos now, I can see how intensely I hated the task. There are only six of them in total, all amongst the worst photographs I have ever taken: blurry, washed-out and indistinct. I fought against having to go back into the house and examine every room, and while I was doing it I certainly didn't want to look at what was in front of me for a moment longer than I had to. That shows in the pictures I produced.

What I also see now is how much I subsequently minimized the misery in which my mother had been living. Asked to recall what I saw, I would have said that I knew the kitchen was out of use, apart from possibly the kettle, and that there was a microwave in the dining room, so in some corner of my subconscious I had been believing that she used that. In the photos I can see an opened can of baked beans with a fork stuck in it. That's what she was eating. Cold baked beans. The microwave had never been taken out of its box.

The pictures don't show the worst of it, either. The pale winter daylight coming in through the windows, however grimily, bleaches out the dirt and the sticky layer of nicotine covering every surface. I didn't photograph the rodent droppings on the carpets, nor the dead ivy which reached in through the bathroom window. I didn't – and I am surprised to see this now – take a picture of the top-floor bedroom, the one I used to sleep in when I came to stay as a child. At some point, water had come through the ceiling, soaking everything. The roof had been fixed, or so my mother had told me, but that was all she had done. The entire room was a ruin. Nothing had been cleared, so the mattress and sheets had rotted away from damp, leaving a black mouldy hole where I had once slept.

Just after my parents split up, I had spent a long time at school embroidering a cross-stitch cushion cover with a design of a Spanish flamenco dancer, all red and yellow flounces, with black wool for her hair. I was immensely proud of my work and gave the finished piece to my mother as a Christmas present. From the moment my mother had moved to Rose Terrace, the cushion had been displayed in that upstairs room. I was always pleased to see it there, not only from pride in my achievement but also because it told me that she too, sometimes, had been pleased by what I had done.

The cushion must have been on the bed when the roof went, because I couldn't find even a single trace that it had ever been there. All that work and pride and love swallowed up into the black hole of rot.

Despite their technical and artistic failings, the photographs did the necessary trick. I went straight to the hospital to show them to Helen, who finally agreed that my mother could be discharged into a convalescent bed. At least that's how we sold it to her, although it was more a device to buy time, while my brother and I fixed up the house or found her a sheltered flat. Even this wasn't an immediate problem, because my mother wasn't recovering as the nurses had expected. Still frail and on oxygen, she was going to be in hospital for a few days yet.

Taking the pictures wasn't the only invasion I had to make into my mother's private world. With no prospect of her being able to return to Rose Terrace, the house couldn't be left as it was, but sorting through her stuff, however much of it was rubbish, seemed even more presumptuous and damaging.

Worse than that, I knew how much my mother would mind. Whenever in the past my brother and I had tried to tidy the house and get her organized, our intervention always ended up with my mother feeling less competent and more depressed. Although she was cheerful enough when we were with her, after we left she'd drink more and retreat from the world for a week or two in a haze of whisky and pity, convinced of her own failure.

Now, with her in hospital and me taking charge behind her back, I was terrified that this interference might be the final blow. I feared taking on the responsibility as well, because this step marked a switching of our roles. However little she had looked after me in the past, I was now going to have to look after her, and part of that had to include going into the house to make it right.

Whatever my reservations, I had no choice, and I wasn't going to be able to undertake this on my own either. Half-eaten and decaying food seemed to be in every room downstairs, and unless that got cleaned up soon, the chaos was going to turn into a full-scale public-health emergency of infestation that I was too squeamish to imagine, never mind sort out. More importantly, I felt I should spend the limited time I had in Worcester visiting my mother in the hospital. This meant I was going to have to do something worse than simply tidying up, which was inviting other people over the threshold to see the mess she had created. I opted not to tell my mother, in the hope that she'd believe I'd done it all on my own.

The social work team – proving once again that nothing

that had happened was any surprise to them at all – gave me the numbers for a couple of specialist cleaners, and a cheerful man called Jim said he had some time free in a day or two when I was coming up for my next visit.

He arrived on my mother's doorstep exactly as promised, with a battered blue van and his son Ed as back-up. A wiry man in his mid-fifties, Jim was cheery and direct, while Ed, taller and quieter, hung around behind him. I apologized at length before letting them in to look around, but Jim stepped into the hall without fear, then came straight back to tell me in his old-fashioned Worcester burr that they'd seen far worse and could get on with things straight away if I wanted. I could have cried with relief. Until now I'd assumed, without ever fully acknowledging the thought, that this mess was beyond any kind of sorting and would be mine to bear for ever.

For the next three hours, while I went to visit my mother in hospital and failed to tell her what was happening in her own home, the two of them worked like an entire army. When I came back to lock up, they'd not only removed any perishables that might attract vermin but had boarded up the back door and even started to work on the waist-high mountain of paper that had engulfed the dining room like a landslide, clearing out bag after bag of junk mail and old newspapers until their van was full. In amongst all of this they'd discovered two packets of rat poison and set some out in the spaces they'd cleared. My mother must have known she had an infestation and got as far as buying the cure, but she hadn't opened the boxes, let alone put the bait down.

Jim and Ed were good at being practical and getting on with the job, but they were also sensitive to what they were sorting through. Anything they thought might be useful, or personal, or simply that I might want to keep, was put to one side for me to check. From the paper midden, this consisted mostly of old bills and other post, almost all in its unopened envelopes, wrinkled with damp, which they stacked into big Tesco bags for life which, fortunately, my mother had also been collecting. These were lined up, one after another, in the sitting room, in the hope that she might get round to sorting them out when she was better.

In its ordinariness this was the most peculiar room in the house. While every other part was crammed with rubbish, my mother had kept this one space entirely uncluttered. The windows were murky, and dust lay on the ornaments on the side table and marble fireplace; damp air had seeped into the sofa cushions, leaving a smell of earth and old shed mixed in with the cigarettes, but even so the patterned brown carpet was clear to every corner, her chair set in front of the television with nothing in the way. The whole room looked just as it had done every time I had visited: a time capsule of normal life that remained even as disorder overwhelmed every other part of the house.

Usually hoarders fill the whole house, leaving no space unencumbered, so in this my mother was very unusual. I imagined her sitting in here in the evenings, able to believe that things were just fine as they were. Maybe this was where she saw herself when she assured me and Helen that she'd cope back at home with just a bit of help from carers. The chaos of the rest of her house didn't have to be imagined.

The call came at 2.15 in the morning. It actually came twice, because I missed the first one. My mobile phone had turned itself to silent, so I heard nothing; there was no ringing to jar me awake. The hospital, urgent, rang again on the land-line, and my husband staggered from room to room, fighting the confusion of sleep, unable to find a phone. When he did answer, he handed it over to me. One of the night nurses on the ward was asking me to come and see my mother.

'Do you mean now?' I asked, confused. Or did they mean in the morning?

I wasn't expecting this call, but the nurse hadn't been expect-ing to make it either. My mother had now been in the hospital for ten days, and when I'd last visited just a couple of days ago, the talk had once again been of discharge plans. Despite this, the nurse said I needed to come as soon as I could, so I set off, hoping that I was capable of driving without crashing when I was supposed to be fast asleep.

I'd only got as far as the high road overlooking Bath when my mobile rang again. Not far from home at all. I pulled over, just past the darkness of the trees, with the orange lights of the city below. This time it was my husband. I hadn't got there in time, nothing near it. My mother had already died, without me, and I was still hours away.

'You could come home,' he said. But it was three in the morning, I wouldn't sleep or rest if I went back, and then I would only have to set off again in the morning, upset and without the saving rush of adrenaline. So I carried on. Anyway, this was what you were meant to do as a child – at least I thought it was. I'd never really had a map of what being a daughter entailed, just as my mother had never really known what to do with me. This was my final chance to get it right. I would carry on to her deathbed, even if she hadn't waited for me to get there before dying.

I knew the route, having been up and down four times

in the last week alone, and now I was so awake that driving was easy. But in these early hours, the terrain was different, stripped of all its usual reference points. Steel refinery tanks towered by the roadside, floodlit and stark, where in daylight there were only trees. Further out, the steeples and towns I knew as my waymarkers had been swallowed up by the darkness. The motorway spooled on: lit, not lit, populated only by lorries and the occasional car. All the landscapes of the day – the Welsh hills and Severn plain, the looming hills of the Cotswold edge – had vanished, leaving me and the car and the road, all the way to Worcester, drowning out thought with radio documentaries on to which I fastened my entire being.

Just as telephones ring louder in the night, fluorescent lights shine brighter too. The hospital glowed like a beacon, or a factory that worked day and night, running on necessity. I arrived split in two, fully aware of the fatefulness of my journey but also able to think lucidly that the good side of turning up at 4 a.m. was that for once there were enough parking spaces. Then I remembered that I was the person at the centre of this serious time, so I wasn't supposed to be caring about such trivia.

The nurses took me in with kindness, seeming almost grateful that I had come. I wondered who did not. They sought an empty room to hold my grief, walking me through the darkened corridors where patients slept in wards on either side, breathing, even snoring, close in company. One nurse brought a cup of tea, while her colleague set off to find who had been with my mother. She needed to tell me that my mother's passing had been as peaceful as possible and that she had not died alone. In my confused state I didn't know whether this was a good thing or not. I felt guilty about not having arrived in time, but at the same time I was fairly certain that my mother had chosen not to wait for me.

I don't remember where the nurses took me under the dim night-time lighting, even though I knew the ward very well by now. Someone must have asked me if I would like to see my mother, and I thought yes, because this was what I was supposed to want, although I'd managed to get this far in life without ever seeing a dead body. I know I must have said yes too, even though I don't remember it happening, because the nurse walked me along the corridor to a corner that had been shrouded off with curtains.

At first I thought they had brought me to the wrong cubicle. An old, tired, dead person now lay there, who looked a bit like my grandmother but definitely wasn't my mother. Her false teeth had been taken out, hollowing her cheeks; her mouth lay open, her skin smooth and grey in the gloomy hush of the ward. I could see her mother and grandmother in that face, but most of all she seemed to be one of the medieval dead. If you visit enough cathedrals, their images are a familiar sight. On top of the memorial lies the bishop in all his earthly splendour, with his cape and crozier painted in red and gold. An impressive monument. If you look down, though, another statue lies beneath, wearing only a shroud. A reminder that death is a great leveller. Sometimes these are skeletons, sometimes cadavers crawling with worms. But often their faces look exactly like this: turned upwards, skin drawn in tight over the face, mouth open. The soul flown.

The nurse slipped away without saying anything, leaving me alone. What was I meant to do? I had no idea. Cry, I thought, but I was too dazed to feel anything at all. It turned out that

I couldn't manage to be a proper daughter even when she was dead. Not that this mattered to anyone except me – my mother was long gone. I looked at the window, latched and shut tight. Many nurses still perform the old ritual of letting a person's spirit out after death by opening a door or window. I imagined that my mother would have taken the first chance she could to flee, desperate to be reunited with the past that had smothered her entire life. Her mother, the dead children, even her father: they would all be there. No wonder she hadn't stayed for me.

In thinking that, I might have been wrong. Back at home, while I had been driving up the endless night motorway, my husband, unable to sleep, heard something in the corridor. Our house is old and so creaks and groans its way through the winter nights, but this, he said, was different. Maybe she did think of me at the end, coming back for one last visit. I'll never know for sure, but it's reassuring to believe I might have meant something to her after all. Only I wasn't at home to know. My mother and I never did get these things right.

Standing in the cubicle, I had no idea of any of this, and so held back, as far away from her as I had ever been and terrified of getting close. This was my last chance to be with her, or what was left of her, and I still couldn't bridge the gap. I had no audience, but in some ways that made it worse. Should I speak or stay silent? Would anything I did or didn't do make any difference anyway?

The only person left to be hurt was me, so I had to try to reach across the gap between us. Very slowly, I walked across the room and touched my mother on the hand, but this now felt as though it were made of the same inert material as the beds, the machinery, the floors. 'Goodbye,' I said very quietly, but even that seemed pointless, so I slipped away between the curtains, leaving her for the very last time.

Five-thirty in the morning is a blank space, empty, particularly in the darkness of winter. I was stranded in the hospital now, with nowhere to go and nothing to be done, so the nurses found me an unoccupied side room where I waited until it was an acceptable time to call my brother and aunt. There was no urgency any more, no need to wake them up to tell them the news that would not now change whatever time they heard it. Only in the day would they pass it on to my uncle and anyone else who needed to know.

I sat in the room with nothing to do. There had been a death, so the hospital system clicked into gear. Protocol had to be followed, and the nurses had left me with a pre-printed booklet containing all the information I needed as the next of kin. I read this three times over, and then every other piece of print in the room as well. None of this took long enough.

I wondered whether the nurses had given me privacy so that I could break down in tears and sob, or even sleep, but neither of these seemed possible. I was as impassive as a brick, but also entirely awake. In the end I spent an hour playing games on my phone to pass the time, feeling guilty about my own banality, but the distraction was more than welcome, it was essential. Anything was better than neutral walls and time eroding in slow seconds. Yet at the same time I couldn't leave: I wasn't yet ready to walk away from my mother. I didn't know which of us would be left more alone when I did.

❀ *4* ❀

bank statement: *grief and hoarding*

BANK STATEMENT

Worcester, 2013

Ink on paper, some water damage
and wrinkling

Gift of bank

THE MOST DIFFICULT part of my mother's dying wasn't that she was dead. That was a relatively simple thing to understand. Beyond that, everything else felt as though it were made of air. I could find nothing clear to hold on to. The death certificate told me that the cause of death was Type 2 Respiratory Failure and End Stage Chronic Obstructive Pulmonary Disease. These were facts, but at the same time they didn't explain why she'd died. In hospital her condition hadn't been improving, but it hadn't been getting worse either. She'd been happy and talking just two days beforehand; even the nurses had been talking about convalescent homes rather than preparing my brother and I for what might come next. I couldn't help wondering whether she'd decided to die. Perhaps anything, even oblivion, was better than immobility, forced dependence, losing her precious home.

For the first few days I felt emptied and numb, but nothing more. My feelings refused to accord with anyone's expectations, including my own. At the school gate, people came up to me and squeezed my arm in sympathy, saying that they were sorry to hear my news, but all I could do was stand and nod awkwardly, afraid that if I said anything at all I would give the game away and reveal that I wasn't mourning properly. I wasn't even sure I was mourning at all.

At least from the outside this looked like grief. Inside I knew the appearance was a sham. Death wasn't going to renew the mother–daughter bond, far from it. I was just as bad a daughter as I had ever been. Possibly I was even worse than before. Who does not mourn their own parent? Only me, it seemed.

I knew what the loss of a parent was meant to feel like. When my father had died five years before, the grief had occupied me entirely. I sobbed until I could hardly breathe at the funeral, his wicker coffin an unbearable sight. Each time an event happened without him for the first time, whether that was making a gin and tonic for my stepmother and me – always his job – or celebrating Christmas, I felt a sharp shock of pain all over again.

In the face of my mother's death I found myself unable to feel anything at all. Dropped into a dim land without signposts, I had to forge my own way through. The only emotions that made their way through the fog were occasional flashes of disconnected irritation. I felt them when I was trying to get stubborn bureaucracies to shut down my mother's accounts, or listening to other people telling me about their own experiences of their parents dying. That only reminded me of what my mother had done when my father died.

Then, too, the phone call had come in the early hours. The next day, I decided to phone my mother because I thought she would want to know. This was the right thing to do, but I'd also hoped that she would be able to sympathize with me, to understand what I had lost. Talking to anyone else who remembered his presence made him less far away – at least that was my hope.

There was a short hissing pause down the phone line, and then she did tell me how terrible it was. For her. In the nearly forty years since they'd divorced, she'd seen him once, at my wedding. Yet her sense of loss and upset was so overwhelming that she didn't even pause to think how I might feel. Almost unable to speak, but raging, I cut the phone call short. Already desperately missing one parent, the last thing I wanted was to be reminded that the other one had always been absent as well.

For days I seethed and boiled with rage, my grief alchemically transmuted into easier, baser anger. I stalked about the house, tears of fury pricking my eyes as I tried to stop myself thinking, over and over again, that the wrong bloody parent was dead.

If I thought about it calmly, I understood even then that it had been the selfishness of depression and alcohol talking. Now I can also see that her life had contained so much pain that any new loss, even of a part of her distant past, was an agony too much to bear. Right at that moment, though, I didn't have a single atom of emotional energy to spare, and could not bring myself to be kind and understanding. What I needed, more than anything, was my mother. But of course she wasn't there; she was still lost in her own world, as she had been for all her life and all mine too. In losing my father, all I got was yet another reminder that I'd never had a mother in the first place.

I never confronted my mother with what she had done. She might have understood, and she would have apologized. But the reproach would have sent her back to bed for days, probably into the comforting numbness of whisky. Then it would have stopped her cleaning up, once again. Weeks of silence and unanswered phone calls would have followed. None of this would bring my father back, nor provide me with the mother I so badly wanted. So I said nothing at all. I packed away my exasperation and upset and got on with living.

Now, I didn't weep. There was no giant hole in my life, no aching reminders that made me howl with tears. Instead, I walked through the days as though they were glue, dazed and unyielding.

Fortunately there was plenty to distract me from my failure to feel. The hospital knew what they were doing when they gave me that neat leaflet of instructions for the bereaved. Every death causes a chain reaction of administrative consequences: finance and inheritance have to be sorted out, coffins chosen and flowers ordered. Undertakers phoned up with questions I'd never even considered before, banks needed certificates, utility companies presented me with bills.

My brother took charge of my mother's funeral while I, having been an executor before, dealt with the will. Only of course there wasn't one to be found anywhere. Now that I didn't have to worry about being respectful, I could tear through the house like a whirlwind. Stacked in one corner of my mother's study, I did unearth a grey metal filing box, tucked away behind one of the armchairs, but this was a remnant of a more organized time, long since passed. Its hinges were stiff with rust, and all it contained was paperwork about my parents' divorce and the purchase of Rose Terrace, and a handful of financial statements to do with my great-grandmother's probate, every one more than thirty years old. No sign of a will at all. I'd expected this, knowing that only some kind of miracle would have allowed my mother to produce a functional will, never mind preserve it safely afterwards.

To find out what my mother had left behind, I needed to turn detective. The bags of post that Jim and Ed had carefully stacked in the sitting room, waiting for my mother's return, would never be looked at by her now. Instead, they became my evidence. I loaded a dozen or more heavy sacks into the boot of the car and brought them home, where they trailed the smell of must and cigarettes and the last ten years of sadness into my own house like a ghost.

I tried to sort all this paper into order but found that I could only work in the shortest of bursts. Sometimes the smell of dampness became too strong to bear, and I had to walk away; more often I was too disheartened by what I found to carry on. As I sifted through bag after bag of miserable and sodden envelopes, I wasn't only reconstructing her finances, I was also revealing my mother's recent life. Very little of this was anything I wanted to know.

For the last few years my mother had been reassuring me that the drinking was under control at last. She'd seemed sober whenever I spoke to her on the phone, so I'd chosen to believe this. Her bank statements told another story, of trips to the local off-licence, twice or sometimes three times a week. Laid out in columns were not only the dates but the times, usually in the evenings. I imagined her at home, wanting to be good, trying not to give in to temptation but, in the end, as darkness fell at seven or eight o'clock, the ghosts or the terrors inevitably became too much. Then she would go and buy another bottle of whisky.

Other bills told even more desperate stories. The boiler had broken two years ago, because that's when her gas bill had suddenly dropped to zero. Two whole years without hot water or central heating. The electricity usage, in turn, rocketed, and in those figures I can see her bending over to plug in those electric radiators, one by one, all over the house.

In the days after her death I could only look at these clues with forensic detachment. I opened envelope after envelope with the remote efficiency of an automaton. Apart from the drinking, what these bags of letters also revealed was that the house had been sliding into decline for some time. Some of the post that Jim and Ed had so respectfully collected was very old indeed, going back eight years or more, the paper flattened and damp, buried at the very bottom of the heap and forgotten entirely.

Not opening the post was a habit of my mother's that went back a while; I already knew that much. The problem with ignoring official envelopes is that small problems can turn into nightmares.

A few years ago, in another bad patch, my mother had managed to ignore a traffic fine. After many letters, this had gone to court, but she'd failed to open the summons too. Finally, the debt had been passed to a collection agent, the amount owed having escalated from a simple £150 into thousands. Somehow – I don't know by what means – this information had got through to my mother and she had paid up. I suspect that a bailiff had come and hammered on the door, but she never told me that bit. All she confessed, in a timid and apologetic voice over the phone, was that she'd taken the money out of her savings to pay the bill. I was furious. Not with her, but with the way that the system had extracted money from a vulnerable woman. I said to her that I would have fought it if she'd told me before. My outrage didn't help anything. Instead, like almost anything else I did or said, it only served to make my mother feel worse all over again.

Most of what I worked my way through was bureaucratic and impersonal: bills, reminders and more junk mail. Envelopes with personal handwriting were rare, and mostly turned out to be Christmas cards from friends I'd never heard of. There were the odd surprises though. Days into my work, from deep in the piles of paper, I pulled out a card in my mother's own handwriting, addressed to me. Opening the dark green envelope, I found that it was my birthday card, another missed day from who knows how many years ago. Its lateness turned out in the end to be perfect timing. My mother died only two weeks before my birthday, and by the time I discovered the card, there were only a few days to go. Her depression and forgetting was transformed into a gesture from beyond the grave; the card finally outwitting her and arriving on time in the end. This almost made me smile. Random chance had succeeded in doing what my own mother could rarely manage to.

Sometimes I'd find my own black scrawl on an envelope, giving me an electric shock of recognition and disappointment every time it turned up in the bags. Occasionally, my letters hadn't been opened at all. More often the contents had been stuffed back in and the envelope sent back into the heap to disappear.

Over the last few years, I hadn't written to her with news, as we spoke on the phone most weeks. Instead, I sent photographs of my daughter, E, and pictures that she'd drawn, trying to conjure a grandmother out of the unlikely material of my mother. Like so many of my efforts, it didn't work at all.

When E was a baby, my mother had found being around her very difficult indeed. I was bewildered and hurt, but this was old pain as well as new. I had needed to see my mother loving this baby as proof that she had cared for me too when I had been so helpless and small. But she couldn't do it. It took her a long time to come and see me after my daughter was born, and when she did finally visit, she found it hard even to look at E, never mind hold her. I've blocked out the rest, partly because I was sleep-shot and disorientated. Mainly, though, I didn't want to remember something that had upset me so much. My husband took one photograph on a later visit which contains all the difficulty of our relationship. I'm sitting on the sofa, holding E, while my mother is standing way behind, keeping her distance. She's probably going for a cigarette, but her posture suggests that small children are fissile and dangerous material, to be avoided.

When my mother left, I wept. I didn't mind so much for E. She was too small to understand, and in any case she had me and T; one grandparent more or less wasn't going to matter. I cried for myself instead. What upset me was that I had seen with my own eyes what I'd always known. My mother had never really known how to care for a child and so I'd never been looked after. Grandparenting can be a second chance, but my mother had no desire to revisit or even acknowledge an experience that, for her, had been hellish the first time around.

I never gave up and kept sending the pictures and photos of E, but now, as I sorted through the piles, almost every single one of these reappeared: some in their envelopes, some just thrown back into the heap. Every time one emerged from the chaos I was wounded all over again. Worst of all was the photograph of my daughter, smiling, blonde, not even two years old. Warped with the damp, with a pattern of mud splattered across it, this looked as though my mother had thrown it to the ground and stamped on it. Except I don't really believe my mother felt enough even to do that. Nothing, it seemed, could make her care.

Things had got better as my daughter had grown. The

problem seemed to be with babies rather than children, and eventually when E was about three or four, she and my mother gradually made friends through the medium of otters. These were my daughter's favourite animal, and my mother bought her otter-themed presents as well as posting pictures and cuttings from the paper. Their connection was tenuous and distant, but I was grateful for whatever little my mother felt able to give.

When I first started to clear Rose Terrace, on the very top of one of the piles in the dining room I had found an otter picture that my mother had cut out from the *Telegraph*, ready to send. It might even have got to us one day. I gave it to my daughter as a last present from Grandma, wanting her to know that this absent, unreadable woman had, despite everything, been thinking of her. I hoped that she'd been thinking of me too.

There was a reason that Jim and Ed, along with all the nurses, were so calm and understanding. Nothing my mother had done was unusual. I wished that I'd known even a small part of this before she died. Then I might have been both less embarrassed about the way she was living and more forgiving.

Because this behaviour is so common, there's a simple word for it too: hoarding. The technical definition of this is 'persistent difficulty discarding or parting with possessions regardless of their actual value', which is a fair description of what my mother had been doing, or not doing, for the last twenty years.

I found this much out very quickly. With Worcester a two-hour drive away, I could only go up to clear my mother's house one day each week, which left me plenty of time in front of my computer in between. I was supposed to be sorting out my mother's financial affairs: totting up debits and credits from the damp statements I'd pulled out of the pile, closing down accounts and asking for refunds until I was able to make a list of her net worth for the Inland Revenue to consider. Instead, I was reading forums and chat boards, leaflets and blog posts, trying to pick my way through research papers and books, trying to understand what had taken place.

While I could tell myself that this was facing up to what my mother had done, the truth was that I was trying to escape from the reality of what had happened, from the spiderwebs, the nicotine, the rodent traps and ruining damp. Most of all I was running away from the deep and unfathomable unhappiness that had brought my mother to live this way.

My own feelings about my mother and our fractured relationship terrified me. The only thing I knew for certain was that if these were released after forty years of clumsy repression, they would drown me. So I reacted as I had always done, and warded off any flicker of emotion by disappearing into a clear imperishable space of words and ideas. I found this a much easier place to inhabit.

I discovered many things in my searches, not least that I was far from the only person to have become interested in hoarding. In fact the subject had recently become a hot topic in psychiatry.

The description of hoarding above comes from the *DSM-V*, the most recent edition of a book which is the bible for American psychologists and psychotherapists and is increasingly being used as the definitive field guide in Britain too. The initials stand for *Diagnostic and Statistical Manual of Mental Disorders, Fifth Edition*, which pretty much sets out the stall for what the book does. If a pattern of behaviour is in the *DSM*, it's a disorder which can be treated; if it's not, then a person is just eccentric or untidy. What is and is not contained in the *DSM* through each of its revisions is the source of much argument and sometimes fury, a discussion which goes on not only amongst professionals but amongst the general population as well. The most notorious example of this is homosexuality, which, despite raging protest, was included as an abnormality in the *DSM* right up until 1973.

Hoarding is a relatively new condition, only arriving in the *DSM* at its last revision in 2013. Until then it appeared only as a subsidiary symptom of OCD, but now it has become a pathology all of its own. Difficulty discarding isn't enough on its own; a psychiatrist would need to observe several other symptoms in order to diagnose someone with Hoarding Disorder.

> – This difficulty is due to a perceived need to save the items and to distress associated with discarding them.
> – The difficulty discarding possessions results in the accumulation of possessions that congest and clutter active living areas and substantially compromise their intended use. If living areas are uncluttered, it is only because of the interventions of third parties (e.g. family members, cleaners, authorities).
> – The hoarding causes clinically significant distress or impairment in social, occupational, or other important areas of functioning (including maintaining a safe environment for self and others).

There are a couple of caveats attached. The hoarding should not be the result of another medical condition, and is not better explained by another diagnosis such as OCD. But once you've jumped these hurdles, a sufferer can be diagnosed with the disorder.

Now I had a definite name for what happened to my mother. The criteria delineated a clear and recognizable pattern of behaviour, and my mother accumulated clutter exactly as they described. She was suffering from Hoarding Disorder.

With that diagnosis established, there were a couple of refinements that the *DSM* wanted me to consider, the first of which was whether 'symptoms are accompanied by excessive collecting or buying or stealing of items that are not needed or for which there is no available space'.

In short, there are two ways of becoming a hoarder. One, the fast-track route if you like, is by actively going out and collecting things to fill the house, whether that's from shops or car-boot sales, skips or possibly other people's rubbish bins. Or even, as the *DSM* suggests, by taking stuff without paying for it.

The other is by the slower, simpler process of not throwing things away. That's the path my mother chose. She didn't go out looking for things to keep; books and newspapers only came into the house because she wanted to read them. But they rarely left. Nor did the broken-down fridges and freezers – three of them – nor the junk mail. The process may be slower, but over time it achieves the same results. The ground floor of Rose Terrace was a huge hoard of papers, carrier bags, ancient food and old fridges, which, in the words of the *DSM*, caused clinically significant impairment in her life.

Finally, the *DSM* asked me to consider the question of awareness. What does the hoarder actually think they are doing?

Indicate whether hoarding beliefs and behaviors are currently characterized by:

– Good or fair insight: The individual recognizes that hoarding-related beliefs and behaviors are problematic.
– Poor insight: The individual is mostly convinced that hoarding-related beliefs and behaviors are not problematic despite evidence to the contrary.
– Absent insight (i.e. delusional beliefs about hoarding): The individual is completely convinced that hoarding-related beliefs and behaviors are not problematic despite evidence to the contrary.

As her conversation with both me and the social workers at the hospital showed, my mother, like many hoarders, didn't believe that there was the slightest thing wrong with her house. Given the aid of just a couple of grab rails and a few weeks of visiting carers, she believed that she would be able to live there as she'd always done. The idea that the carers might refuse to come inside, or the house might collapse around her from neglect, never appeared to enter her mind. There's no question that, under the rules set by the *DSM*, my mother would easily have qualified for a diagnosis of Hoarding Disorder with poor or perhaps even absent insight.

By dying, my mother swerved the need for intervention of any kind, but with a medical label it might have been easier for me to get her some help. Or at the very least the social workers would have believed me when I said the house was uninhabitable. I might have felt less as though the entire sorry state of affairs was my responsibility.

At the same time as knowing that the label could have helped me when my mother was alive, and would undoubtedly help others in the future, I found the *DSM* profoundly frustrating. The accumulation of stuff warps people's lives, often for decades. Hoarders are alienated from their families, they are evicted and lose custody of their children, their marriages fail, their health suffers, all because the heaps of rubbish take over. But all the *DSM* told me was what I had already seen. It refused to say what I should do about it or why this disaster had happened.

The guidance leaflets, research papers and books didn't seem to find this a problem. Most of the academic research only wanted to pathologize the condition further. Hoarding Disorder is listed and tested and checked with standard questionnaires to see if it is co-morbid with other diagnoses. The brainwaves of sufferers are recorded as they are forced to throw away other people's stuff and then their own; markers unique to the neural architecture of hoarder brains are sought; hoarders are poked, prodded and measured in an attempt to find a biochemical reason for their behaviour. Yet throughout these processes, the researchers seem remarkably reluctant to ask the sufferers of Hoarding Disorder what they think is going on.

The real story was always missing. I wanted to know how people ended up in this bleak place. I wanted to hear about the events that hurt them so badly that their only refuge from the pain was to bury their memories in a tidal wave of belongings. The psychiatrists didn't choose to see any of this at all. It's much easier to measure brainwaves, even if that won't help people get any better.

Even the self-help books, which did at least offer remedies, weren't interested in why. The accepted treatment for Hoarding Disorder is Cognitive Behavioural Therapy (CBT), in other words a focused approach aimed at acclimatizing the hoarder to the idea that throwing away their possessions won't be as painful as they think. The books and leaflets addressed at sufferers and their families all used this approach. With some neat mental retraining and a handful of checklists and quizzes designed to lead people towards a realization of their errors, thoughts can be recast, piles of stuff will be sent to the tip and all will be well with the world.

The apogee of this approach was a leaflet aimed at counsellors and therapists which described best practice for working with hoarders. Its conventional CBT-based approach left little room for actual insight. 'People may be attached to possessions which have personal meanings,' suggested the caption to a line drawing of a photograph in a frame and a fountain pen. You don't say.

The thoughts of hoarders themselves appeared in speech bubbles scattered across the leaflet. When one of these told me that a man called Harry thought he had a problem with tidiness, my exasperation boiled over into rage. The many and varied experiences, memories and associations that have brought people to hoarding scarcely got any kind of mention except as an aside. The physician had become king (or queen), and the patient's thoughts and experiences were no longer worth reproducing, or possibly even listening to, unless reduced to the most mundane truisms.

That this leaflet incensed me was the first sign that I was grieving. My soul couldn't provide the sadness that other people were expecting; instead, I flared up against diagrams and inanities that shouldn't have mattered to me at all. But I did so because I was seeing this intellectual stupidity as being entirely aimed at my mother. No one wanted to hear her unique and complex story, or even to help me discover it.

Instead, she had been reduced to a problem to be solved, a product to be inserted into a system which believed it could teach her to think better and more correct thoughts. If only she could do this, then all of her problems would have evaporated into nothing and her carpets would have been clean again.

How did psychiatry, in the face of the magnificent messiness that is the human mind, come to such a simplistic and Gradgrindian worldview? Even I would prefer to be a hoarder than be treated so mechanically.

There's also a particular irony in treating hoarders in this way. These are people dramatizing the turmoil of their own inner lives through the state of their homes, people for whom objects above all have meaning and significance. They seem to me to be natural Freudians, but instead of finding the symbols of their internal drama in dreams, they find them – and make them – in the world around them. But the pragmatic psychologists who practise CBT don't want to understand what a hoard might be saying; they and the hoarders stare at each other across a gulf of incomprehension.

There's another, far more straightforward reason to dislike the way CBT is used to treat hoarding, which is that it doesn't work very well. Even the most successful studies show that, after a year or two, only 20 per cent of hoarders show a sustained and continued improvement in their living conditions. And these are the people who want to change, who have volunteered to be part of a research project because they, unlike most hoarders, are aware that they have a problem. The ones who don't think they have a problem wouldn't even begin a course of treatment, let alone change as a result. What's more, reading between the lines, the benefits of the programme may not entirely have come from the CBT element. The hoarders were treated for a year or more by a therapist they saw once or twice a week and who sometimes visited their homes. This wasn't eight weeks of by-the-book reframing of thoughts, it was a proper long-term relationship with a therapist who, I can only guess, began to understand the hoarding and all the history it represented. Even then, it only managed to improve the lives of one in five of them.

Nothing in these papers could help me. I didn't want to know which bits of my mother's brain chemistry might have been failing her. All I wanted was to discover who she had been underneath the things which had piled up around her.

Even so, my research hadn't been a total waste of time and emotional energy. What I did get from both the academic papers and the self-help manuals was an acute appreciation of the physical state of my mother's house. Hoarders' homes are rated on a scale of one to nine. One is that state just a little bit beyond messy, where it might take a bit of effort and some thinking to tidy the stacks of paper and misplaced objects. Nine, meanwhile, is a space as crammed as a warehouse, where some or all of the rooms are unusable and the fabric of the building itself has been damaged. I found it hard to say where Rose Terrace might fall on the scale. While the house was structurally unsound in a whole variety of ways, my mother had been using the majority of the rooms, even if most other people might have chosen not to. Let's call that a seven.

This scale is often accompanied by questionnaires designed to open the hoarder's eyes, so that at last they appreciate the state in which they have been living. For me, what these did was recall, very clearly, the final state of my mother's house.

A question about insects reminded me of the thick cobwebs which hung across the dining-room ceiling in a way I had never seen before. Each one had become weighted with years of dust and nicotine, which left them draped like swags of thick grey fabric. Only this single room was affected: the spiders clearly preferred it there and nowhere else, although I couldn't really see what the difference was myself. In any case the spiders themselves were long since departed, leaving only their abandoned homes. Maybe even they couldn't stand the filth. Either that or the smoking had killed them.

In many cases not even the thorough inquisition of a questionnaire can persuade a hoarder to acknowledge the scale of their problem; very many of them radically underestimate the mess they live in. To counter this, one researcher – Professor Randy Frost, who pioneered the first research into hoarding in the early 1990s – created a pictorial scale by amassing empty cardboard boxes, papers and clothes in a faculty flat at his university. Rather than describing their mess, hoarders can point at the staged photograph which looks the most familiar.

Scaled again from one to nine, his pictures of rooms carefully stacked with stuff are undoubtedly useful, which is why they are reproduced in every single book about hoarding that you will ever read. Researcher after researcher reports how much more accurately hoarders describe the actual state of their homes when they indicate one of these pictures rather than conceptualizing the mess in words. Those who treat hoarders have found that they tend to think visually rather than in words, and so for them photographs are easier to comprehend than text.

They may help psychologists and sufferers, but the

pictures didn't work for me at all. I could make no connection between my mother's filthy house and these clean and sanitized recreations. Only in the photographs of real-life hoards did the images start to seem familiar, like tourist-board shots of a place I had once visited. Seeing a black and white picture of dark stains of rotting food running down the front of a fridge door, I found myself thinking, 'Oh, a kitchen just like hers.'

One reason I could see my mother's life in these pictures is because every hoard becomes generic and universal. The squalor depicted is overwhelming, the possessions so many and compressed that they can only ever be anonymous. It's impossible to read anything into these heaps and piles when no single object is identifiable. There are no photographs, no personality on view at all. It's always paper and boxes, plastic bags and junk, rubbish and rotting food, as though all the hoarders have folded up their own individuality and buried it deep amongst their great wall of possessions. These towering heaps of stuff make upset visible, but that's all they express. Without words and explanations, it's almost impossible to know what distress these messes represent.

The more I read and the more images I saw, the more I started to feel that Rose Terrace wasn't so bad after all. The toilet had always been usable, and used; almost everything that my mother had kept was paper and clothes, not food or other people's rubbish, or even her own bodily waste. This last is apparently not uncommon and is known as 'wet hoarding'. To my relief, my mother no longer had any pets either. That would have been the hardest thing to bear. The picture that stayed with me longest showed someone's sitting room. At the centre were the remains of a dead dog, reduced to no more than a skeleton and a dark stain on the carpet where it had lain down and died in front of the sofa.

The cleaning I'd been doing was straightforward in comparison: almost everything I found could be picked up without too much revulsion once I got used to it, and I didn't have to wear a mask or a biohazard suit. But that's what the cleaners and social workers had been saying to me from the start. *We've seen far worse. Don't worry. It's more common than you think.*

None of this satisfied me. What my mother had done may have been common, but in its particularity it was also extraordinary. I needed to know why this disaster had happened to her and what she had meant by the mess she had left behind.

timeline: *her own story*

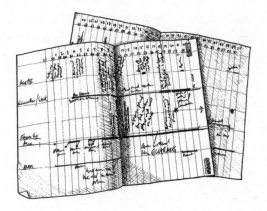

HANDWRITTEN TIMELINE OF A LIFE

Worcester, post 1987

Two sheets of A4 paper, marks where
previously held together by sticky tape;
writing in seven colours of pen.

Provenance unknown

Heading up the M5 four days later to start the clearance of Rose Terrace, I was as apprehensive as when I'd first visited after the policeman's call. My logical mind understood that my mother had died four days ago, but at the same time I knew that if I were going to Worcester, it could only be to see her. Driving up an everyday motorway of Eddie Stobart trucks and flat cloud, I couldn't help remembering the footsteps that my husband had heard after her death. It didn't seem likely that my mother would haunt me, but I could easily believe that she would refuse to leave the house she had loved so dearly. I half expected her to be there waiting for me when I opened the front door.

I'd planned my visit with care, preparing for every single ordeal I might find on arrival. A crate in the back of the car held rolls of black bin liners, rubber gloves and a selection of the most industrial cleaning products I could lay my hands on: bleach, mould spray, nylon scrubbers and disposable floor wipes. My green credentials had been ditched; all I wanted was to get this house clean. I'd also learned from my own renovation of a mouldy, abandoned house and bought a bulk pack of disposable plastic gloves from the builder's merchants. I had a flask of coffee and a can of something called Odour Destroyer Spray. On top of the crate sat my battery-powered radio, ready to ward off ghosts, atmospheres and too much thinking.

After I pulled up in the grey light of mid-morning, I sat in the car and tarried, just as I had on my first visit two weeks before. This time I phoned my husband and told him straight that I didn't want to do this, but now that I'd gone to the trouble of driving all the way there, he couldn't say very much apart from that I would feel better if I did it. There was nothing to do but agree. I only had a short day here, and I was wasting it already.

When I finally got the padlock to unclasp and pushed the door open, I stood on the threshold for a few seconds, but all my fear had evaporated. The worst had already happened, and I knew what I would see in front of me. There were no ghosts, no surprises. All that remained was the dark and the mess, along with a strong smell of damp.

Fetching my box of ammunition from the car, I set up a basecamp in the hall and tried to take control. First step was several long squirts of air deodorizer into each corner of the room. There was no way that this was going to get rid of the seeping smell of damp paper, cigarettes and mould, but it was a start. My next step was the radio, which I turned up loud, then balanced on a stack of papers. That done, I wondered where on earth I was going to begin.

I took a few steps into the dining room, but foliage pressed up against the window, and the sticky layer of dirt on the glass meant that only the faintest traces of the morning's light got through. Through the gloom I thought I could make out fresh rodent droppings on the few clear spaces of carpet. There were probably things living in these piles that I didn't want to meet. Ahead of me the kitchen was even darker and messier, with a pool of mucky water on the floor. Jim and Ed had tried to clear that up last time I'd been here, but the puddle had somehow regenerated. I couldn't see enough to work but didn't dare switch any of the lights on for fear of the whole house fusing in some terrible coming together of electricity and water.

The stairwell was at least getting light from the landing window above. I looked at the books stacked three deep on every tread. These could be packed away to go to charity – I'd brought some cardboard boxes too – but when I picked a couple up, the pages were buckled with damp and impregnated with the smell of cigarettes. I put them back down on their pile.

The mess had overwhelmed the house and was now threatening to do the same to me. I'd come in full of good intentions but was starting to see how my mother might have felt defeated by the hoard, unable to know where to begin. Her stuff emanated its own inertia, defying me to make a difference here in any way. Even if I picked up a bin liner and filled it with rubbish, then filled another five, my effort would leave no visible trace. So why bother beginning?

I wandered into the sitting room, where there was at least the space to think. Wondering about packing up some of the ornaments which had survived, I picked up the glass bird from the mantelpiece, then put it down again. It seemed pointless to clear away in here, the last remaining part of her home which was cared for and orderly, when the only thing I wanted to do was get rid of the mess. Somehow.

My drifting was interrupted by the rap of the doorknocker echoing into the hall, followed by a cheery 'Morning!' as the door was pushed open. Jim and Ed were back to rescue me.

I'd rung Jim last week to tell them that my mother had died, so they already knew that today's work would be different. No longer were they trying to replace the mess with normal life, although I'm not sure that this would ever have been possible.

Instead, their work would be damage limitation, taking out
the remaining rice and pasta, dried herbs and cans from the
kitchen, removing the mouldy paper and anything else that
might deteriorate further. Then I could deal with whatever
inert matter remained.

After saying how sorry they were for my loss, they set to
work, bagging and carrying and lifting and moving, until the
two of them had once again got rid of more in an hour than I
could have managed alone in a week, or even a year.

I tried to be useful around them but quickly realized that
I was getting in the way. For half an hour or so I sat on the
damp sofa in the sitting room and picked through the contents of the metal filing box. I'd searched it once already to
make sure it didn't contain a will; now I examined each piece
of paper with care, looking out for life insurance policies or
deeds. But there was nothing relevant to be found. Ancient
history all. Shutting the rusty lid, I put the box to one side,
wondering what I should do as Jim and Ed stacked bin bags
two high in the hall and then marched them out to the van. I
wasn't contributing much to the cause.

Going back upstairs, I threw a broken blind fitting, an old
perfume bottle and a couple of unidentifiable pieces of plastic
into a black bin liner of my own, and added another stained
and faded towel to the recycling pile I'd begun earlier. Then I
looked at the pile of papers that poured, like a landslide, out
of the door of my mother's study and on to the red carpet of
the landing.

The study was tiny, originally a box room with space for
no more than a chest of drawers and a single bed. Where this
would have stood, my mother had put her grand Victorian
bank desk, with its carved rosewood drawers and green

leather top. Along the wall behind where she sat was a row of white IKEA bookshelves, assembled and installed by me and my brother on a previous clearing-up trip many years earlier. I have a distinct picture of the three of us putting the shelves together on a sunny day with light streaming in through the sash window, but things must have been in a bad way if my brother and I had come up together on a joint mission to tidy Rose Terrace. Had we known what was to happen later, the chaos wouldn't have seemed so terrible at all.

On a good day, when she had first moved in, this room must have been a lovely place for my mother, sitting at her desk next to the sash window which filled almost the whole end wall, framing the view of tiled roofs and pale stone spires like a luminous painting. Now, as I stood in the doorway with a roll of black bin liners, I could see that it was a long time since my mother had sat at the desk, or even reached it. The room was filled with an indiscriminate sea of paper and books, spreading out from a steep stack on top of the desk, flooding across the floor and over the threshold towards where I was standing. More paperwork spewed out from the open drawers of her desk, some settling on top of the bookshelves in drifts.

Even so, clearing this room still felt like the easy option. I could work in light streaming in from an unobscured window and, amazingly, could see almost no damp. The water that had devastated the bedroom above had not come through this ceiling, and while it had been the leaking radiator in the corner of this room which had rotted the ceiling in the hall, in here all it had done was eat up a small corner of carpet. Somehow, sandwiched in between all the deepest damage to the house, the study was still intact. What I had to deal with here was a more ordinary kind of mess, not the dank mouldering squalor that filled the downstairs, nor the depressingly personal detritus in her bedroom.

At first I only found rubbish, filling bin bag after bin bag with old receipts, blank and battered sheets of A4 and instruction leaflets for long-defunct appliances, keeping only old bank statements, legal letters and anything else that I thought might be useful one day. These were few and far between, so I threw things away as though I were on a production line, the radio burbling away next to me for company.

As I made inroads into the pile, I started to realize that there was a kind of order to be found in here, even though it had been disguised as chaos. My mother's study contained every single piece of paper that mattered. These weren't the bank statements or utility bills, although I carried on collecting these, just in case. What I began to dig out of the heap were clues to my mother's past life. The further I got into the room, the more I found, as though the desk had a magnetic charge and had been drawing them all in towards itself.

Many of these papers were simply the kind of thing that you expect to find when clearing a dead person's house. I pulled out my mother's old passport, issued in 1967, with me included from the start and my brother an afterthought, added in a year later. There are stamps from holidays in Spain and France, and in her picture she's smiling. This is the relic of an ordinary life, with an intact family, holidays and good times. Perhaps that's why she kept it so long.

More surprising yet were the photographs. I was struck by one kind in particular. Black and white, they had been set into card presentation cases, which meant I had to open them up to see what was inside. Each time, I would find my mother and father, probably before they married, pictured at a dance

*My mother in her passport photo,
looking forward to a foreign holiday in
about 1967.*

or a party, surrounded by friends, laughing and happy. He possesses a good job and prospects, she is beautiful and at this moment, saved for ever in the shot, they are the king and queen of the world. In these pictures my mother is a person I'd never known, sparkling with life and the excitement of being young. Her hair is short and curled, the dresses skim her narrow waist then flare out into a skirt made for dancing. The war is over, there is fabric and optimism to spare, and my mother appears glad to be alive, my father pleased to be spending the time next to her.

One by one the photos stacked up next to me in a pile on the stairs. I was surprised how many of these my mother had

My mother as a teenage schoolgirl.

My father and mother at what might be his college ball in the late 1950s.

kept. Of course she was a hoarder, so she wouldn't throw them away, but I can't help thinking that she'd saved these ones in particular as a reminder that life hadn't always been bleak. Once upon a time she'd had a future to look forward to. Except these aren't only happy photographs, they are also mementos of my father. Perhaps it wasn't only my brother and me that she'd lost after the divorce. I'd never thought to ask this question before, but in the pale January light I looked at my father's optimistic face in yet another picture and wondered whether she'd carried on loving him even after they'd split apart.

The other thing that struck me about these photographs, and it hit me hard, is how much she was smiling out of them, radiating not only charm and glamour but also a straight-forward happiness. In all the time I had known her, I couldn't remember her looking like that, not once.

On holiday in 1970. My mother has two children under five and looks exhausted.

By lunchtime, I'd scarcely shifted enough papers to get in through the study door, but I'd already had enough of dust and memories and needed a break, so I decided to walk into Worcester. I wanted lunch and fresh coffee, as well as some kind of battery-powered light so that I could see into the dark corners downstairs. Most of all I wanted to breathe fresh air and walk amongst order and normality, in the company of people who had no idea what had been going on in my mother's house. Then I might have the strength to start again.

By the time I returned, Jim and Ed had already filled their van with black bags. There wasn't time for a second trip before the end of the day, so they set off to the tip, already booked to return when I did next week. With another hour at least before I needed to leave, I went back alone to my work in the study.

Every so often, between the sheets of blank paper and other rubbish, I would pull out a piece of paper in my mother's handwriting. She hadn't been dead long enough for this to shock me yet, so I'd glance over what they said and then, mostly, keep them. Many were notes she'd made about the history of the house, recording the names of previous occupants and owners, interspersed with a few ancient scraps which seemed to be from when she and my father split up. Most surprising was a list, my mother's handwriting filling page after page with the details of how the contents of our old house would be divided after the divorce, with cash values. This was their marriage set out in stuff: she got the green sofa, the cookery books and an electric blanket; he took the Wedgwood coffee set, the lawnmower and the piano. Every last item is enumerated and allocated, down to the box of shoe-cleaning brushes and the tea towels. The fury and hatred of their separation has rendered their marriage down into no more than its physical relics. Even my brother and I have been written out of this story. To inventory the house, my mother has organized her list by rooms, including bedrooms one, two, three and four. One of them must have been mine, but it doesn't even bear my name. Our family has disappeared; all that remains are the solid objects and the spaces in which they live. This list marked the point where my mother chose inanimate matter rather than people.

Much of the correspondence I found seemed to relate to either the divorce or Rose Terrace. My mother must have taken all her pent-up emotions, from losing me and my brother and even missing my father as well, and invested them all in her new home instead. A house, after all, wasn't ever going to leave her, however badly she treated it.

With each new piece of paper, I kept trying to skim over the words, not get too drawn in to what I found. All I wanted to do was sort things: keep or not, rubbish or heirloom. On the pile or in the black bag. Done, move on. I could read them later, if I wanted to, but right now I was desperate to get the place cleared. My intention held until I found the two sheets of lined paper stuck together to make one great strip. On this, lengthwise, was a complicated chart of lines and numbers in my mother's hand. When I started to decipher its meaning, I realized that it charted the story of her life, at least from her own perspective.

Along the top of the sheet ran the years, beginning with her birth in 1937 and progressing through the decades to end in 1987, when she was fifty. My age now. Down the side were four labels: Health, Education and Work (sharing a row), Family, Men. In between, set out across the grain of the lines in a range of different colours, was my mother's autobiography, distilled into a diagram. Some events were dots or squares; others, like her time spent in different jobs or schools, were lines that stretched across years. There were also quite a few names in the Men row, both before she married and after the divorce. Some of these I remembered, some I did not; I couldn't bring up a picture of Ronald, who, the timeline told me, was the one who had tricked her out of her savings. They succeeded each other, one following the next without a break. My mother hadn't just been attractive to men, she'd needed to be so, and that, it seemed, had never changed.

That apart, there weren't many surprises. What the paper told me was the unhappy story that I'd always known, only this time with dates.

When it begins in 1937, my mother, Patricia Gilmour, is the second of five, already trailing behind her sister Anne, as she would do for the rest of her life. Alastair, Maggie and Mike

My mother's parents, Antoinette and Allan Gilmour, in the year before she was born.

follow her into the world, but Alastair doesn't stay long, dying in 1941 after just thirteen short months.

Though nothing more was written down, I knew that this pain had remained with my mother until her own death more than seventy years later. Alastair's death was one of her first memories. He slept in a cot in the same room as her, and one morning my three-year-old mother had woken up and her brother simply hadn't. She could never forget her own mother's howls when she found her dead son, nor the sight of her kneeling in front of his cot banging her head against the floor, trying to make this terrible event unhappen.

I did find some surprises in the paper's coloured lines. I knew that my mother had been to boarding school as an adolescent but not that she'd been sent away once before, when she was only seven. 'St Margarets' said the note above this green mark. 'Boarding. Remember wetting bed and happiness at coming home on train.' Another piece of pain in my mother's life and all that remained of it now were eleven short words. At least she only stayed there for a year. After that were just 'various schools, Scotland'.

My mother's childish perspective doesn't even notice the war. She'd told me that, living as they did, deep in the Scottish countryside, it didn't really impinge on their lives. No bombers came near them, while cream and eggs were always plentiful.

For her, what happened after was far worse. In 1946 their house is sold. 'On the move', is my mother's note, which sounds quite jaunty, only I know that this happens because her father, Allan Gilmour, has drunk away all the money.

Next, if I shift up two rows to Health, is a thick red block marked Polio, which stretches across half of 1947. Once again, I know more than the paper tells me. That year was a polio epidemic, and my mother spent long weeks in the isolation hospital, with no toys and enforced bedrest in a vast, cold ward. Her family were only allowed to visit once a week, and even then only to shout hellos through the window. When they could come at all. I imagine high windows and intense loneliness.

What I know also makes me look down to the bottom row, where she has recorded the men in her life. The dark line that records her father stops here too. 'Last seen in the hospital.' They'd both had polio, and had been in the same hospital, but she was only allowed to see him just once, when she was nearly recovered. Straight after that, she was told that her parents were going to separate. That was the last time she ever saw him.

With her husband's Gilmour money gone and little of her own, Antoinette was now entirely dependent on her mother, Carrie Jenkins. It had been Carrie who decided that all four children should go to boarding school, and she who paid for it. My mother always swore that this wasn't for educational reasons, but because Carrie wanted her daughter free to be her travelling companion. The result was that my mother went straight from the polio hospital to Sibford, the same Quaker boarding school that Carrie had attended thirty-five years before. She spent the next year there without once coming home. My mother detested the school, and for the rest of her life she hated her grandmother for sending her there, but at the same time she did not rebel. In a rare piece of introspection by email many years later, she described this to me as 'not the best of times but school was just what happened so you put up with it'.

She did at least enjoy the holidays at Sibford, when there

was playing out, and trips, and bikes. Reading this, I was relieved to find some light in her account. Then in the sixth
form, Worcester Grammar School for Girls was 'a waste', but
underneath she wrote, 'Had a number of boyfriends – a good
time.' Some shreds of happiness were still possible.

The strange thing about the diagram was that events
weren't drawn with their proper weight. Sibford was a great
long yellow streak across half a page, but the crashing catastrophe of Alastair's death became only a small black dot on her
family line. Twenty-three years later, in 1964, my sister Fiona
was born and died on the same day, and her entire life and
meaning had also been compressed into the same tiny full
stop.

I was lucky enough to live, which meant I got not only a
black dot for my birth but also a green line that stretched
out into the future, although my mother also marks her time
with us as a fine black line of broken nights for year after
year, culminating, at the divorce, in a breakdown. After this, I
am no longer a steady line but a set of dashes instead. There,
but not there: part of her life, but also absent. Real, and not
real.

Folding up the paper, I put it to one side. I was in no state
to think about how my mother had felt about me. Anyway, I
had a whole house to sort.

I returned from this visit with only what I brought: my crate
of cleaning materials, the radio and a feeling that the work
was going to carry on for ever. Had my mother lived round
the corner, I would have gone back every single day, week
after week, until the entire house was empty and every trace
of her misery had disappeared. The four-hour round trip

meant this was a fantasy. I could go up to Worcester once a week at most, and even then only in term time. I certainly didn't want to bring E with me to see how her grandmother had lived.

One evening, I found myself in front of the Channel 4 series *The Hoarder Next Door*. Watching programmes about hoarding had been one of my guilty pleasures for several years before my mother died. It's easy to see why: in every one of these shows, hoards are put into skips, houses are turned from dumps into sanctuaries and filth is banished for cleanliness. I might not have been able to sort out my mother's life, but I could at least watch the process happening to other people, a vicarious pleasure available in my own front room.

There was a double irony to my viewing because I had worked on the very first hoarding clean-up show on television. Until then, hoarders and their problems had only been observed by a dispassionate camera with commentary from an off-screen voiceover, in programmes such as *A Life of Grime*. For *The Life Laundry*, on-screen experts waded in to help people get organized back into normality. That format set the template for every single hoarding show that followed. The chaos is intensely scrutinized as the camera tracks slowly over heaps of clothes and paper, filthy sinks and stacks of boxes, empty cans, used plates and broken electrical devices, all usually covered in a thick layer of dust and debris which suggests how long they have been there. The hoarder acknowledges their problems to the camera, and then the team help them to clear up and throw away. There are usually one or two difficulties and false starts, but skips are filled and trips to the dump and charity shop are made. Then – and this is where the series do vary – the house is either cleaned up and returned to its owner or, as was the case with *The Life Laundry*, the programme goes even further and redecorates the house in a symbolic fresh start for its owner.

Hoarding proved to be compelling viewing, and twenty-six shows were made for the BBC between 2002 and 2004, opening the floodgates for a wave of similar formats from *How Clean is Your House?* to *Britain's Biggest Hoarders*. The basic trope remains the same though: messy is made clean in every single show, time and again, and then everyone lives happily ever after. At least that's what they'd like us to believe.

In America the shows reached a whole different level of success. *The Life Laundry* was exported as *Clean House*, and then the genre took off. *Hoarders*, on the A&E network, was their most-watched new series ever when it launched in 2009, generating copycat formats such as *Hoarders: Buried Alive* and *Confessions: Animal Hoarding*. Whatever the name and premise, the narrative never alters, with a team of experts and cleaners arriving to effect an almost instant makeover on a hoarded house.

The American shows differ from the British formats in a couple of ways. Family and friends are brought in far more often, not simply as witnesses to the transformation, which is their function in the UK programmes, but as active participants, clearing and exhorting and often despairing throughout the process. In many cases they are also the people who have asked for help in the first place.

This probably happens as a direct result of the other main difference. The US series have a much greater sense of what television people call jeopardy – the sense of urgency and dramatic tension that's needed to keep a viewer watching right up to the end. Almost all their participants are faced with the threat of losing their hoard to compulsory clearance by the local authorities. In the most extreme cases they are about to have their homes repossessed and demolished because of the squalor. The programme is their very last resort, because if these hoarders don't clean up, they will lose everything. In contrast, the narrative drive in the UK shows tends to be whether the British hoarders can clear their houses enough to be able to invite their friends round for tea for the first time in years. It's a different world.

What all these programmes have in common is that they make clearing up a hoard seem like a straightforward process. The hoarder is initially defensive and uncooperative, but is talked round by the professional declutterers and psychiatrists until they agree that everything they have collected is rubbish and fit only for the skip. In reality – both on and off the screen – the process is far more convoluted. This was made explicit in *The Hoarder Next Door*, where regular therapy sessions are alluded to and continue for months before the hoard is touched.

Hoarders, meanwhile, accomplishes its much more dramatic transformations in only a few days, but often with an uncomfortable sleight of hand, where the house owner is shown, forty minutes into a one-hour show, still resisting the clean-up. Suddenly, after an ad break, it takes place anyway and the rooms are empty. This process is often so inexplicable and unspoken as to suggest that they tranquillize their punters and clean up ruthlessly for the sake of filming an ending. I wouldn't put it past a TV producer. But the programme does acknowledge the reality of how hoarding works; as well as what's shown on screen, they also offer six months of further psychiatric and organizational aftercare. Like most television, what you see is a bit of a con. But that doesn't stop the millions of viewers from watching.

These programmes are so popular because it isn't only hoarders whose houses are too crammed with belongings. Almost every single one of us keeps things we don't need, has sentimental attachments to useless objects that live at the bottom of our cupboards that never come out, own ancient cardboard boxes which have lived in our attic for years and whose contents we could not even name. We have storage containers, garages, trunks full of unnecessary things. We need the hoarding programmes as reassurance. By watching people whose houses have been rendered utterly uninhabitable and whose lives have been overwhelmed as a result of the volume of their clutter, we, the viewers, can tell ourselves that these are the people with the problem, not us. Those on screen are hoarders – they are filthy, dirty and wrong and so need to be reformed – while however much we own and however long it is since we last moved the sofa to hoover underneath it, as viewers we are on the other side of the line and we are OK.

Or are we? Perhaps we also know this isn't really true. We hold fears about the things that surround us. Are we really in control of the quantities of stuff that we own? Would we be able to walk away from our things, or even survive without them? While we may not all be in danger of hoarding, almost everyone has irrational possessions, a cupboard full of functionless keys, small bits of plastic and broken tools, or simply too much stuff. Minimalists are just as much in the thrall of things, if anything even more so because they fear what excess might do.

We cannot be certain that we are in control. Given half a chance, or just a moment's inattention, our possessions will rise up and drown our lives, just as has happened to these poor people on the screen. We need to watch the hoard being vanquished, week after week on television, in order to reassure ourselves that we will be saved.

The other transformation implicit in these shows is the belief that, if the hoard disappears, the rest of a person's damaged life will be healed as well. The alienated father will be visited by his children, the divorced wife will find happiness again, and everyone will live happily ever after, regardless of what has taken place in the past. It's the CBT mindset all over again. If hoarders can only be taught to sort through their belongings and throw things away, then their anxieties, their sadnesses, their deep belief that they are not worthwhile will somehow get chucked into the skip along with the old newspapers.

I had believed this too, or at least I wanted to. That's why I found watching these series so satisfying. If I could get my mother's house sorted, then she too would be transformed. She might even become happy enough to care about me.

Finally, after many years of watching it happen to other people, I was clearing up a hoard just like they did on the television. Only now, when I switched on *The Hoarder Next Door*, I found it too painful to watch. My mother had gone, which meant that redemption was no longer possible. Now there could never be a happy ending.

photo album: *what loss looks like*

ALBUM CONTAINING BLACK AND WHITE PHOTOGRAPHS

England, early 1930s

Pages of black paper, covers of black imitation leather with embossed lettering on the front

From the estate of Antoinette Gilmour (née Jenkins)

O N MY NEXT visit to the house, I was all alone. Jim and Ed had other work to do that day, different people's sorrows to bag up and clear away, but I knew the drill by now. I arrived in several fleeces and a hat against the raw February cold, always magnified by the still dampness of the house, then set up the radio and refreshments. The only way to fix the leak in the kitchen had been to turn off the water at the mains, so I knew to sip my Thermos flask of coffee frugally, because my only chance to get to a toilet would be on my lunchtime walk into the city. This was becoming a routine. I always needed new, stronger cleaning supplies, or at very least more bin liners, but, after a couple of hours in the house, I was also desperate for the fresh air.

Even with the portable lantern, I was still afraid of the dark mess downstairs without Jim and Ed there as moral support and to defend me against rats, dead or alive. So I went back to the study. This time, with a walkway cleared into the middle of the room, I could reach the desk and the bookshelves for the first time.

Getting further into the layers didn't mean that what I was finding was any more organized. The five drawers of the desk were rammed with a jumble of letters, torn pages of books, receipts, unused pieces of paper and bookmarks, along with tins, buttons and an assortment of other odds and ends. Some of this was no more than rubbish, but other discoveries were entirely inexplicable. Where had the badge for the Palestine Police Force Veterans Association come from, and why?

One item that the heaps would disgorge regularly was photographs from every part of my mother's life. As well as the black and white dance souvenirs I'd found earlier on, there were handfuls of glossy prints from the seventies, their colours faded like ancient tapestries. Occasionally, I would pull out a picture that would startle me.

One I recognized immediately, because a copy had been framed and on display in my room ever since I was a student. Beautiful, happy, about nineteen, my mother is sat in front of a plate of food and smiling at a private joke. She's in my

In my father's college rooms; dinner
served on classic 1950s crockery.

father's college rooms, and the amusement is that he's actually cooked her a meal.

When I first got that print, it wasn't my mother that I was interested in. The plate in front of her is an Empire Ware design, almost certainly bought from Woolworths. As a student, my main obsession was collecting 1950s tableware of exactly this kind. The picture was not so much of my mother as of one of these plates caught in their heyday, as though I had discovered an image of a rare animal out in the wild, with a member of my family standing next to it. Now, when I looked at the picture again, I felt very guilty. I should have paid more attention to my mother when she was alive. Instead, like her, I had concentrated on stuff.

The longer I worked, the more often the pictures came up. Further down the pile, I found a set of pastel-coloured scenes from my own childhood. Here is me on a tricycle; there I am eating ice cream with my brother. The moments they showed happened more than forty years ago, but my mother hadn't held on to these photographs for all that time.

She couldn't have done. One of the smaller but still significant losses of her life had been the pictures of our time as a family. My father was, always, in charge of the camera, and he used slide film, the results of which he filed tidily away into dedicated boxes. Each slide, neatly numbered, had its own slot with an index on the lid where he would write down what was shown. Holiday in Palma; S and P bedtime story; East Leigh with Auntie Joe. Of course my father was going to keep this archive when they divorced, but this left my mother with nothing to remember those times by at all.

In my late teens I acquired a handful of prints from those early years before the divorce, which turned up when my paternal grandparents died. Even then I understood that my mother had also lost her photographs and with them her version of these times. So I made two copies of the picture of me and my brother sitting on the low stone wall, eating melting ice cream wafers. Twice I pedalled across the lawn on my pale-blue tricycle with a tatty panda riding pillion in the basket on the back, and twice I stood dressed in my best Viyella frock for my brother's christening, looking up at my grandmother's hat. There were only seven or eight in total, but I treasured them as proof that this part of my life really had existed. And I passed a set on to my mother.

These emerged now with their corners bent, warped from the weight that had sat on top of them. She certainly hadn't been treasuring my gift. Like so much in her chaotic, over-flowing house, to my mother these photos represented not happy memories but the reappearance of a part of her life that she, at best, didn't want to remember, but which I think she in truth found too painful to think about. I'm sure she wanted to be grateful to me for finding them but nonetheless found it easier to let them disappear into the chaos of things.

I can see this now, but as I worked through the piles I felt a small stab of hurt every time one appeared. The only consolation was that my mother hadn't looked after her own photographs either. A big part of what I found in and around the desk were her own faded, glossy prints. Sometimes I'd find a wallet of these together, but individual pictures would also turn up between two other pieces of paper or stuck to the bottom of a drawer. These discoveries were almost as disappointing as finding the ones I had given her, but in a very different way.

Although it was only a couple of weeks since her death, I

already knew that I was sifting for clues, looking for ways of discovering who my mother had been for all those years. These photographs were a blank-faced dead end, a refusal to answer. After the divorce, it seemed that my mother never took any pictures of people, nor let anyone take pictures of her. She preferred wide landscapes of mountains and plain, or a beach overshadowed by palms. There are pictures of animals too – a parrot staring back at her from a thick-leaved tropical tree, or an elephant cooling its feet in a shallow stream. Once or twice my grandmother and aunt wave from the distance, although these distant figures could be someone else altogether; they're too far away to tell. No one else ever appears.

I couldn't see any purpose in keeping them, so put them to one side in a stack and checked with my brother, who simply commented that our mother had been a bad photographer and so he didn't want them either. Now I feel that I discarded them too fast. These empty landscapes were a message of a kind, after all. The woman who took these shots isn't the same one who'd been smiling down at her plate at nineteen. What my mother's pictures tell me is that, long before she started hoarding, she had already begun to retreat from the world.

As the morning went on, I gradually began to tame the desk until I had found the green leather of its top for what was probably the first time in years. Fetching my spray and polish, I wiped it clean, trying to bring back its shine. This was the first part of the house, however small, that I'd actually managed to restore.

I couldn't face yet another drawer of unsorted paper and memories, so I turned to the easier project of the book-shelves. These hadn't been hoarded so much as abandoned;

yellowing paperbacks and empty ring binders had been left here untouched for years while the tide of papers lapped around beneath them. Their contents were quick to sort through, and within an hour I had three shelves cleared and wiped: real progress at last.

When I got to the bottom shelves, my progress stalled. Here, kept safe but also hidden until now by the sea of paper, were things I wanted to keep. The first was a pair of black-covered photograph albums, tatty-cornered and old. I opened them hoping against hope to find myself inside. But these were much older, the small photos black and white, recording a time that I was never around to remember. I flicked through them and realized that these belonged to my grandmother.

The irony was that, although she shuffled and disregarded every relic of her adult life, allowing it to disappear into the hoard, my mother had been a very good custodian of the more distant past, both her own childhood and the time before. After her own mother had died, she ended up as the keeper of the family history in the form of her mother Antoinette's two photograph albums. These I stacked in a safe place to take home with me. But when I thought about it later, her choices hurt. Why hold on to the memories if her childhood had been so bad? Why didn't she keep souvenirs of me safe instead?

Back at home, I sat down to look through the pictures. The small black one belonged to my grandmother alone, and it's the album in which she grows up and becomes an adult. She inhabits a privileged world. The book begins with finishing school, high in the Alps, and most of the snaps are of her and the other girls skiing. These are followed by tennis parties and walks, fancy dress and riding. Next, she is sent to the

Antoinette (centre), wrangling turkeys against her wishes.

agricultural college in Scotland that she'd never wanted to attend, but there are clearly larks and beautiful summer days as well as hard work and pigs.

Carrie Jenkins' decision to send her daughter to agricultural college seems out of character, because the one thing my mother always said about her grandmother was that she was a raging snob. Tennis parties and finishing school seem much more her style than turkeys and muck, but possibly she hoped her daughter might meet someone with land.

If that was the motivation, Carrie had done the right thing. Soon after college, Antoinette met Allan Gilmour, who appears in the album as a drooping and self-absorbed-looking boy holding a gun and staring out into the distance. The Gilmours were much more established than the Jenkins family. Antoinette's father, Harold, although well off, had been managing director of the Mining Engineering Company. In contrast, Major Angus, Allan's father, was a landed proprietor

*My mother in Scotland, aged about
three, with Anne behind her.*

with an independent income, owning a vast Victorian house
and estate. Allan married Antoinette two pages after he first
appears in the album. The wedding party are pictured standing outside the Jenkins family home, Oldbury Grange, just
outside Worcester. Carrie Jenkins looks very satisfied indeed
with the upward mobility that her daughter had secured.

The last few pages of my grandmother's first album are full
of their first child, Anne, along with holidays spent fishing
and skiing. My mother appears very briefly at the end, but it's
the second album, twice the size and leather-bound, which
records her growing up.

The first pages go exactly as a woman of my grandmother's
age and class would expect. Anne and my mother are dressed

in frilly white frocks; they smile out of the back of Silver Cross prams and dance with fat-legged glee in swimsuits on the lawn in summer. There are grandmothers and nursemaids, studio photographs of the two of them together. A new car arrives, and in one picture Allan proudly holds a giant salmon. As time goes on, they are joined by Alastair. Anne holds him uncomfortably on her knee, then she and my mother sledge and grin in a giant snowstorm. Alastair grows and walks held by reins.

Then everything stops.

On the next page time has fallen in on itself. My aunt Mags, born the winter after Alastair died, is now nine or ten, my mother grown into a teenager. Each of the girls has had their

One of the very last photographs of Alastair, at about ten months old.

photo taken professionally; there is one photo-booth picture of Mike, the youngest child, in a suit. That is all. The following pictures are of Anne's wedding. My grandmother never put another family snapshot in the album again.

What has happened in between is the time when it all went wrong. Alastair dies, then they had to sell the big Victorian house. My mother and her father go into the polio hospital. Antoinette gives up on her marriage and moves back to Worcester, and Allan disappears from their lives entirely.

Antoinette was so heartbroken by what had happened to her life that she couldn't even pretend to be happy for the camera. She'd rather have no photos at all. It's not hard to see why the lively girl out camping had turned into the faded and vague Granny that I remembered, and I can also understand why my mother felt valueless and unwanted. The accumulated pain was too great for either of them to withstand.

When I told my mother's remaining siblings, my aunt and uncle, that I had these albums, they both asked me if I could send them copies of some of the pictures, in particular any of them as babies. In my replies I evaded the question, not wanting to be the one to have to say there is nothing there.

This rent in time is what loss looks like from the outside, and loss is the one thing that unites hoarders, though you'd be hard-pressed to guess this from the professional literature. The fatuous leaflet mentions it, but only as an aside. A woman called Danielle says, 'I think it's trauma . . . too many of them . . . loss, if you are dealing with loss, it scrambles your brain.' Or, as translated by its writers into their preferred jargon, self-reported trauma levels were over 50 per cent higher in the hoarding group.

That's about as close as any psychologist or researcher seems to get to admitting that loss makes hoarding, which is curious, because whenever hoarders tell their own stories, it's the one thing they always mention. So often these people have lost houses, had all their toys destroyed in front of them, been shuffled from home to home in only the clothes they had on. Husbands have died or divorced them, parents disappeared. Time after time, what they say is that the hoard really began to accumulate after the death of a parent or child. Their friends and children report the same things. When one woman clears the hoard after her grandmother's death, what she finds underneath are the clothes of her little boy who died at four years old. He just stopped breathing when she was giving him a bath. A daughter understands the hoarding because when her mother was ten her own mother died and the father remarried. His new wife didn't want the children, so they went to live with an aunt and could only bring what they could carry. Everything else they owned was put on a bonfire in the back garden, and the children had to watch it all burn.

My mother lost a brother, a house, a father; she was sent away from her family. Then, when she thought herself safe, it happened all over again: another dead baby, the house gone, a second family broken for good. That relentless stream of catastrophes weighed down on her for the rest of her life.

Loss is a negative, an absence, so it ought to be light, but I don't think it ever feels that way. My mother filled her house with things partly to create that weight of hurt which she felt in a physical form. The rubbish that filled her house was the external expression of her inner turmoil. With the hoarding, she'd turned herself inside out, so that all of her problems sat on the outside for everyone to see. Or at least they would have done had she ever let another person through the front door of her house.

Hoarders often live alone, and the hoard can be a defence against intrusion. In even the biggest house, if the sitting room, the chairs, the bed are all covered in clothes or books or cardboard boxes, there can still be not enough room for anyone else to come in. But keeping people out isn't the real motivation. What the stuff really does is take up the empty space where the missing might have gone. Loss is a hole, and possessions are the easiest things to hand if you want to plug it. If the gap is really huge, that's when people start to collect even more. Sometimes there is a lot of absence that needs to be filled up.

I only realized how this equation worked when a friend of mine who shares care of her eleven-year-old daughter with her ex-husband admitted she was finding the weekends on her own very difficult indeed. One Saturday, cleaning up for visitors had sent her into a panic. With the house so neat and organized, she felt her daughter's absence far more intensely and painfully. She realized that she only ever tidied up when the two of them were home together. When her daughter was gone, the idea of the floors being clear and the rooms unoccupied by stuff was almost physically upsetting. She needed the emptiness left by her missing daughter to be filled.

As well as manifesting the problem, the hoard, paradoxically, can be a distraction at the same time. By creating one vast, tangible emergency, the hoarder manages to divert attention away from the unhappiness and the loneliness and all the past sadnesses they are trying to forget. By the end of her life, my mother was too defeated and tired to want to look at her past any more. The chaos of Rose Terrace didn't only take up space, it also stopped anyone from asking difficult questions and so dredging the misery back up to the surface again. For years my brother and I only focused on what we could see in front of us, just as the hoard meant us to do.

This sleight of hand may have worked for my mother as well. The agonies of her past were eclipsed by a single big disaster in the present, one which confronted her every day when she got up in the morning and was still present when she went to bed. The hoard was unpleasant, draining and I am sure never made her feel good, so it was never my mother's friend. Even so, its presence might have been less awful than being alone in an empty house with her demons. In a strange way the mess may have kept her company.

The photograph albums stayed with me long after I'd closed their pages. I'd understood my mother's sadness in the gaps, because that same hole existed in my own life as well. What's missing are any memories from the time when my mother and father separated. This isn't a reflection of my being too young, because I could write pages about the time before, when my parents were together, but what follows is a void, the mark of a time so awful that my brain shut down rather than think about it ever again.

I'd spent my whole life proving that I was the polar opposite of my mother in every way, that I had inherited nothing that she could pass down: not her looks, not her behaviours, not her thoughts. What her things were telling me, over and over again, was that this simply wasn't true.

Every time I found a likeness to my mother I was faced with the same question. Did our similarities mean that I was destined to become a hoarder too? I had good reason to worry.

The research shows that the condition does run in families, so the odds were stacked against me. The specialists argue about whether this represents a genetic predisposition or a learned behaviour, but the distinction is a moot point to someone wondering, as I was, whether they could escape being buried in stuff.

The books and articles had given me list after list of the characteristics associated with hoarding. Hoarders are visual people, who identify very strongly with the objects they own. They invest these things with meaning and association, and their lives echo with loss and abandonment. So far, I fitted every single one of these descriptions.

There was one more attribute to consider, which was that hoarders are often very distractible. They fail to clear up because they find it almost impossible to finish the job. Most of the time, they can hardly begin; although they may start to sort through a pile of paperwork or an overstuffed drawer, before too long they're sat down reading what they found, or the project has been abandoned because something across the room has caught their eye. People who work with hoarders call the results 'churn'. Hoarders rarely manage to sort through their possessions in a meaningful way; instead, they just move items from pile to pile, one heap to the next. Everything changes, but it also stays the same.

This may be partly the fault of their visual natures, as it tends to be objects in their field of view which distract them rather than thoughts or fears or other jobs in a different room. Equally, it may be the way their brains are wired. Some researchers believe that one root of hoarding may lie in either impulse-control disorders or ADHD. No one has managed to prove a direct relationship, but the links do seem significant.

Once again, in looking for my mother, I find myself. The very first thing written on my medical records was 'Hyperactive'. It's easy to see why I got the label. As a small child, I slept only between 11 p.m. and 5 a.m., spending all the hours in between badgering my mother with questions: my own contribution to that dark dotted line of broken nights and difficult days which sent my mother towards depression and divorce. These days I would be tested for ADHD and probably given drugs, but back then there was only that single word, which I would read upside down from my notes while my mother talked to the doctor.

Was my mother hyperactive, inattentive, distractible? Just the same as me? Was this the key to why she ended up hoarding? At first I found this hard to imagine. When I call her up in my mind's eye, my mother is always languidly smoking a cigarette, sitting still. She certainly never had my relentless energy. But when I look at her timeline again to piece together her working life, I can see someone who was restless, getting bored of one thing after a few years and moving on to the next, never settling into a career. At college, she trained as a PE teacher, and worked in schools for the five years between graduation and my birth, although at five different schools. After the divorce, she briefly returned to teaching but soon switched to working as an estate agent and then selling life assurance. After her grandmother Carrie Jenkins died, she had just about enough money not to work, so didn't, although she busied herself for a few years with being a city councillor in Worcester. But she never stuck at anything for very long at all. Reading back through her papers, I find it painful to see that she could never settle to something, was never able to find a work or a purpose that absorbed her. Without that, and with her children living elsewhere, she never truly found her place in the world.

Going through these inventories of dysfunction, I found myself indicted as surely as my mother. There only seemed to be one problem with this diagnosis, which was that I didn't hoard at all.

The difference possibly lay in one final attribute that the lists always mention, and that's indecisiveness. This might be part of ADHD, or something separate, but whichever way, hoarders often find it hard to make decisions. Imagine being a hoarder starting to sort through a great stack of amassed stuff. Not only are all the other piles an ever-present visual distraction, but when you pick up that first piece of paper, a decision has to be made about where it goes. Is it a bill which requires action or just a piece of junk mail? Do I need this? Might I ever want the information it contains? Even if it is clearly important, where do I put it? By this point, it probably does seem easier just to hold on to everything. That saves you from having to make any decisions at all.

One thing I can do is decide, and this might be the single trait standing between me and a hoard of my own. The possibility is pent up inside me like an electrical charge, but this ability is what stops it leaking into the world.

Maybe I wasn't the real problem. E is vague and distractible. She loves art. And she hates making choices. I worry that all that uncertainty and indecision has resurfaced in the next generation. Can I help her or will she, when I am dead and gone, end up in the same chaos as my mother?

deeds: *houses and homes*

COLLECTION OF LEGAL DOCUMENTS

Worcester, 1924–80

Typewritten on paper

From the estate of Mrs P. Walker

Even back at home, where the heating worked, the windows showed the world outside and I could walk across each room with ease, there was work to be done in sorting out my mother's estate. The administration of death is a cruel trick, presenting the bereaved with an obstacle course of complex and interdependent bureaucracy just at the point when they have been so stunned by loss that even making a cup of tea seems to be an insurmountable effort. At least that's what I told people. In truth, I relished the labour, the forms and the spreadsheets. It gave me lists to tick off and a sense of achievement at the end of each day. It allowed me to tidy up my mother's mess on the six days a week when I wasn't at Rose Terrace. Best of all, it stopped me from thinking.

Amnesia was still my best coping strategy. I still told no one about the state of her house, and if at all possible didn't even mention that my mother had died in the first place. At night, I dreamed of baggage in waiting rooms. What was in the cases? I didn't want to look.

I still couldn't uncover a single emotion that I knew to be my own: not love nor hate, or even pity. All I felt was a glassy numbness. Only once did this alter. At my desk, surrounded by old bank statements and letters from insurers, I had begun to read the probate forms on my computer screen to find out what was expected of me.

Section 3.1 Did the person who died leave a will? If no, go to Section 4.

When I'd searched Rose Terrace for my mother's will, I hadn't for a moment expected to find one, but even so my mind flooded with fury. Why hadn't my mother written a will? How dare she do this to me? She'd been such a useless mother I couldn't even expect this one simple act from her, a way of making her children's lives so much easier after her death.

In fact it's fairly easy to sort out someone's estate even if they don't have a will. The form made this clear. But I wasn't interested in logic. This single missing document had become the emblem of every time my mother hadn't looked after me, each act of selfishness over the years. I sat tight still, unable to focus on the screen, trying to push these red, raging furies back under. I ran away, taking myself out for a long walk in the drizzle, stamping my rage out on the damp pavements until it had been entirely discharged and I could breathe again. I didn't dare allow a lifetime's worth of suppressed hurt to break through the brittle surface; its force might sweep me away like a rip tide.

The absent will had been an inconvenience, but other more crucial documents were also missing from Rose Terrace. My brother and I were starting to think about selling the house. This required a faith in its eventual resurrection, the belief that one day Rose Terrace would be mended enough to show an estate agent. Right now, Jim and Ed were still the only strangers I would consider allowing into my mother's house, and I couldn't imagine this changing for a long time. Even so, I began on the paperwork, which was the easiest part of the enterprise because it didn't require letting anyone else through the front door.

The problem was that a sale relied on my proving that my mother had owned it in the first place, and that wasn't something I could do. I'd been through every room in the house, brought every single potentially useful piece of paper back with me but still hadn't come up with any idea as to where the deeds might be. I had plenty of paperwork about the house, but this was all to do with its Grade II listing, an ancient guarantee for tanking the cellar, and my mother's reams of notes about its history and past owners. For a few panicking days I didn't think we were going to get anywhere, possibly for years.

When I turned to the internet for help, I discovered, to my relief, that my mother's missing documents didn't matter. Even though Rose Terrace hadn't been sold for thirty-five years, its ownership had nonetheless been recorded on the online registry. The paperwork was no longer required. Naturally, this discovery caused the deeds themselves to appear. The probate process had triggered a letter from my grandmother's solicitors, saying that they had been holding them in lieu of a mortgage which had been paid off many years ago. The papers were irrelevant, but I asked if they could be sent anyway, just in case they told me anything.

When the package arrived a few days later, it didn't contain the aged and intriguing parchments I'd been hoping for but an unruly jumble of crispy sheets of yellow paper covered in typewritten legalese, pale-blue mortgage forms with official stamps in shillings, flimsy carbon copies of old contracts, none the same size as another. I couldn't help being disappointed. From my childhood, I remembered the grown-ups talking about deeds and how they were so precious that they needed to be kept in safes or lodged with the bank for security. As the only means by which ownership of a piece of property could be proven or transferred, they had been powerful items which made hoarders of us all. But these stiff papers were now powerless and obsolete.

My mother must have seen the deeds at some point, because the people who inhabit them – James Loveday Griffiths, the warehouseman and fly proprietor; Mary Frevillier, who inherited the house before she married; and Sydney Millichip, who, like my mother, died without making a will – are the same ones I found in her handwritten notes scattered around the study. She'd taken the history back much further, to the buying of the fields on which her house had been built in the late seventeenth century. I found the same set of information written out three separate times on different sheets of paper. As so often in my mother's life, she'd started but not known how to finish. Her work on this history, even if it never found a form nor an outlet, was a sign of how much she adored her home. The final record wasn't what she cared about; it was the doing of the work as a means of expressing this devotion that mattered.

The building was, after all, the last great love of my mother's life. As safe as bricks and mortar, she must have thought, but she should have known better than to believe this. Our family had lost houses over and over again, and the pain runs down through the family line as surely as if each one had been a bereavement.

I inherited these emotions long before I understood the actual events. Unsurprisingly, the feelings leaked into my consciousness through the medium of stuff. As a teenager, I was in love with old things but, having no money, searched through jumble sales for 10p finds. The pieces that I loved from the 1920s and 30s had already become genuine antiques, sought after and known, rarely turning up in the village hall or market stalls where I shopped, so I was forced to invent my own treasures: bright-yellow curtain fabric printed with coffee jugs and onions, battered brooches from the Festival of Britain to wear on my lapel, garishly patterned china perched brightly on my windowsill. Over time, I learned to love these 1950s styles for their own sake, but back then they were only substitutes for the treasures I really desired.

In my mind, the attic of my great-grandmother's house, Oldbury Grange, would have been full of the finds I coveted the most: swirling Edwardian dresses packed into trunks, art deco tea services, glittering costume jewellery and peacock fabrics from which I could create extraordinary clothes. These were all unattainable. Carrie Jenkins had sold Oldbury Grange

Oldbury Grange, my great-grandmother's house just outside Worcester, in the heyday of her time there.

141

when I was a tiny baby. I'd been sucked into the family dream of a lost great house which would have satisfied all my desires.

Every part of this fantasy was, of course, a complete illusion. To start with, while Oldbury Grange had possessed several helpful attributes, including a Regency facade, an Austen-esque name, two house cows and a small amount of land, the house was never the stately home of my imaginings. More to the point, it had never been handed down through the generations. Carrie and Harold Jenkins had bought it when Harold's firm, the Mining Engineering Company, moved its factories from Rotherham to Worcester in 1925; after forty-odd years, the attic wouldn't have contained much more than plywood, a few flimsy pieces of furniture, an old gramophone and some dust. Bought with Northern industrial money made good, there were no ancient treasures to lay up for future generations.

I never articulated my thoughts about Oldbury Grange to my mother because she would have stamped on them quite hard. Her world contained no room for sentimentality about Carrie Jenkins. Even so, my mother was responsible for these longings, because the lost house ran as an undercurrent through many of her stories. Once upon a time, she told me, a great mansion had been theirs, but lost through profligacy and alcoholism. On top of that, almost the only reference she ever made to her father was that he'd drunk away the family home. Her implication was clear: their fall from grace and gentility had been entirely her father's fault. In fact my mother's telling conflated two separate events. The house that her father, Allan Gilmour, had lost was a solid Victorian villa in the small Perthshire village of Grandtully.

Oakbank House can be seen in the background of a few of my grandmother's photographs, from the time when their family

*Oakbank House in the late 1930s as my
mother might have remembered it.*

life was safe and comfortable, and taking snapshots seemed like
a normal thing to do. A handsome double-fronted house with
big gardens, its stone-clad bay windows looked out over the
valley of the River Tay below. This was a solid start to married
life, and my grandparents moved in just after their wedding.

The ghosts of what happened there can still be traced in
the records. The electoral roll shows that Antoinette and
Allan arrive at the house in 1936, a year after their marriage,
and with Anne either just born or on the way. When the war
begins in 1939, they are still in residence. But on 15 May 1945,
just one week after VE day, their comfortable life has begun
to unravel. Lawyers have been called in, and Allan Gilmour's
estates sequestered. In other words, he was bankrupt.

By the time the electoral register resumes at the end of that year, my grandfather and grandmother have left the house and are now living down the road at the Grandtully Poultry Farm. Antoinette's unwanted training at the agricultural college must have come in useful for those chickens. She needed to find some way to scrape a living, despite her feckless husband.

Just two years later in 1947 comes the terrible epidemic of polio which incarcerates Allan and my mother in the isolation hospital. After that, Allan was responsible for the poultry farm on his own; Antoinette and the children had gone, returning to Worcester and Carrie. In the end, even the chickens slipped through my grandfather's grasp. Three years later, he has moved to the Loch Rannoch Hotel, more than twenty miles from the scene of his failures. Then he disappears from the records entirely.

Allan Gilmour did drink away a house, just as my mother said, and probably a poultry farm too. At the same time, I can't despise my grandfather, because I can see how he had suffered. Alastair had died less than four years before. Knowing what the loss of a child did to my parents' marriage, the devastation it wreaked on my mother, I can imagine what misery his loss inflicted on her father.

The shape of my mother's story echoes my own. She is a shadowy and inexplicable figure to me, but her own father must have been even more faint a presence than that. She too spent her life looking for a ghost she had never really known. Our experiences mirrored one another's in other ways as well. I wasn't only pining for Oldbury Grange because I'd half understood our family myths: I too lost a beloved house when I was a child, just as my mother had done.

For the first eight years of my life, barring an initial six months in Watford, our family lived in a big Victorian house high up on a ridge at the edge of Oxfordshire.

Edgehill House was a square Victorian villa built from harsh orange Cotswold ironstone hewn from a quarry at the end of our garden. Once upon a time, this ridge had been deep underwater, and its stones teemed with the spirals of ammonites and shells like tiny fingernails embedded in the rock. In more recent times the two sides of the Civil War had battled on its steep slopes.

The house was old-fashioned, draughty and inconvenient, but I loved it entirely. More than forty years after we left, in my mind I can still walk around every room with the eyes of a seven-year-old. I can return to the space under the sink in my parents' room where I would sit behind the towel and listen to my father shave in the morning, or find the sticky patch under the radiator in the kitchen where he had begun to pull

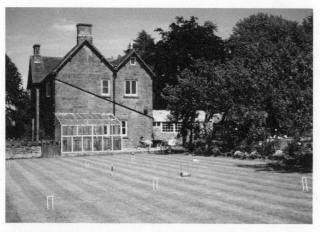

Edgehill House seen from the garden; my mother is sunbathing on the terrace.

up the bright 1950s linoleum tiles, only to discover that they had been laid on sticky black bitumen and were impossible to remove. Their intended replacements sat in their boxes by the cellar door for years after. I can still see the views out of each window, where the snapdragons grew in the flowerbed near the monkey puzzle tree, the cupboard by the front door where my favourite blue mackintosh and hat lived, the gap in the hedge where I could squeeze between the yews and the beech trees and become invisible to everyone. At least so I believed.

Going back into the house again in my mind, each room appears in front of me as I wander about; I creak on the floorboards, push open the doors. Here are the white bannisters, the tall wardrobes and pink candlewick bedspreads in the spare room. But my mother is nowhere to be found.

My father, of course, is everywhere. He sits at his desk in the study where he is not to be disturbed, or puts on the *Sesame Street* record that he brought back all the way from America for us. He's fastening my brother into the baby bouncer which hangs in the double doors that lead into the sitting room, and I am furious at being too big to fit into it when it's really mine. And that's just one room; he inhabits the whole house in the same way. He is coming in through the front door, reading me a story upstairs or mowing the lawn outside and burying me in the heaps of clippings. Even those boxes of tiles by the cellar door are a memory of that rare time when he was defeated by a job.

In comparison my mother is as elusive as a ghost. If I concentrate hard enough, I might find her washing up at the kitchen sink, her back to me, looking out of the small window into the garden. Perhaps she is at the dressing table in her bedroom. Or has she just left her presence in the form of the silver

*Summer 1967. My father is taking photos
while my mother reads the papers.*

hairbrush and powder pot, the face creams and the perfume
bottle that is the distilled essence of her? Maybe I have wandered up here on my own and am picking through the stuff to
look for some traces of her. Even then, my best chance of finding her was in things. I had to start this work young, because
my mother slipped out of my life long before she left the house.

Being half-shade, my mother found other people too solid
and too whole. Most of all, I, her daughter, was too awake
and alive to be borne. After the death of my sister, I had been
the thing she most desired, a living, breathing child, one full
of life and energy and vigour. The problem was that I was
too much of what she had longed for. My excessive existence
reminded her of just how insubstantial she was. I didn't make

her happy; I made her scared. At the same time I made her sad, or at least guilty, because she knew that she was failing me. She could see I needed more from her; the problem was she had no idea where to begin.

With my mother only half present and clearly preferring my brother when she was there, and my father out at work all day, the house itself became the solid constant in my life, the meaning of home. When my parents divorced, my father stayed in Edgehill House with us. But my new stepmother couldn't stand the place: stranded out on a high windy ridge where there were scarcely twenty other houses and no one to talk to; where the tiny kitchen was a throwback to the 1950s, the heating pipes squeaked and muttered in the night and there wasn't enough furniture or heat to fill the vast Victorian rooms. A place where the remnants of my father's past life with my mother lurked in unswept corners. It wasn't for this that she had swapped her neat flat in a European capital city, her family and her friends. We moved away within six months of her arrival.

My stepmother never understood what this did to me. I wasn't given to saying very much back then, but it took me twenty years of trying to forgive her, and I'm still not entirely sure I've succeeded. Just as Oakbank House represented safety and security for my mother, Edgehill House was the place where my life had taken root.

What strikes me is not only that my mother and I spent our lives grieving for the homes of our childhood. What I realize now is how much Edgehill House looked like Oakbank. Both built out of solid stone rather than brick, they have the same double bay windows and high gables; they are surrounded by the same flat lawns.

My mother was trying to go back. She bought Edgehill House in the hope that life could be restored, that she could recreate for herself the security that she'd once felt in her early life in Scotland. But the dream proved impossible. Divorce ripped through her life for the second time. The big Victorian house was gone, and the safety of gables and stone walls and rolling lawns had been lost all over again.

napkin ring: *the boy who died*

**SILVER NAPKIN RING, WITH ENGRAVED
DECORATION AND DEDICATION**

England, 1937

Manufacturer Henry Clifford Davis,
Birmingham

Presumed gift of Mrs Caroline Jenkins

D RIVING UP TO Rose Terrace the next week was a relief. This was a February without snow or rain, just a pale-grey sheet of cloud as though the weather itself had given up trying. I liked the season for being unremarkable in its dull light. The trees were silhouettes, the grass faded, tussocky and brown.

When my father died, suddenly and unexpectedly even though he had been diagnosed with cancer, spring had been in full flood and all the hedgerows were sodden with blossom, white and heavy, so full of life that they hurt. That year, too, a strange crop of spiders had hatched, stripping one particular kind of bush back to the stalk, the bare stems smothered in glistening webs. We drove back and forth from the hospital with the hedges flickering between life and death as we passed, and I thought that I would never be able to stand spring again.

This time there were no landmarks at all. I saw nothing that would remind me with each new winter that this had been the time when my mother had fallen and then died. A season that would be easy to forget. At least that's what I was hoping for.

As I drove alone and unobserved, my thoughts arrived one after another like the motorway traffic. I felt sorry for my mother and her life, or at least for my version of what had happened to her, and at the same time relieved that she could not be depressed for one moment longer. I was upset that I hadn't made her happy when she had lived, and also angry that she squandered her beauty and her taste and her brilliance. At last I was no longer responsible for her, and I savoured this lightness, but then this reprieve made me feel guilty all over again. Each of these thoughts came and went, arriving and then fading away, until by the time I was reaching Worcester the practical problems I needed to solve pushed this parade to one side.

I'd only just managed to wrestle the padlock off the hasp when Jim and Ed arrived, lifting the atmosphere as soon as they appeared on the doorstep. Without ever mentioning the subject, we had all decided not to talk about what had happened in Rose Terrace. This made everyone's job easier. For the two of them, neither of whom ever said more than they needed to anyway, it was a survival strategy born out of experience. If they didn't find out about the person who had lived here, they could stay detached and impersonal, reducing their task to a set of bags, trips to the tip and concentrated heaving. Understanding might have made their labour more difficult.

For my part, I was grateful not to be asked to explain any further. I was done with that now. No account I made to anyone would change what had happened. Action was better than words.

When they were looking for more black bags or simply stopping at the bottom of the stairs for a breather, Jim and Ed told me about other houses, where the newspapers had been piled up to the ceilings, with only the narrowest of walkways to pass through; of garages stacked so high that the door could no longer be opened; houses that had taken months to clear – each story an understated kindness, telling me that they understood.

I'd intended to carry on clearing the study, but Jim and Ed

were calling me down more and more often to look at stuff and decide whether or not I wanted to keep it. The familiar shape of my mother's dining room was becoming visible. Out of the chaos emerged the old black teapot and eighteenth-century wine glasses. I imagined Jim and Ed as gentle-handed archaeologists, unearthing the fragments of a civilization from that heavy heap, and these fragile objects seemed particularly miraculous finds, like a Greek vase or an Egyptian perfume bottle excavated intact. All of them had once lived on the alcove shelves, now collapsed on top of one another at the far end of the room, yet the basalt china and delicate two-hundred-year-old glass had survived.

I spent my time in the sitting room, sifting through the pieces that they dug out, deciding what I wanted to save, or at least wasn't yet ready to throw away. Only the most unreactive materials like china and metal had survived the damp, with all the fabric and books pretty much ruined. Even so, far more remained than I had anticipated. At least my mother had left me plenty of newspaper to wrap it all up in.

While Ed finished off the dining room, Jim had started work on the hallway. Later that morning, he called me over to where he'd cleared away a mountain of papers and bags and boxes. The front of my mother's sideboard had been revealed, and the doors could be opened for the first time in years.

Inherited from Carrie Jenkins, this piece of furniture was an exuberant Victorian creation, with carved doors and drawers that billowed out in front like a matron's bosom. My mother's name for it, the chiffonier, suited it much better than 'sideboard'. Stained a deep brownish-black, it dominated my mother's hallway. But this was also exactly the kind of amusingly ugly furniture that my mother and I had both enjoyed.

In the good times the chiffonier had kept not only its Victorian looks but also its traditional function, storing a miscellany of silverware, mats, cutlery, glasses and tablecloths. When I had visited back in the better times, I would lay the table while my mother cooked, and the chiffonier would be where I found almost everything I needed. Now, any exposed wood was sticky with dirt, nicotine and tar. Mice, finding it hard to get around the house on the floor, had chewed through the back of each drawer to make a runway. When Jim pulled out one to show me, the back fell off in his hands. I had thought that the chiffonier might be the one piece of furniture that I wanted to take home, but this, like so much else, was only ever destined for the tip.

Inside, barricaded against the decay and danger, many of its contents remained surprisingly untouched. Here were the last remaining heirlooms of the Victorian family: a silver sugar shaker shaped like a Gothic church censer, the crystal glasses, the bone-handled fish knives that had once belonged to my great-grandmother. Only the linen napkins and tablecloths were too stained with damp to be saved.

I was tempted to get rid of the lot, but didn't dare throw out the whole family history, not yet. I settled down in front of the cupboard to survey the contents properly. One side was filled with cut crystal, from tumblers and sherry glasses to three odd miniature tankards made for hot punch. Some of these, I knew, had been left to my mother by an aunt that wasn't hers. When my parents had split up, my father's only aunt had been so outraged that she cut all contact with him. In her eyes, my brother and I only existed when we were staying with my mother. She held this fury, undimmed, until her death, when she left a will in which she refused to acknowledge my father but bequeathed my mother a selection of cut crystal glasses.

The problem was that as I picked the glasses out of the cupboard one by one, I had no idea which had once belonged to her. Over the years, they'd become mixed up with other legacies from my grandmother and great-grandmother. My mother was no longer here to ask, and the crystal, while it had survived both family arguments and then the damp and disorder of the house, could not speak. All my aunt's fury at my father had now evaporated into the atmosphere, never to be recaptured. As I wrapped them up one by one in yet more newspaper, I couldn't help thinking that this was a useful lesson. Sometimes a thing can return to being only itself and not remain freighted with memories for the rest of its time on earth. I found this a relief when so many of my mother's things had far too much to say for themselves.

I discovered yet another of these stacked behind the glasses – a small tankard of solid silver, with 'Patricia Gilmour'

My mother's christening tankard, after cleaning.

157

engraved on its face. This must have been my mother's christening mug, but I'd never seen it before.

Thick with black tarnish, its shape was battered and dented as though it had been kicked down stairs; yet another emblem of the misfortunes of my mother's life. But this wasn't the most resonant item that the chiffonier contained. Only when all the other contents had been removed did I find the napkin ring, in the far back corner of the cupboard. The surface was so blackened that at first I thought it too had belonged to my mother, but when I brought it into the sitting room and let daylight fall on to its surface, the letters were very clear. They spelled out 'Alastair'.

Alastair as a small baby, with his nursemaid.

What I'd found wasn't a precious object or a happy memento kept in a safe place. The napkin ring was a problem, a reminder of losses and failings and pain which had to be hidden away lest all the horrors it held exploded back into my mother's present-day life.

This family sadness carried far more weight than the tiny black dot which my mother had marked on her timeline. Losing a child is an unthinkable grief however it happens, but Alastair's death cut even deeper because he was the only boy, and my mother's family prized boys above all else. My grandmother Antoinette's life had been blighted to the core because she would always be compared to the golden child, her brother John. He could do what he liked, but when my grandmother, deft and brilliant at sewing, asked to study fashion, she was sent to agricultural college instead. This experience didn't turn Antoinette into a feminist, far from it. She'd internalized so thoroughly these lessons about where girls stood that she could only repeat her own experiences when she in turn had a family. Alastair was the prize, the heir, the longed-for boy; his death the greatest sorrow imaginable. The napkin ring was the only solid marker of his thirteen months of life in the world.

I took the napkin ring home and cleaned it, but this didn't render it any less impassive. For a few days it sat on my desk while I glanced at it warily now and again in an apparent stalemate.

As an object, divorced from the story, it wasn't very impressive. The edges were finished into over-fussy scallops, while the engraving said 'Alastair, December 1939'. He was born in November, so this date must have been his christening. Beyond this, the silver seemed to be entirely mute.

159

This frustrated me intensely. The ring represented the crux of my mother's unhappiness and how it began in her childhood. I felt that if I could only understand this one object I would have the key to understanding who she had really been. But all I could uncover was dry facts.

No one cares about napkin rings these days. I can't imagine that many people under fifty use one at the dinner table, still less a silver one engraved with their name. Keeping your own napkin distinct and separate between meals is an obsolete idea. The rings did have a taxonomy, because that's how museums and collectors like to organize the world of things, so it's possible to trace them from their origins in 1800, through changes in shape and ornament, right up until their present-day obscurity.

Each individual ring also tells the story of its making and sale in the hallmarks stamped on its body, a code which is always pleasing to crack. As a child, I was fascinated by the tiny hieroglyphics on my own napkin ring, and now I could tell that Alastair's had been made in Birmingham in 1937. This meant that it had sat on the shelf in a jeweller's for a couple of years before it had been bought, and that the customer was most likely my great-grandmother Carrie, making a trip up to the big city from Worcester.

I seemed to have reached a dead end where nothing more could be found, until I realized that the point about napkin rings was precisely their futility and irrelevance. It has never mattered what they do, because these are not tools but ritual objects.

As Alastair's was, the rings are traditionally given at birth or as christening presents. In many ways this is absurd. No child uses a napkin at the breast or bottle, and they'll be wearing a bib for a while after that. Yet this gift must be given. When E was born, my father was insistent that he had to get an engraved napkin ring as her christening present, even though there wasn't going to be a ceremony. I gave in for a quiet life, rolling my eyes at the absurdity of it all. To this day, the ring sits in a drawer in the dining room, pristine in its small square box. Only now do I understand why it mattered so much to him. The gift was essential, because in a certain kind of middle-class family, which ours was, the napkin ring acted as a sign of who belongs and who does not. If E did not possess a ring of her own, she could never truly be one of us.

The use of a silver napkin ring at the dining table is a small ritual of kinship and exclusion which is acted out at every meal. Not only families require this performance. RAF squadrons and Royal Navy ships use sets of silver napkin rings in their officers' messes, where it's a tradition that senior naval officers have their individual rings engraved with the names of every ship on which they have served. There's even a law firm in the city where a new partner gets not only a share of the company's equity but their own silver napkin ring as well. The partner's dining room holds a rack of cubbyholes where these are stowed after lunch every day, revealing very clearly who belongs and who does not.

Each of these is a close-knit community that wants to signal who has a right to a place at the table. The corollary of this is that guests are inevitably singled out as separate and other. In my own family they were given plain rings of yellow bone or green plastic that had been handed down from my grandparents. But not silver and not named. Visitors are temporary and unrelated. They are not us.

After my parents divorced, the arrival of my stepmother

posed a problem for this unspoken system. Arriving not from the English middle classes but the strangeness of Belgium, where they do so many things differently, she came to us without a silver napkin ring in her luggage. Yet it was imperative, at least from my father's point of view, that she should belong. She was issued with a spare one of his instead, engraved with the wrong initials, but silver nonetheless, and thus my stepmother was initiated into our family for good.

There's an inverse logic to this too. If a person has disappeared or died, their napkin ring acts as proof that they were once alive, that they once formed part of the family. That's what I found hidden in the darkest corner of my mother's chiffonier. The thin ring of silver was solid and lasting evidence that her brother was still, and had always been, a Gilmour.

As such, the napkin ring was a profound, potent item which exercised a dark spell over my mother.

'It should have been me.' She had told me that more than once. Everything had happened the wrong way around. Alastair was the child that Antoinette had wanted to live, and my mother knew that she should have died instead.

This single realization, more than anything else, was at the centre of my mother's lifelong feelings of being wrong. Alastair's napkin ring, that simple circle of silver, became a reliquary, holding all my mother's distress about losing her father and being unwanted by her mother. My mother could not bear to face these feelings for fear of them tearing her apart, so the ring which represented and contained them needed to be hidden away at the very back of a cupboard behind glasses and boxes and Great Granny's ugly fish knives. Even that wasn't safe enough. Then the doors had to be barricaded with newspapers, boxes and rubbish to make sure that those thoughts and memories, that intense and unshakeable pain, remained confined inside the chiffonier with no hope of escape.

The problem was that these emotions were still living under her roof, always at risk of bursting out. This was one of the reasons for building the hoard: Alastair's napkin ring had to be buried in a white noise of meaningless rubbish. So much of what my mother accumulated – all those plastic bags and envelopes of junk mail – didn't have any significance of their own. Their job was to bury the objects that did, to prevent the terrifying misery of the past from ever being discovered again. In my mother's study, notes, receipts, stationery and blank pieces of paper diluted the difficult letters, those souvenirs of divorce, loss and failure, the inventories that listed, mercilessly, everything that had gone wrong in her difficult life. She hid the napkin ring behind a wall of newspaper and old fridges as though she were sticking her fingers in her ears and chanting nonsense in order to drown out words she did not want to hear.

The one thing that my mother could never do was throw the napkin ring away. To do that would mean killing Alastair all over again.

Now I was required to deal with everything that the ring meant. I offered it to my uncle and aunt, but neither wanted it. Both were younger, born after Alastair had died, so for them he had never really been a presence. My uncle also said that it was a very unhappy time in his mother's life, and he didn't want to live with a constant reminder of that loss.

This must be how normal people think, people who aren't hoarders. My mother in contrast had to hold on tight to what had happened, however bad it had been, and now the problem had been handed down to me.

I put the napkin ring in a drawer to wait while I decided what to do with it and what that act would mean. It wasn't a frightening object for me, more sad, and that mainly because of what it had represented to my mother. The problem was that I was far too close to her way of thinking to be able to throw it away. That would mean that I had discarded Alastair's small life for ever, because there would then be no more record that it had ever happened. I could not allow that. At the same time, I didn't want her memories sitting there in the drawer, weighing down on the present.

Many people might find it difficult to throw away possessions with such intense family associations, but for hoarders this problem is replicated in every single object they own. Nothing can be permitted to leave the house, because every single item, from a dustbin to a plastic toy, is unique and contains intense quantities of memory and meaning.

This is how I live too. Every item in my home has a biography that I can tell, and each one can elicit meanings and associations. But when I start to look at the furniture that surrounds me, what it often carries are memories of my mother. Most of these aren't valuable heirlooms. Often, like the battered 1950s armchair in the corner of my bedroom, their stories are much more haphazard.

In the mid-eighties I left university for an unfurnished room in Archway, and this must have been in one of my mother's good patches, because for a change it was she rather than my father who was able to help. I went up to Worcester in search of not only bargains but ideally the kinds of 1950s kitsch that was already priced like antiques in London. Even though she didn't share my tastes, my mother stepped up to the challenge. We spent four days in her car, speeding from auctions in the depths of Herefordshire to people in far-flung villages who'd been advertising good-quality beds in the small ads. Together we appraised, haggled and judged, found bargains and laughed at the people who wanted too much for what we knew to be rubbish.

Two of our best finds, however, turned up very close to home. Just a block away from Ceci's the delicatessen, at the bottom of my mother's hill, was Browning's, full of bric-a-brac and second-hand furniture. I got a dressing table and wardrobe, classic post-war Utility designs, for £10 the pair, and along with them came a Parker Knoll armchair. Thrillingly, when we took off the red floral stretch covers, the original 1950s upholstery was preserved underneath. I couldn't have been happier, and my mother was delighted to help, even if she'd never have chosen it herself.

Returning to clear Rose Terrace, I discovered that Browning's was still in business. The sign outside offered house clearance, and I did consider asking them to take away some of my mother's things, in what would have been a pleasingly circular transaction. But Jim and Ed told me that they could deal with furniture as well as rubbish, so I let them, too tired to take anything but the easiest option.

All these thoughts – the happy interlude spent buying furniture with my mother, Browning's, taking off the stretch Dralon covers, and now even my memories of returning to the shop – are attached to that one chair. In this I am no different to many of the hoarders who fill television screens and online forums, for whom every object is just as meaningful, leaving them unable to throw a single thing away.

How had my mother felt about her own things? Was she just as over-invested? Did thoughts and memories hang about every single object she owned as well? I have to believe it was the same for her. Otherwise why barricade Alastair's napkin ring inside the chiffonier with such a weight of stuff? She did not want to face up to the memories it contained, but at the same time forgetting them would be the most terrible thing of all.

another album: *my family and other penguins*

BOOK OF PHOTOGRAPHIC PRINTS

Worcester, 1940

Photographer: Brendan Kerney

Photographs printed on cream paper; brown card binding

Commissioned by Caroline Jenkins

B<small>Y RIGHTS</small>, I should have brought far more books home from Rose Terrace. My mother had loved reading and right up until her death had worked in the Oxfam bookshop in Worcester, arguing with the managers and being opinionated about what should be kept and what disposed of, as well as giving me first option on any books about architecture and buildings that came her way. She also treated the shop as a personal lending library, borrowing paperbacks one after another and then returning them for sale. The literary part of her mind was as sharp as it had ever been.

Rose Terrace had been groaning with books: heaped in the dining room and teetering in unsafe piles up the narrow stairs, buried in the flood of papers in the study. Too few of these survived. Those downstairs were so wrecked that they had to go to the tip – I kept only one from all those stacks, and even then it still smells of nicotine and damp. Upstairs on the study bookshelves they survived better, but there were few here I wanted to save. Most were old detective novels or 1970s thrillers, untouched since they'd been put on the shelves back when my brother and I were tidying up. Wedged between the yellowing paperbacks and unused ring binders, I had dug out a handful of things worth preserving, bringing them home in just two small cardboard boxes. My keepsakes were a miscellaneous selection: anthologies of poetry and Victorian editions of Dickens, as well as two copies of a volume celebrating the centenary of Jenkins of Rotherham, the family firm.

Sorting through these at home, I found one more surprise. Thin, with an anonymous brown cloth cover, the book looked unassuming at first, but when I pulled it free from the press of books, this turned out to be a bound album. Produced by a professional photographer, it contained twelve pages of sepia-toned portrait shots, eighteen pictures in total. The whole album is meant as a memento, filled with cherished photographs to keep.

When I opened it up, though, the contents were not at all what I expected. Every single picture was of cats. To be precise, just two cats, Nicky and Li, their names given on the front page: Great Granny's cats, posing at her house. They sit and they stand, one licks a paw; sometimes they look at the camera, or their glinting eyes stare out into the middle distance as they lounge on a chair. In a few pictures, trees and fields recede behind them for a bit of variety. The photographer

Nicky and Li being imperious around Oldbury Grange.

has extracted about as much variety and information as can be got from a pair of disdainful Siamese, but that isn't a great amount.

These pictures showed me that Great Granny had loved Nicky and Li, so much so that she paid for them to be captured for posterity. But that wasn't the only story that this album told. These pictures were taken when her grandchildren were tiny: Anne was just four, my mother two and a half, while Alastair was only six months old. Yet there are no expensively printed albums of their toddler days, or at least not that I've found, and I'm sure my grandmother would have kept them if there were. All that remains are the tiny black and white Box Brownie snaps that Antoinette pasted into the albums I now own. For Carrie, cats were of much greater importance than children, and these photographs made sure her grandchildren knew that.

Apparently inconsequential, the book nonetheless contains an enormous emotional punch, so much so that I had to wonder why my mother had held on to it for all these years. The napkin ring had been a more obvious heirloom and so harder to get rid of, but why didn't she just throw this album in the bin? She didn't care about Nicky and Li; in fact, she'd probably have preferred not to be reminded of them. The obvious answer is because she was a hoarder, and so that's the very last thing she would have been able to do. That's not the only reason though. Had I asked my mother, she would have claimed to be wryly amused at the glimpse that the album gives into Carrie Jenkins' character. That's what she would have wanted me to believe.

The more I cleared away her stuff, however, the more I was coming to understand that my mother held on to these

171

reminders because she didn't want to get rid of the hurt. She did not want to have travelled those lands and have no souvenirs. Even more than that, her childhood of dead children, hospital stays, boarding school and disappearing parents had become an integral part of her selfhood, a deep dark mass that sat inside her. Without that core of despair, she would be flimsy and insubstantial, a ghost.

Worse than that, my mother might have feared that there was nothing to her but this pain. Getting rid of it would mean that she, Patricia Gilmour, would have been entirely obliterated, just as her grandmother had removed her from the photographic record and replaced her with a pair of Siamese cats. In the way that her mother would have preferred her dead and Alastair alive. Oblivion was an ever-present danger, her constant terror. Better to be here and in pain than not exist at all.

There's one extra layer of absurdity in the album. The date on that first page is May 1940. At the point when the Germans are racing across Europe and the British Expeditionary Force is being evacuated from Dunkirk, my great-grandmother's most pressing concern is having professional photographs taken of her cats.

Great Granny spent the last forty years of her long life in the company of Siamese cats, as Nikki and Li were followed by a succession of bad-tempered pairs, right up to those I met as a small child. By this point, she had sold the big house, Oldbury Grange, and built a modern 1960s bungalow in the corner of the garden. I recall lots of brickwork and wood, and the cats walking along the low, irregular stone walls of her garden.

Carrie probably did prefer her Siamese to people. Cats, while supercilious, were nonetheless more reliable than human beings, and demanded less. While she might seem to have lived a charmed life of big houses, ample funds and travel, she had also been very unfortunate, the main cause of this being mountains. Her husband was a keen climber who died in 1933 in a car crash in South Africa, on his way to a remote range in Lesotho. Harold had passed his love of climbing on to their only son, John, who died fourteen years later in the Alps. This left Carrie with only her awkward and unwanted daughter Antoinette. She lived another thirty-three years with this bitterness, dying when she was ninety-two.

This isn't the only explanation for why she loved Nicky and Li, along with all their equally sulky successors. The love for a particular animal seems to have been handed down our family line for four generations, all the way to E with her intense affinity with otters. Either that or the need to identify with a totem is a throwback that we, more than other families,

Carrie Jenkins with her children, John and Antoinette, c. 1918.

have not been able to leave behind. Several years ago, I visited the Tomb of the Eagles on Orkney, a Neolithic chambered cairn which had been excavated by the farmers who owned the land. A small museum in one of their barns was crammed with cases of stone tools, pottery sherds and tiny fragments of skeleton, human and animal, every piece a bleached, wind-burned ivory. These had all been found together in the cliff-side tomb, where the split grey stone of the islands had been used to build a chain of small spaces, holding the dead of many generations. With them had been buried the remains of sea eagles, or earns, the great birds of the cliff and sky on these islands. These people wanted to be proud and elegant, to soar through the world and hunt without fear. They were the eagles, and the birds, in turn, were part of them.

Alongside the tomb and its contents, a later Bronze Age roundhouse had also been found, built from the same flat Orkney stones and shaped like an igloo with its narrow passage entrance. My most vivid memory of all is the farmer standing in the middle of this house, explaining how his predecessors had cooked their food using stones heated in the fire. As he spoke, his black and white sheepdog walked around the house a couple of times then settled itself into a small niche in the entrance corridor, a place that must have been built for some Bronze Age dog to bed down in too, patiently guarding his family each night. Some instincts remain unchanged, even over thousands of years.

Only now we live in more individual times, and each of us has to choose our own totem. This isn't only true for my family. Philip Pullman shows his characters with their individual daemons, and J. K. Rowling allows her characters to conjure up their own patronus. The trait continues down our line as well. E has her otters, while I share my great-grandmother's rather obsessive love of cats. To me, they feel exactly like Pullman's daemons, a part of myself that I am tied to with an intense and emotional connection yet that lives totally separate from me. When they feel pain, I feel it too. Reading about the death of a cat can reduce me to tears, when I don't readily cry about anything else.

While Carrie Jenkins and I favoured cats, my grandmother Antoinette found her soulmate in the form of a bird, the penguin. I brought one of her totems back from my mother's house: a foot-tall penguin, made from some polished tropical wood. This had stood on the side table in Rose Terrace, but in its previous life it stood proudly on the windowsill in my grandmother's hall. I've held on to the ornament not simply because I like it or because it represents Granny's deep and longstanding obsession with penguins, but also because it's standing in for something much more significant: her picture.

Over the fireplace in my grandmother's small sitting room, always, hung an oil painting of a group of penguins standing around on an ice floe, with the pale Antarctic skies behind. Painted by the renowned wildlife artist David Shepherd, the canvas was vast and imposing, stretching almost the entire width of the chimney breast. Looking back now, it seems a very odd choice: that great big slab of cold hanging over the only source of warmth in the room. What I also see now is that the birds represented my grandmother's essential view of life: a cold, bleak existence in which we all stand as isolated individuals on our own blocks of ice, staring out into the distance until it ends.

Her love of penguins was a constant, but it was only when her own mother, Carrie, died, leaving her money of her own at last, that Antoinette could afford to go and see them in the wild. My cousin, Mags' daughter, then in her early twenties, was approached as a travelling companion for the first trip. Being fresh out of university and broke, she said an enthusiastic yes to what looked like an all-expenses-paid trip to Australia. What my grandmother booked instead was a fortnight on the Falkland Islands, with flights there and back on an RAF Hercules transporter. My cousin was suddenly very busy, and Mags went instead. Antoinette didn't mind; she was going to have the trip of a lifetime regardless of who went with her. Less than ten years after the war, no one went to the Falklands out of choice, so the penguins thronged there unregarded and not afraid of people at all. My grandmother spent day after day sitting on a rocky outcrop in a sturdy woollen overcoat and hat, looking like Paddington's Aunt Lucy, surrounded by penguins going about their daily routines, as happy as she had ever been.

Several more journeys followed. There was a certain irony in this, because exotic travel was what Carrie had inflicted on Antoinette as the price for financial support, but my grandmother's need to see penguins clearly outweighed any misgivings she may have had about history repeating. She took my mother with her on her next trip, and then on several more to see animals in the wild all over the world. These were the journeys which produced my mother's flat photographs of empty landscapes and wide beaches, so it's hard to say whether she enjoyed them or not. I suspect that, like me in Naples, she travelled hoping for some recognition from her mother which she never received wherever they ended up.

The photographs and the wooden penguin survive, but the painting has disappeared, taken over to the West Indies by Anne after her mother's death. Anne herself died only a couple of months before my mother, so who knows where those birds on their floe live now, or if they even survived in the tropical humidity.

The only person in my family who didn't seem to want an animal totem was my mother, although she did, after a few years in Rose Terrace, get a cat. She would have hated to be like Carrie Jenkins in any way, but those spoilt and resented Siamese had nonetheless taught her that cats ought to be elegant and communicative, so she compromised with a small chocolate-brown Burmese, the runt of the litter. Lucy came from an oriental cat rehoming service at a year old, after belonging to a family who were about to have their first child and didn't believe that cats and babies belonged in the same house.

'Ridiculous,' said my mother.

She liked talking about Lucy in the evenings when I was staying with her. After supper, my mother would sit down in the deep 1930s armchair that had once lived in my grandmother's house, and almost immediately Lucy would walk in and settle down on her lap, paws tucked in, eyes closed but ears still alert.

'How are you, Lucy Poosey?' my mother would say, scratching her under the chin. Then she'd look at me. 'I call her that because she's like Henny Penny, always thinking that the sky is about to fall in.'

This was one of two things she said about the cat every time I visited. The other was how picky Lucy was about food. My mother blamed her original owners, who'd owned a fish and chip shop and, my mother firmly believed, gave her the leftover fish at the end of the evening.

'She won't ever eat fish with the skin on. It must have come off with the batter before they gave it to her.'

The smoke from my mother's first after-dinner cigarette curled up towards the ceiling. She and Lucy would have been sitting here like this whether I was present or not.

In truth, Lucy was spoiled, and my mother enjoyed feeding her Marks & Spencer's tinned tuna as a treat. This seemed to make them both happy, so I never said anything. Contentment was a rare quality and had to be conserved.

Eventually, after many years of companionship, Lucy disappeared, at a time when things had already started to get bad for my mother. I imagined that she'd gone to hide in a dark bush to die, as cats do. I would have wanted to find her, to mourn. My mother didn't seem to care at all.

'Lucy's gone,' was all she said over the phone. Her voice was flat and empty.

I couldn't bear this, and not only for the sake of the cat. If I disappeared, would this matter so little to her as well?

What I see now is that my mother was trying to protect herself from the pain that yet another loss would bring. What I thought of as my mother's peculiar quirks turn out to be the stock in trade of hoarders. An American writer recounts asking her hoarder mother where her dog had gone. The mother replies that he ran away from a kennels while they were on holiday. 'What did you do about it?' asks the daughter. 'Nothing,' is the affectless, one-word reply. The more she is questioned, the more she clams up. She does not dare to engage. These people become hoarders because they have suffered so much loss already that the disposing of even a single object would be too hard to bear. So when they are faced with something or someone they love disappearing, an experience that threatens to be real and emotional and painful, they can't cope with it at all. Their only response is to shut down.

When I returned to the chaos of Rose Terrace the next week, my brother took the train up from London to meet me. The house was no surprise to him: he'd seen the state of it when she'd been in hospital and had already spent a day clearing it on his own. Now he was visiting to choose what, if anything, he wanted to keep of her things. What I needed from him was reassurance. Was I doing the right thing by our mother in throwing so much away? I needn't have worried, because he was even more ruthless than me, picking out only two or three ornaments to take back in his rucksack, content for the rest to disappear for good.

After the first hour of packing towels and clothes into rubbish sacks, I asked him how he felt about my mother now that he was back in the house. He paused, then the corners of his mouth half twitched with a smile. 'She was dealt a bad hand, but she played it very badly too.' Then he went back to filling his black bin liner. He didn't need to think about it beyond that. I envied him the ease with which he could leave the detritus of the past behind him, without feeling the pull of memory or what might have been. He too was upset and angry, grieving and confused, but none of what he felt resided in the things my mother had left behind. I wished that I could face them with this clarity.

With him there, I had more stamina, so twice we filled my car with broken electrical equipment, old textiles and wood to be recycled at the tip. For weeks I'd been wanting to clean the back windows of the house, each one thick with dirt and sticky tar. Now I dared to climb up ladders and on to windowsills and worktops in the knowledge that he would be there to find me if I slipped and I fell. I cleaned the inside of the windows while my brother worked outside, and together we performed the most satisfying magic so far. As we got through roll after roll of paper cloths, the sunlight slowly came back in through the windows, falling on to the stained carpets, the half-cleared heaps of newspaper, the thick grease in the kitchen. Seeing the ruins so clearly should have made things worse, but the splashes of clear light brought in a normality that had been missing from the house for years.

I foisted one job on to him entirely, and that was investigating the cellar. Jim and Ed had been down for a quick look early on, and the plumber had been in too when he'd come to turn off the water. They'd all said that the small room had been empty, and that should have been enough, but the problem was no one could find the electricity meter, and we'd looked everywhere else that it could have been. My suspicion was that the basement extended much further, right to the front of the house, but I'd only managed to get as far as opening the small door under the stairs. From there I could look at heaps of dusty tools, boxes of nails and old paint cans which my mother had stashed on the stone steps which led down into darkness and the space below. I couldn't even manage to get over the threshold.

Despite the demands from the electricity company for a meter reading, I put off the job from one visit to the next. This wasn't just because I was afraid of spiders; going down there had a symbolic meaning as well. If my mother had identified herself so totally with Rose Terrace, her person and the house becoming as one, that meant the cellar represented her unconscious, containing all those dark and unhappy emotions that she had spent a lifetime trying to repress. Knowing why I feared the place didn't make me any more able to open that door.

I would have happily done every other bit of cleaning and clearing that remained, quite possibly with my bare hands, as long as my brother dealt with the cellar. Unburdened by excessive metaphor and over-thinking, he was happy to oblige, so I handed him the lantern and waited. At first he came back and said that there was only the small room that Jim and Ed had found, but being an older sister I sent him back and eventually he found the meter far away in a whole new space under the sitting room. He also discovered the other reason I hadn't dared to go down. The rodent poison put down by Jim and Ed on their very first visit had been eaten, but as yet we'd found no corpses. The dead rat I'd been dreading was also under the sitting room, and starting to smell. My brother disposed of it while I went upstairs, moved some papers around and pretended that none of this was going on.

The rat wasn't the end of our day's labour. The garden was an overgrown wilderness, with ivy and thick branches pressed up against the kitchen window and brambles reaching through the hole in the back door. My mother had planted a bay tree by the fences, only a few easy steps away from the kitchen, but now it was a thirty-foot giant sprouting up into the sky, its leaves unused for years. I could hardly get beyond the back door before being defeated by growth and could not imagine how it might be cleared.

With my brother there, it seemed possible to face this too, so together we took turns to saw through branches and flatten the thickets of stems. I'd armed us with the right tools – a solid pruning saw, secateurs that had once belonged to Carrie

Jenkins and, best of all, a tough-bladed scythe from my local agricultural supply store. This allowed us to smash through the undergrowth like explorers in the Amazonian jungle, making the work swift and satisfying. After just a couple of hours, we had a heap of waste to be shredded and a view of the sky above for the first time in years. We could even make out the round shape of the lawn edging beneath our feet.

I never said this to my brother, but as we worked away I was also looking very carefully at the ground we cleared. Somewhere in this I expected to find a small cat skeleton, the last remains left where Lucy had gone to curl up and die. By the end of the afternoon, we had exposed every corner of the garden, right up to the shed at the very end, but there weren't any answers, not even a single skull. Lucy had gone for ever, and I would never know where, but that wasn't the biggest disappointment. I had also begun to realize that my mother's house wasn't going to tell me everything I needed to know.

bone china: *the life of things*

PART DINNER SERVICE (PLATES, BOWLS, GRAVY BOAT, SUGAR BOWL AND CAKE PLATTER)

England, *c.* 1980–95

Bone china with gilding to rim

Manufactured by Royal Worcester Ltd

Purchase

With my brother taking so few of my mother's things, the fate of what remained was my responsibility alone. Underneath the junk and in the calm of the sitting room, far more had survived than I had expected, but for once I wasn't able to decide what I wanted to keep and what we might sell or give away. The only thing I knew was that everything had to be cleaned before I would let anyone else look at it. I returned home with not only five boxes of ornaments and glass but also two whole dinner services.

The plain bone china I knew intimately because my mother had used it every day, whether eating alone or cooking for other people. Although it had been made by Royal Worcester and came from their factory just a ten-minute walk from the house, the style wasn't one you could buy in the shops. As usual, my mother had been fussy. She didn't like any of the patterns that Royal Worcester produced, from their fancy florals to the plain green and gold banding that Antoinette had chosen for her best set, but at the same time she refused to eat from clunky earthenware. Only bone china would do. The one design which pleased her, this delicate white ware with the single gold band around the rim, came from the seconds shop. These were, of course, a very particular kind of second, only produced when a well-made piece had a blemish in its white glaze. If the flaw wasn't too visible, the result wasn't discarded but given a quick circle of gold paint and put out for sale in the factory shop. What was on offer depended on what had gone wrong. My mother, living so close, went in most weeks and so managed to build up her set over the years.

I'd never seen my mother use anything but the Royal Worcester, so was surprised when Jim and Ed found another complete service lurking in the kitchen cupboards. Made by Spode, the pattern was a 1960s interpretation of Regency in a sludge green, with a neoclassical frieze of sunflowers in the centre and swags of ivy leaves around every edge. The result is relentlessly ugly, which is probably why my mother's set was complete, right down to the last tureen and milk jug. This must have been the best dinner set given to her and my father as a wedding present, then taken by my mother as her portion after the divorce. My father had the everyday china, a brown Hornsea earthenware, but my mother held on to the Spode, even though I am fairly sure she hated it.

Both services arrived in my house filthy. The Worcester

My parents' wedding in 1962. My mother will keep the china they received for more than fifty years.

had been living in a cupboard with one door missing and the other hanging off, leaving it covered in the same sticky dust that had attached itself to every other ornament, door handle and skirting board. The unwanted Spode had been shut away in a corner cupboard, behind working doors. This should have protected it, only the stacks had been ignored for so long that an older, more delicate kind of dust had crept in, so the pieces were covered in a thick grey fluff instead.

I stacked the boxes in the corner of my study, only bringing out their contents to be washed in the daytime when E was at school, or in the evening when she had gone to bed. I wanted her to remember her grandmother in otter egg cups and cuttings from the newspaper, not filthy washing-up water and grime. The china came out brown with nicotine and dust, sticky to the touch. No one could ever want to eat food from plates that looked like this. Every piece was rinsed, then scrubbed, then rinsed again under the tap. I ran one sink after another, as only two or three items were enough to turn the water the colour of river mud. Yet when I finally set them to dry on a tea towel, every expanse of smooth glaze shone again; the light glinted off the gold.

Each piece gave me hope, for the first time since my mother had died. Here were items that had lived through the darkness of her hoarding and not only had they emerged intact but after I worked on them it was impossible to tell that anything bad had happened at all. This allowed me to believe that the house might one day be restored and made safe, turned into a place that someone other than my mother would want to inhabit. I wanted to wash anything I could lay my hands on in order to make this redemption happen over and over again.

More than that, as I cleaned and scrubbed and rinsed I

187

could feel myself deep in the thrall of magical thinking. If the china could be made good, and the house could be returned to its former glory, then if I carried on with this work I would manage to set my mother's life to rights as well. I knew, of course, that these thoughts couldn't ever be true, but that didn't stop me working.

When I'd brought the china home, I hadn't intended for it to stay. I'd thought that I was cleaning the services only to return them to Worcester, where they could go to auction along with the few bits of furniture which hadn't been ruined by damp or mice. I didn't mind boxing up the Spode service, in all its green ugliness; as I couldn't remember seeing it before, it held no meaning. The Royal Worcester was another story. Every piece of it had become entangled with my mother. She had chosen the style, spent time selecting each individual plate and bowl from the seconds shop, picking over the stacks to make sure that any mark or mishap was on the underside, that the rim sat flat and that the base didn't rock when she put it down on the table. Then she'd infused it with yet more of her personality by using it day in, day out: white plates on dark-green mats set against the deep polish of her mahogany dining table, whether she was serving home-made summer pudding to a visitor or eating Marks & Spencer's quiche on her own. And so the white china ended up in my dining-room cupboard. Were I to sell it, a part of her soul would have disappeared, but for as long as I held on to it, a bit of her lived on alongside me.

This sense that objects can be filled with personality and meaning, maybe even life, is common in hoarders. Should you believe that a thing has feelings, or soul, it becomes much harder to discard.

This relationship with animate objects is the most ancient of all. Ever since the first tool was created, people have believed that things have been living and feeling and meaning, that not all their powers are bestowed by humans. Across the other side of the Orkney Islands from the Tomb of the Eagles is the village of Skara Brae. It too dates from the early Neolithic period but survived for more than four thousand years because wood was rare on the low, storm-swept islands, so everything had to be built from the slate stone – not just the thick walls of the houses but also the furniture they contained. Each house holds beds and a hearth, but in pride of place, facing the door as you enter, is what archaeologists call a dresser. These three-tiered stone shelves are where the inhabitants must have kept their possessions, but storage alone could have been achieved by a stone box or a pit. The dressers are a kind of altar. Here, long before writing or money or consumers, things were revered.

Some of these very particular objects survive. Polished stone axes, dating from the same moment in the Neolithic period, have been found all across the British Isles. These weapons have a glossy surface which would have taken days or even weeks of labour to produce. The polish protects the stone from cracking, so the work had a practical purpose, and some of the axes bear the nicks and scratches of daily use. Others, though, are as sleek and flawless as the day they were made, and these are made from a kind of jade quarried from the highest peaks of the Alps and traded across the seas. These axes were not made to chop down trees; their work was to mean, not do.

To their owners, the precious jade-stone weapons may almost have been alive; archaeologists suggest they would have had names and biographies. When they came to the end of their uses, they were either broken and disposed of in streams or on sacred hills, or given a burial, like people.

Long after their makers had been supplanted by societies with bricks, horses and metal ploughs, these axes maintained their aura. One survivor, in the British Museum, had been pierced at each end and then mounted in silver so that it could be worn on the body. This was not done by some primitive tribe but in the nineteenth century, the work of a Scottish Army officer who hoped it would cure his kidney disease, as though he had intuited its powers across thousands of years.

These greenstone axes weren't a rare exception. Some archaeologists now believe that meaning, not function, drove technological progress. The first metalworkers were not impelled by the need for practical tools. Instead, they produced sceptres, beads and neck torcs, things which spoke and meant rather than did. Being strange and magical, liquid and solid, born from rock, metal had powers, and these could be passed on to the human who wore it, making them closer to gods.

There's something else worth noting about Skara Brae. Storms career across the flat islands of the Orkneys all winter, and the people who lived in the village needed shelter above all else, so the houses were sunk into a huge mound of organic matter. Archaeologists call it a midden, but what this means is that people lived deep in their own refuse, which warmed and protected them. The villagers tunnelled into it to get from house to house, and it may even have been a symbol of regeneration, a central part of their view of the cosmos. Burying yourself in rubbish hasn't always been a bad thing. Sometimes it can be a survival technique.

*

Objects kept their powers long after the Neolithic period. The relics of medieval saints could protect against disease or bring a child to the infertile, and this ability to act wasn't the preserve of sacred things alone. On some Scottish islands, a boat from which a fisherman had drowned was beached and left to rot rather than returning to sea with its innocent companions. This idea bled into law: ships could be tried in a court, while in Europe glaciers were excommunicated for damaging valleys.

The intellectual revolution of the Enlightenment was meant to kick out magic, replacing it with science. From this moment, things and people occupied separate realms. Only people could act and do; objects, in contrast, were entirely inert. There was no more place in the world for bones that healed or objects that killed. Life had drained from the world of stuff.

Nearly three hundred years later, this is still how we prefer to think about our things. Magical objects, which act and live for themselves, are only allowed to persist in very particular corners, such as religion, where wine has the power to be both blood and itself at the same time, and bread can be both flesh and forgiveness. Modern art also has a strand of this thought at its core, believing as it does in the transformative powers of the gallery. This can turn an ordinary object, whether a urinal or a screwed-up ball of paper, into a work of art, as surely as bread turns into body.

Apart from these rare exceptions, magical objects only exist where we, the descendants of the Enlightenment, are not. Anthropologists seek them out in the dense forests of Papua New Guinea or the townships of South Africa, and the analysis of how spirited things work in other societies fills shelf after shelf in their libraries, although without much agreement being reached. The only certainty is that the West is different. For us, things are things, inanimate and without soul; only people can make them do anything.

From this perspective, hoarders seem to be throwbacks to the people of Skara Brae with their magical axes, a primitive tribe who see life in papers and plastic bags rather than trees, greenstone and gold. There are parallels. One of the recurrent beliefs of tribal societies is that taking possession of someone's detritus – their nail clippings, hair cuttings or lost teeth – can give a witch powers over that person, because these leftovers contain a portion of their soul. The most extreme hoarders hold on to exactly these things, and their urine and faeces too, for fear of what might happen if they let any part of themselves go.

At the same time, hoarders are not freaks in every respect; much of their world is a more amplified version of our own. When they insist that discarding a photograph of someone might bring that person harm, or that a Tupperware box might be upset to be put in the bin, we catch a glimpse of a vitality which we normally refuse to acknowledge and yet which surrounds us, teeming under the surface of our supposedly inert world. Perhaps this is one of the reasons why hoarding frightens us so much, because it forces us to confront our own irrationality.

The other reason we find it hard to perceive these qualities in things is because we are missing the words to describe what is happening. In English, the goods and chattels which surround us can only be dead. When anthropologists want to discuss cultures in which things have life or act, they are forced to employ foreign terms. These are fetish objects, filled with *mana* or *qi*. Or they fall within the great catch-all term of 'magic'. As we are no longer peasants or Neolithic hunters, and use science rather than the supernatural to explain the world around us, this makes the idea as strange and remote from us as using a foreign word would do.

Yet we need to speak about how we live with our possessions. We are not surrounded by inert tools which change the world only when we pick them up; our lives are spent in a complex dance of association with solid objects which not only resonate but can contain spirit and change us. We hold irrational beliefs about them and treat some as though they were animate. Without the words to describe this, we find it easy to pretend that this thronging mass of lively stuff does not exist. But it does.

E is in the last years of primary school, and the power of things is already at work in her life. For her, it's pencil cases which matter the most. These are almost the only non-uniform possessions allowed on the premises, so for inconsequential objects they must do a lot of work. It's important to have the right brand if you want to be cool. I can tell E time and again that possessions don't matter, that what you do is far more important than what you own, and if the in-crowd think that self-worth comes from possessing that one piece of turquoise plastic they must feel very insecure inside. Whatever I say, though, having the right pencil case will still matter to her very much indeed.

Almost every single thing which surrounds us resonates with social meaning in this way. Entirely practical objects which carry no symbolic weight are becoming fewer and fewer in number. A simple sink plunger bought from the ironmongers might be one of them, but it's entirely possible that in New York or Tokyo there already exists a designer sink plunger whose material and design speak of the taste of its owner, along with their spending power. More and more we need our possessions to mean as well as do, to speak on our behalf. Our stuff defines us, it tells the story of our lives so far and who we would like to become, as well as who we really are.

The most important of these, like cars or houses or books, become incorporated into our wider being. We are all partly made of stuff, and in our heads the border between what is mine and what is me can be very fuzzy. For E, not yet possessing very much of her own, this crucial function is performed by her pencil case. For adults, paintings and houses, souvenirs and heirlooms, photographs and furniture can all become part of our selves. This interchangeability of self and stuff is the bedrock of all advertising. A gleaming new car, television or bottle of perfume offers the buyer a new personality; power, charisma or beauty comes as part of the purchase. But money doesn't have to change hands for an object to become incorporated into who we are. We can also take in the second-hand and inherited by cleaning, altering and repairing it. In the case of the Royal Worcester china, my mother had made it hers by using it every day for twenty years or more; I, in turn, cleaned it up, turning the pieces into something which had belonged to both of us, and which also embodied the way in which I had tried to repair her life after she had gone. No wonder I found myself unable to pass it on.

Almost all of us live among objects which are vital and animated in this way, tangled up with our memories and self as though each and every one of us were a hoarder. Heirlooms allow us to live alongside the dead as surely as if we mummified the bodies of our forebears. Souvenirs retain important experiences or journeys. Old drawings, toys and pieces of clothing can bring back a fleeting childhood, even when the children themselves have long left home. Although I threw away so much of what my mother left behind, I have her black teapot and the Royal Worcester china, the Arab robes, the red bird and many boxes more, all charged with an electricity of memory which makes them impossible to discard.

The strangeness of these things is demonstrated by the way that they occupy a space outside the conventional monetary system of value. They are, in the jargon of economists, non-fungible; that is, we would not be prepared to exchange them for other, similar objects. Pets and children are the classic examples, but much of what we own, once it has been brought into our homes and appropriated, becomes much less fungible than it ought to be; things filled with human spirit even more so.

One way of measuring the life things contain is what I think of as the *Antiques Roadshow* test. People bring in what are mostly cherished possessions and tell the story of how they came to own them. These are then identified and analysed until the moment every viewer is waiting for: the valuation. It's not only the sum of money which matters. What makes the revelation compelling is the conflict between this and any personal value that the item contains.

Within the show, there is an implicit understanding that some things have such personal significance that they have no place in the system of value and exchange. This might be because they have little value, but often it is because their power is too strong. An elderly couple have brought in his grand-father's medals from the First World War, where he served as one of the earliest pilots.

'Of course you're not going to sell them,' says the valuing expert, and the man nods in agreement. The medals are the embodiment of his grandfather's bravery, and this connection to his ancestors trumps any possible sum of money.

Where this becomes most revealing is in the marginal cases. A vase does not carry that emotional weight, so when an ornament or knick-knack is brought in, the owner may say at first that they would never sell. Should the value turn out to be huge, however, tens of thousands of pounds or more, the sum becomes so potentially life-changing that the object may end up back in the marketplace. It turns out we can value the emotion something contains. Our connection to great-granny may be worth more to us than five hundred pounds, but were we to be offered five thousand, then the scales will tip. This difficult reckoning is what gives the programme its appeal.

For hoarders, almost every one of their possessions has the same level of emotional investment as the pieces featured on the *Antiques Roadshow*. All have been removed from the normal economy of use and disposal. Nothing is fungible, not even a plastic bag. Each one is as unique as a work of art, and no replica or substitute will do.

All of these beliefs can be explained in terms of human agency. We transmit meanings and lives into things, and they do not act of their own accord. However irrationally we behave around them, their powers have originated from us.

But things can also have a more problematic, less explicable presence in our lives, possessing a strangeness and vitality that doesn't rely on human intentions and interpretation. They can soak up the personalities of people, or the presence of history itself, and in doing this they become alive with a spirit entirely their own.

Once again, hoarders reveal what we do not always acknowledge in our own lives. Often they speak as though the hoard itself has been making the decisions and they are just bystanders in their own house. 'The things just started coming in,' said one woman on a hoarding programme as she gazed around her living room, even though it was she who had been buying them from charity shops and eBay. Even officialdom can find itself sucked into this viewpoint. One report described a hoarder who had ended up sleeping on her sofa because 'she could not make enough room on her bed; the stuff had claimed ownership'.

For all that our culture would like to believe that only ancient peoples, remote tribes and hoarders think this way, our everyday lives contain a host of objects which live and act in just this way, and these surround us almost from the moment we are born.

Very many of us spend the first years of our childhood close to one magical thing. Most children pick out one of their cuddly toys to be special, a comforter and constant companion: what psychiatrists call a transitional object. These soft toys are imbued with the life and protective powers of our parents. When our caregivers cannot be next to us, when they leave us in a dark room on our own, these comforting beings allow us to keep the safety of the grown-ups close by, so long as we hold on tight. Mine was a panda, who sits in my study to this day.

Bears and pandas may have been left behind on our childhood beds, but the idea that people's personalities might seep into their possessions stays with us when we move into the wider world. Whole auctions are built around the idea that some kind of ectoplasm leaches from a famous person into their possessions. Marilyn Monroe's dress is worth more than any ordinary piece of clothing; the same is true of John Lennon's piano. The more charismatic the person, the greater the value, as though their energy has entered the object like a static charge.

It's easy to dismiss this as a foible of silly people with too much money, but the basic belief that a person's spirit can live on in the things that they own is one we all hold. Scientists have done a variety of experiments to prove this, but I managed to demonstrate it quite easily at home, in a short conversation with my husband.

Me: So you've got a mug.

T: Yes, fine.

Me: But it's Fred West's mug. Can you use it?

T (horrified): Of course not. I'd have to throw it away.

He then spent the next few minutes debating whether it might be too contaminating to be put in our kitchen bin and so whether he would have to smash it, in order to prevent anyone else using it without knowing its toxic history, then dispose of the pieces beyond the boundaries of our house, and whether putting it in a public bin would be unfair on the person emptying it. However it was done, the mug had to go, in as final a way as possible.

Almost everyone would feel the same. The mug is, of course, without personality or morals, and with our logical mind we know that. At the same time, it's almost impossible to escape the sense that a profound transfer of energy has happened, making the mug so dangerous that it cannot remain on the earth unguarded. It has become an object as powerful as a Neolithic jade axe. Anything which has once been this sacred or profane cannot simply be disposed of; instead, it has to be ritually destroyed.

These beliefs are ingrained into the very structure of our society. Even the government is prepared to spend considerable amounts of money on the understanding that the souls of the dead live on in things. The force of this belief can be seen in the stories of two sets of Arab robes.

Up in our top bedroom sits a suitcase of green canvas with tan leather corners, theatrically old-fashioned. This isn't a family relic, but its contents are; I daren't put them in the attic lest they rot. It contains the garments that my mother was so concerned to rescue from my grandmother's house before her sister Anne got to them: the set of men's Arab dress and full-length burka, the veil that conceals the full head and body down to the ankles, leaving its owner to look out on the world through a thick embroidery grille. These were originally bought by Harold Jenkins, Carrie's husband and my great-grandfather, in the 1930s when he was travelling the world in order to sell mining and oil-drilling equipment.

The robes are fascinating, particularly the burka, which is the colour of a shiny aubergine and made not from cotton or linen but a modern rayon which slips through the fingers like water. The headpiece is densely hand-stitched and close fitting, but cascading out from this the fabric is pleated into irregular folds, for all the world like a Fortuny gown. Fashion and modernity have been woven into a centuries-old tradition. In holding the garments I am also connected to the curiosity of my great-grandfather and his travels to what were then distant lands. Even at the most specialist auction, his souvenirs

Harold Jenkins, intrepid traveller and keen mountaineer, on a family camping holiday in the early 1920s.

would be valued at only a few hundred pounds, but should the *Antiques Roadshow* ask, I won't be selling them.

In 2015, however, a set of Arab robes and a man's headdress sold for more than £35,000. The difference didn't lie in the headdress but the fact that they had been owned and worn by that mythical figure, Lawrence of Arabia. The man, T. E. Lawrence, was long dead, but part of his spirit and bravery still resided in the clothes that he had worn. This belief wasn't only held by one or two rich collectors but by the state itself. At the auction, the robes were sold abroad, but the government put a bar on their export. Lawrence's essence was so important that it needed to be preserved in his relics for the entire British people, for ever.

On offer in the same auction was a dagger that had once belonged to Lawrence. Like the robes, it is a relic which contains the spirit of the man, but this weapon also demonstrates another way in which we still believe objects can carry power. They preserve time and events in material form.

Lawrence didn't use this dagger in battle or daily life; it was a presentation piece, made to commemorate his role in the Battle of Aqaba in 1917, when he was a strategic advisor to the Arab armies in their victory against the Ottoman Turks. His intervention, like the whole battle itself, was crucial in driving the occupying Ottoman forces out of the Arabian peninsula, yet his role left no physical trace or record. The dagger was commissioned as a means of turning an ephemeral moment of history into silver and steel, thereby ensuring that it would never be forgotten. This freezing of time is the work commemorative objects do.

Retirement gifts are the most common examples in everyday life, preventing a lifetime of employment from evaporating into oblivion the moment someone stops work. The archetypal presents, across a wide range of companies and cultures, are the gold watch or the carriage clock. If we were to articulate why, the answer might be that people look at a clock or a watch regularly, and know that they were appreciated, but the choice is far more meaningful than this. The worker who retires has given years of his life to the company, but instead of disappearing these are transmuted into a ticking piece of solid time that could last across generations.

Medals perform the same mysterious alchemy, transforming transient acts of bravery into solid discs of bronze or silver gilt. By far the best way of ensuring that time is kept for eternity is to choose metal. My mother's house proved to me that the stuff is a survivor. It will not react or shatter, nor, if the right kind is chosen, will it corrode. Still and unchanging, it can make a single small moment in time last for ever. Alastair's napkin ring held the sadness of his going for decades, allowing it to sound out in the atmosphere long after everyone who remembered this one small boy had gone.

This slowing or even halting of time is something for which hoarders yearn. One of the great appeals of stuff is its inertia, the way it does not age or decay as quickly as human beings. Alastair's napkin ring and my mother's tankard could have waited in the darkness of the cupboard for centuries and emerged essentially unaltered. In the face of loss after loss, hoards are a reassurance to their creators and owners that not everything must pass. Their contents remain patient for as long as anyone might want, unchanging.

In my work of sorting out my mother's house and goods, I too had been trying to slow down time. I was negotiating with her death – its finality but also its precipitate suddenness. My mother had not been ill enough for me to consider that she would die, so the time I spent in Rose Terrace was a way of slowing down my mourning until I was ready to believe in her permanent absence. These things were precious because they had once been hers, and the fact that I was handling her possessions without her being present was a constant reminder that she had gone. At the same time, they kept my mother close to me. These frontiers between us and stuff, between the living and the dead, become porous in the unreal and disconnected time after someone dies. I had to believe that a part of her spirit had really remained in her table and chairs, in her hoard, in the very fabric of her house. This was how I might still find her. Death had turned my mother into a cold body, but in the same act it had brought her things to life.

This sorting and processing of stuff has become part of the modern ritual of grief and mourning. Under the skin of rationality, it's common to feel that the dead persist, a piece of their selves remaining in the possessions they have left behind. Surrounded by their stuff, we can keep them present in the world for just a bit longer until we are ready to acknowledge that they have gone for good. Sometimes magical thinking is required in order to survive.

five hoovers: *in the museum*

VACUUM CLEANER (ONE OF SET OF FIVE)

Britain, 1920–2010

Metal, plastic, fabric

Manufactured by Hoover

Bought or inherited 2000–10

M Y MOTHER HAD died after Christmas, the busiest time of the year, which meant waiting six weeks for a crematorium slot. Now the funeral was finally looming, and I made plans with my brother, approved readings and ordered flowers, but in truth I did not want it to take place, because that would mean that my mother's death was an acknowledged fact. I needed my loss to be a fresh wound, otherwise there was no excuse for the tumble of inexplicable emotions that still possessed me.

For the last few years she'd called me on a Thursday morning. That week, after more than a month of forgetting, I found myself for a split second expecting the phone to ring. Then I remembered. Even if phones had existed where she was now, I wasn't sure she would have called. My mother had always been too tangled up with the dead to pay proper attention to the living. Reunited with them at last, she wouldn't be thinking of me.

The next day, I drove back up to Worcester for that week's visit. What I couldn't shake from my mind as I headed up the motorway was the picture of arriving at the front door to find my mother waiting for me in the hall, berating me for everything I had done to tidy up in her absence. Of course when I reached Rose Terrace, I opened the door to silence, nothing more.

*

Each trip brought new discoveries, and this time it was vacuum cleaners. Long before I stopped visiting the house, I knew that my mother had too many of them, but back then I found it wryly amusing rather than annoying: the woman who has a stack of hoovers but can never clean up. At the same time, her collection had always held a promise of hope. If my mother was able to go out to the shops and buy a brand-new Dyson, it did at least prove that she wanted things to change. She intended to clear up, even if she never quite managed to make it happen. The number of hoovers fluctuated, or so it had seemed. At some point I remembered some particularly ancient examples, and then those seemed to go. Only now, with the upstairs landing and study clear enough for Jim and Ed to access the cupboards, did I realize that this hadn't been true at all. None of the old ones had gone away; my mother had simply put them out of sight.

The newest, a Dyson, was sitting in the bedroom, immobilized by heaps of clothes and still with its original box. I wasn't sure it had ever been put to work; simply the promise of cleanliness and order had been enough. Her original, first-model Dyson in yellow and black stood on the landing outside. By the time Jim and Ed had finished hunting through the cupboards, these had been joined by three more hoovers, each older than the last.

The oldest one wasn't much more than a fabric bag on a stick with a brush at one end, as though someone had decided to electrify a carpet sweeper. I looked at the frayed, fabric-covered cable and hoped that my mother had never actually tried to use it. This must surely have belonged to Carrie Jenkins, adopting the most advanced technology available to the well-off housewife in the 1920s. However ancient and provisional it seemed now, this machine had once been the height of modern living. The second was a slightly more advanced version of the bag on a stick: still functional and brown, but more solid and able to stand up on its own. I had vague memories of seeing this in my grandmother's house when I was a child, but it must have been antique even then.

The third was very different. Not only was the design more streamlined and neat, with the working parts boxed in, but it was made from white plastic rather than metal. The vacuum cleaner had become a piece of domestic equipment rather than engineering. Was this the hoover of my mother's early married life, or her new start after the divorce? Whichever way, I didn't remember it at all. The older Dyson must have arrived when she moved to Rose Terrace, keeping her brand-new house in shape, at least for a while.

I set the hoovers out in a row on the landing. Here were all the periods of my mother's life, and before, exhibited in terms of cleaning equipment. There was a certain elegance to the line-up. I wish, now, that I'd photographed them, but at the time all I wanted to do was escape from the overwhelming heaps of stuff and get rid of the evidence as fast as I could. I certainly didn't want any lasting reminders. Had I taken the picture, I could have displayed it next to another family image, although not one I'd found in my mother's house. Taken at my christening, it's a portrait of the female line in our family. I'm in my mother's arms, and by her stands her own mother, Antoinette. On her other side is Carrie Jenkins, my great-grandmother, making four generations of us in a row, like evolutionary stages of the same organism.

I've thought many different things about this picture over the years. One is simply that it's great to see the four of us

Antoinette, my mother, Carrie Jenkins and of course me at my christening in 1966.

standing together. I also used to see it as a striking image of how I supposed my mother's side of the family operated. Being a feminist, I imagined it to be a matriarchy. The family was dominated by women, but I no longer believe this happened because the women were strong. Although Carrie Jenkins and I could probably take on all comers, I'm not so sure about Antoinette and my mother. The truth is that the matriarchy existed because all the men disappeared. Husbands died young, or left, or met other women. Sons and brothers died too, until only the women remained.

Now that I'm older, the picture reveals another, more disconcerting message. It tells me what I will inevitably become.

At my christening, my mother was straight-backed and young, but it's easy to see that Antoinette is well on the way to becoming her elderly mother; they share the same hunched shoulders, pushed-down hat and suspicious expression. My grandmother is the exact image of my mother before she died. One face transforms into another with the inevitability of time. This picture reminds me of the biological facts: however much I fear turning into my mother, it's going to happen whether I want it to or not.

The hoovers felt different to all the other contents of Rose Terrace. The heaps of paper and post, the bags, newspapers and the books had just accumulated, but my mother, it seemed, had chosen to keep the five hoovers, in an orderly and deliberate way. What's more, she'd done so long before her house had begun to overflow with indiscriminate stuff.

But was I right to see these hoovers as a collection, or were they simply another part of the hoard? It was impossible to say, but I was far from the only person to ask this kind of question. The fuzzy boundaries between hoarding and collecting appear to unnerve many people and volumes of writing exist, across a range of different disciplines, which want to codify what sets a collection apart from a hoard: order, series and planning. A collection excludes things, while a hoard is omnivorous. Hoards are hidden while collections are on display.

I've always been a collector, at first of china and now vintage posters. In both of these – the stacks of dust-collecting plates and the heaps of old and sometimes tatty paper – I see echoes of my mother's hoarding. The posters in particular edge dangerously close to her territory because, numbering in their hundreds, they vastly exceed our available wall space. Never displayed, they are kept secret, in darkness, like a hoard.

Whatever my mother had intended with her set of hoovers, I could understand why she had singled the five of them out for different treatment. Each one contained a promise that it

211

would clean up the mess and thus make her life better. This kind of message is, after all, what our consumer society assures us with every new purchase, that we will be improved as people both practically and spiritually. We are bombarded with these messages through advertising, packaging and social pressure, so these are the meanings of things with which we are most familiar.

But for this kind of consumerism to work, people need to throw away the old products in order to make room for the new and improved. This was the part of the equation that my mother had decided to ignore. Each new vacuum cleaner had not displaced the one before, instead it had just been added to the stack.

She'd done this because the message of improvement promoted by advertisers and manufacturers is, in the end, the least important part of its story. Once items are assimilated into our homes this brand meaning evaporates, replaced instead by the personal mythologies and relationships that we all weave around the objects we own. This second, more personal life of commodities is rarely recognized or discussed, yet it is what binds us to our own possessions.

So what did my mother mean by her collection of hoovers? What did each one represent for her? I wanted to make sense of her life by sorting out her house; maybe she too hoped, after death, to redress her relationships with her own mother and grandmother. She might have hoped that all the difficult things which had gone before could be vacuumed up and made to disappear – a kind of magic which would of course work so much better if she used their own hoovers to perform the redemption.

*

For the rest of that day, as I sorted and chucked, filled bin bags and took them downstairs, the hoovers sat on my mother's landing, taunting me. I found their mismatched parade entertaining. But when Jim asked me what I wanted done with them, I couldn't come up with a single good reason why they should stay other than that they gave me a certain amount of pleasure. Together they looked like a museum display about the history of vacuum-cleaner technology, and museums were, after all, places where I felt very much at home.

In my twenties I had spent three years studying and then working in the Victoria and Albert Museum. My course resided behind eighteenth-century Britain. In these galleries, huge three-sided rooms, like sets for a television play, had been constructed to frame the plasterwork, fireplaces and dainty furniture of the period. Our studies took place behind these false walls, in a warren of leftover spaces. Entrance was via a tiny door next to a vast marble staircase, which looked as though it ought to house a cleaning cupboard but in fact, as was entirely natural in the Alice-in-Wonderland world of the museum, led to a long chain of offices, a kitchen and seminar rooms.

I quickly learned to see this arrangement as normal. Surprises like this were concealed in every part of the building, and my staff pass took me wherever I wanted to go. With the right key, a tiny cubbyhole door opened to reveal a cast-iron Victorian roof, each truss lavishly decorated with flowers and curlicues; there were dark rooms hung with medieval tapestries, huge hallways with casts of cathedral doors and Trajan's Column, and long galleries stacked with helmets and spears where no visitors ever went. This was the stately-home attic of which I had always dreamed; I could have spent my whole life in its tangle of corridors, rooms and dead ends and still found something new to discover.

I wonder whether I liked the museum so much because walking around its corridors and galleries was like inhabiting the inside of my own head. Stuff is piled up all over the place but with some attempt at categorization and order. I never needed to create a hoard, because my interior life had already been laid out in objects and space, in the form of the museum itself.

At first sight, it's hard to see museums and hoards as being kin. Like collections, museums are orderly, controlled, socially approved; they select the objects that they want to keep. In fact the two have a great deal in common. Museums are, after all, based on the basic principle of a hoard: that things are very important indeed, and therefore worth preserving. Like a hoarder, their entire existence is dedicated to the importance of stuff. What's more, both museums and hoards, in the end, are graveyards for what they contain.

When an object arrives in a museum, its status changes in two important ways. First, it loses its function. A desk will never again be used to write a letter, a dress will not be worn, a teapot used to brew up or pour out. A set of cutlery, given by the manufacturers, has never touched food and will never do so. Items in a hoard have reached a similar dead end; if they cannot be found, how can they ever be used?

This state of affairs is also permanent. Once a piece enters the collections of a museum it will very rarely leave. Like hoarders, museums don't really like to throw things away. Deacquisitioning, as they call it, is a rare and troubling occurrence. An online group for curators and archivists calls itself

Socially Sanctioned Hoarders. One contributor defined their job as acquiring artefacts, most of which are kept in storage just in case someone wants to look at them. As the hoarder says: *I'd better not get rid of it; that might come in handy one day.*

Like the hoarder, too, the museum can never have enough exhibits; it is always collecting more. When I studied there, the V&A was stuffed with far more items than it would ever be able to display. The curators would open doors to lead us through tiny back corridors, where we would squeeze past furniture, tables and desks stacked three high, banked up as though they were in a warehouse, each one carrying a thick carpet of dust. None of these pieces was glamorous enough to put out in the galleries, but they were also too important to discard, and so they remained, cluttering the place up, forcing the staff along the tiny paths between them, just like a hoarder negotiating their way between stacks of bags and boxes. Hoarding professionals call these paths 'goat trails'. There didn't seem to be a name for them in the museum; that was just the way things were.

The excess of stuff hasn't gone away, but what's changed is that museums have become more open about admitting their problem. Many institutions now offer tours of their stores and archives, allowing people in to see the scale of their predicament. The V&A has gone one better, bringing some of its hoard into the body of the museum itself.

I had returned there to see if I could find out any more about the black teapot from my mother's dining-room shelves. Cleaned up to reveal its black mourning sheen once more, it had found a new home on my own bookshelves, still determinedly making its point that all taste is relative and that wonderfully ugly is an under-appreciated genre of design. I knew it was Victorian and that, being black and un-glossy, it fell into a category called Basalt Ware, first pioneered by Wedgwood, but the pot had no mark or stamp on the bottom to identify its maker. Eventually, I'd thought back to the endless stretches of 1930s display cabinets in the Ceramics Department of the V&A and wondered whether there I might be able to find if not its twin then at least its cousin.

Up the broad marble staircase in the main hall, past impassive saints in their niches on the way. Into the eighteenth century, then first right to another set of stairs which led to the top floor. But when I arrived in Ceramics, all my landmarks had gone. I entered the first room to find a great wall of glass, holding piece after piece of china, each in its own transparent box, one shelf above another until they almost touched the high plasterwork ceilings. Museum displays are usually sparse and selective, each individual object the tip of an iceberg, indicating the vast mass of similar stuff which lives in the obscurity of the stores. Here, the curators were confessing that they had too much. The reinforced glass was a necessary defence; without this, their holdings might spread throughout the building, unrestrained and unstoppable.

This display wasn't entirely intended to overwhelm, or even as a means for the curators to admit to their hoarding problem. The intention was also to help someone like me, who'd come to the museum with a specific piece of research in mind. As much as possible was on display because everything, potentially, had some interest to a researcher. Even so, I couldn't find a direct match for my mother's teapot, nor anything related. What I did find, though, were some very familiar objects indeed: a set of 1950s tea plates demonstrating a wide range of designs from the period. I knew them very well because they'd once lived in my kitchen, but what they revealed to me now was that a museum collection may not be as rational and orderly as its curators and visitors might wish to believe.

While studying in the museum, I'd amassed a considerable collection of all kinds of bright 1950s earthenware, haunting the junk shops and flea markets of North London to buy plates, bowls and jugs, and anything else I could lay my hands on for 10p a piece. The collection grew far beyond what my flatmates and I could use, stacking in corners and filling walls, until I had over a hundred different patterns and colour ways. Eventually, I decided to research their history for my master's thesis, in part because I couldn't find anything written about them. What I had, the museum did not.

For more than thirty years the Ceramics Department had ignored any mass-market products in favour of art pottery: unique pieces by individual craftspeople. These knobbly brown pots were the enemy. I couldn't understand why anyone would want a plate with a texture like porridge when you could have one which was chequered in bright green and yellow, or decorated like Formica, or printed with poodles or televisions. The museum had collected them because they wanted to improve the nation's taste, and back in the 1950s that meant craft, Japanese glazes and dull colours.

I became interested in mass production just at the point when the Ceramics Department was beginning to realize that they had been blinkered in their collecting. The light-bulb moment had been when they realized that possibly the single most significant piece of pottery design since the war had been the mug, yet their cases didn't contain a single one. The curators went on a buying spree. When I offered them some duplicates from my collection of 1950s tableware, they happily took more than twenty, filling another gap in their collection.

These were the plates I now found on display. I'd won the argument, and the gaudy designs I loved were now valued as equally as the muddy studio pots, but the museum's shift uncovers a whole world of difficult, perhaps unanswerable questions. What are museums for? Whose is the culture that they display? There are no right and wrong answers; every museum, every department could make a slightly different case, but what the questions show is that a museum collection can never be complete, nor neutral, nor omniscient. Rather they are always partial and irrational, stuff accumulating for not entirely logical reasons. Just as my mother's house and the stuff in it had become a part of herself, museums create our national identity out of objects: paintings, furniture, modern art, rare textiles and, of course, 1950s plates. Like any individual person, the national character has its quirks and oddities as well as its strengths.

Roy Strong, who was director of the museum when I first arrived, called the V&A an extremely capacious handbag, but I've always believed that, more than any other museum, the V&A is our national attic. It's the place where the British as a nation put things that we have no further use for but cannot bear to chuck out. As a result, it is among the least coherent of all museums. Things end up in the collections simply because they exist. In the furniture galleries sits the Great Bed of Ware, a lumpen piece of carving which has no pretensions to being good design but whose vast size made it a celebrity even in Shakespeare's time. Once he had mentioned it in *Twelfth Night*, it could never be broken up. The stores of the museum hold, amongst many other things, plaster casts of medieval cathedral doors, Elton John's spectacles, Punch and Judy puppets and the original lifts from the Savoy Hotel. The accession process must be a version of what goes on in everyone's lives. 'Well, they're too good to throw away, so what shall we do with them?' 'Better put them in the loft, then.' It's very close to being the national hoard.

Of course museums believe that they do not accumulate things with the illogicality of a hoarder. They should be immune to magical thinking, objects arriving unencumbered by their biographies and associations. As a design museum, any new acquisition at the V&A, whether that's a pair of trainers or a poster, a Victorian dining chair or one of my plates, is chosen only as a pure example of its form. No one needs to know that the plates I donated were found at a junk shop in Tufnell Park and then used by students for sandwiches and toast before arriving in the museum, nor that their history before that had been lost. We are meant to admire their pattern and shape, see how their design developed from their predecessors and influenced what came after. Memory and meaning are meant to be kept out of these hushed galleries. But they slip through the doors anyway in the form of the Great Bed of Ware and its many kin: objects whose associations are far more important than their designs.

Sometimes magic can be the entire reason for an object being in a museum. T. E. Lawrence's robes and dagger, important only because they retained his actions and charisma, ended up in the National Army Museum. If the V&A holds our national identity, then the NAM is our medal drawer, keeping ephemeral victories and deeds of bravery in the minds of future generations.

A more sombre aspect of the national soul is contained

in the Imperial War Museum. Founded even while the First World War raged in 1917, the museum exists to ensure that the bravery and sacrifice of those who took part would be remembered for eternity. More than any other museum, the IWM is animated by the spirit of hoarding; it acts as a container for memories which were considered at the time to be too awful ever to be forgotten but which the country could not bear to look at in its daily life. Within its walls, the horrors of war are contained safely. Here is the dark face of the national hoard, a place of loss and covered remembrance where things too terrible to discard can be kept without having to be contemplated every day. The attic of the V&A is, in comparison, open, sunlit and benign.

Even the basic principle of a museum is based on a magical relationship with things. Museums hold objects because they are evidence. It's possible to create a logical argument for this: a Victorian teapot like my mother's can tell us about the colours and design that people preferred, about the popularity of tea, methods of production and the prevailing taste in decoration. At the same time, we acknowledge that the item itself also has a kind of presence, revealing an aspect of history that cannot entirely be expressed in words. The sentiments of history and the feelings of the people who used it have, in some way, inhabited the items they display, and an object which has survived from those times gives us a direct connection to the past.

The museum becomes a shrine where we pay our respects to these relics, each one containing a vibrant spirit which needs to be revered in the hushed, sparse conditions of a church. We stand before them without feeling the need to understand how they fit into the history of design or culture, what their makers intended or why they have been collected; all that is necessary is to take in their aura. In their presence we become more alert to the power of stuff. Behind the scenes, the curators are people who have spent their whole lives feeling the deep pull of objects in the way that my mother did, and as I still do.

In this we were, once again, twin sides of the same coin. We both liked objects that could be kept for ever, that would never abandon us; we both wanted to lay out our thoughts in things. The difference was how we went about it. By going into museums rather than hoarding, I channelled these desires in a more socially acceptable and also more orderly way.

However long and hard I thought, nothing I discovered would turn the chaos of my mother's house into a museum. The parallels did reassure me, though, helping to make her seem more normal. They also gave me a way of coping, as gradually I realized that I was employing my own urge to structure and curate on the contents of my mother's house.

Leaving the hoovers behind, I set off in the afternoon twilight with the car full of my mother's things. As well as ornaments, some books and the photo albums, I also brought back the little tan briefcase which contained all the paperwork I'd found in the study. I drove down the motorway to the rattling of glass and china and the squeaking of boxes wedged against the car door. I didn't know what I would do with any of them yet, but I wasn't ready to decide. The real question that her things were posing was how did I want to remember her? I didn't yet have an answer.

Despite the insistent clatter and rustle of the objects, it was the case which occupied my mind. It not only held the obvious souvenirs like photographs and notes but also any piece of paper I thought might give me some clue about my mother's life. The thought I couldn't shake from my head, all the way home, was that what I'd been making in that small suitcase was a museum of my mother.

pride: *a philosopher in a barrel*

PLACE SETTING OF CUTLERY, 'PRIDE'

Sheffield, 1953 (designed), 1960–1 (made)

Designed by David Mellor, manufactured by Walker & Hall Ltd

Electroplated nickel silver, stainless steel and bone

Gift, 1961

MY MOTHER'S FUNERAL came and went. The same journey on now-familiar roads, but this time I was in my
best clothes with T and E alongside me in the car, and there
was nothing to clean when I arrived.

I made it through the day numb and apart, as though
watching myself through a sheet of glass. My brother had
done a good job. People assembled; we had honoured her
passing. He delivered a eulogy, but I, the only other surviving
child, had not been able to find a single word of my own. If I
could not speak the truth, I didn't want to say anything at all,
and I wasn't sure I'd ever know what the truth had been, so
I avoided the issue entirely by reading a poem. T cried, but I
could not manage a single tear.

I believed that the ceremony had passed over me like wind
over a lake, ruffling the surface but changing nothing, but as
the days passed afterwards I could breathe a bit more easily.
Then came another emotion which I could not admit to
anyone, and that was joy.

So taboo was this bliss that I had to save it for my trips up
and down to Worcester each week. I watched the sun glance
off windscreens, stopped for coffee on the way up and savoured the taste. Back in the car, I turned the stereo up high,
became obsessed with new bands for the first time in years,
playing my favourite songs over and over again.

There were plenty of reasons to be happy. I'd always loved

driving and motorways: far better to be going somewhere than not. The work of clearing Rose Terrace had also given me purpose. E was growing up and needing me less, so my year had begun with the dull ache of knowing I had to find an occupation. Within just a few weeks, my mother's death had filled that gap, giving me not only tasks to perform but an answer when I needed to justify how I spent my time.

This alone would have kept me going, but other, less straightforward, forces raced within me as well. I had been released, even if I did not know what ties had been binding me. Reasons didn't matter; this was the real me at last. No longer was I squashed into the shape my mother wanted, half a person and still unloveable. She could no longer hurt me. As I raced up and down the M5, I imagined particles of energy streaming away behind me as though I were a comet. I had known that grief might send you insane, but I never expected this to take the form of mania.

Even if I couldn't explain what was happening inside me, this state of mind had its upsides. When I made my weekly visits to Rose Terrace, with my boatload of cleaning chemicals on the way up and an extra cargo of cigarette-smelling salvage on the way home, I was no longer overwhelmed by the scale of the task. Instead, I tore through the dereliction like a whirlwind, able to face anything. Jim and Ed were now beginning to recover clear space downstairs. Boxes and bags lined up in the hallway, awaiting a trip to either the tip or the charity shop. Finally, I could see the old lines of the house re-emerge from under the paper and junk.

My next job was to scrub the dense fog of nicotine and tar from the paintwork now that it could be reached. I became obsessed with finding the perfect cleaner, working my way through different sprays and liquids, cloths and scrubbing sponges until I finally decided that heavy-duty floor cleaning wipes cut through the brownish film of stickiness best. I bought pack after pack, and kept finding new parts of the house to work on: the doors and their frames, the bannisters and their newel posts, the shutters which framed the sitting-room window, wiping over and over until I revealed the yellowed paint underneath.

Chemicals couldn't restore everything. As I worked, I began to get properly angry with my mother for the first time in my life. I was furious at the amount of work she was forcing me to do, when it was her who had made the mess in the first place. I worked harder and faster, wiping paintwork, floors and doors that no one except me would ever notice. The state of Rose Terrace was too obvious a parallel for the damage she had done to her own life. Now, every damp stain, every broken hinge and grimed windowpane had become my problem. This cleaning was the last chance I was ever going to get to rectify both of our lives, and I wasn't going to waste it.

As I went through the house like a storm, one particular absence began to bother me. The only thing I still hadn't found was my mother's cutlery, the silver-plated knives, forks and spoons that she had used every day. I'd expected it to turn up in the chiffonier, where it had always lived, so when it didn't emerge from there, I began to worry. My mother hadn't got into this state by throwing things away, so it seemed absurd that something so substantial should be missing entirely. Jim and Ed would never have disposed of anything so heavy and important, not when they had rescued each photograph, every personal postcard and bill from the heap for me to check. Yet the cutlery still failed to appear when the whole dining room had been cleared, and as I stripped the kitchen back to bare cupboards, it hadn't been hidden in there either. It seemed to be lost for ever.

What made this worse was that this set was almost the only possession of my mother's that I really cared about. Every other object in Rose Terrace could have succumbed to damp, rot or rodents and I wouldn't really have minded, not as long as I had found her Pride. The design was beautiful, a mid-century reworking of plain English eighteenth-century forms, each fork and spoon the perfect weight to hold, with long handles and elegant lines; the knives with oval bone handles and a delicate stainless-steel blade. They were my mother in the form of household goods: slim, beautiful and understated, with a deep relationship to the past. But I also needed to find the cutlery because its history was so deeply intertwined with my own.

In my late twenties, living and working in London and perpetually single, I had decided that I was a career girl, too modern to get married. Outwardly I celebrated this with ironic certainty, but inside I saw myself as too odd, opinion-ated and fat to ever be considered as a wife. The big drawback with not having a wedding was that I would also not have a wedding list. I could mostly buy whatever I needed or liked, so this wasn't a catastrophe. I only pined for two items that seemed out of my reach: a fish kettle and a complete canteen of cutlery.

Being practical, I solved the cutlery problem for myself. Over several years, I painstakingly built up the canteen of knives, forks and spoons that I so desired. I achieved this by getting my parents to buy it for me each Christmas, one place setting at a time. The service I chose was Pride, by David Mellor.

There were many good reasons for wanting this design over any other. I loved the 1950s, and my entire flat was a dazzlingly coloured, china-stuffed homage to the decade, including a refurbished English Rose kitchen with a black and white chequered lino floor. Pride had been designed in 1953, so would feel right at home. I had studied design history, and the service was a classic, still in production. What's more, I'd studied at the Royal College of Art, and Pride, in turn, had been David Mellor's graduation piece when he'd been awarded his own degree from the college. Being a classic design, a set was, of course, held in the V&A.

More important than any of that were my sentimental reasons for choosing Pride. Whenever I visited my mother, we would have our meals round her oval Regency dining table. Each place would be neatly set with the white Royal Worcester china, and either side of that would be the knives and forks of Pride. I knew how crisp the silver looked laid out against the dark wood of the table, how well each one sat in the hand. By collecting the set myself, I would be carrying on the line. This was a rare positive connection with my mother; for once I wasn't running away from any likeness but choosing to celebrate it instead.

In picking Pride I'd left out one very important fact. The cutlery that my mother used at home had been given to my parents as one of their main wedding presents. My mother had taken it as part of her share after the divorce. In all the years I collected my own Pride I had in effect been asking my father – who at this point had been divorced for almost twenty years and was still unable to speak a single kind word about my mother – to give me a present that represented his broken first marriage. I never realized this until after he died; he never

229

pointed it out to me either, but only ever bought one setting before seemingly losing interest.

In contrast my mother was keen to buy me another setting of Pride each year. When I had enough knives and forks, she moved on to ladles, serving spoons and teaspoons, until I could have furnished a small state dinner with my holdings. She was probably enjoying the simple pleasure of sharing something she herself enjoyed with her daughter. It wasn't something I let her do very often. It's unlikely she wanted to spite my father. She never shared his urge to erase the unfortunate past. Quite the reverse: she could never manage to let it go.

At the age of forty, I finally got married, forcing my parents to be in the same room as each other for the first time since they had divorced. To my relief, everyone behaved. And at least I didn't need to put any cutlery on the wedding list.

I had no practical need for my mother's Pride, but I was still desperate to find it, as a tangible sign that there had once been a bond between us. Had my mother, in her depression and hoarding, even managed to destroy her connection with me? I didn't want to think it could be so.

My mother's kitchen had been the filthiest room of all. I'd cleaned it on every visit to Rose Terrace, yet still the work was not done. First, I'd scraped the muck and water off the floor, then repeated that the next week when the leak had returned. Jim and Ed had thrown out the rotten food and papers, then together we'd taken every single sticky glass, plate and saucepan out of the cupboard to be cleaned. With my brother, I'd cut the ivy back from the window, then cleaned the grime and smuts from the glass so that the light could come in for the first time in years and I could see what might be saved.

Very little could be retrieved. Her expensive food processor and Kenwood Chef had to be sent to the tip, their plugs green with moisture, too sticky and ruined to be recoverable. Chopping boards and wooden spoons went in the bin too, splitting and rotten, along with plastic pots, cracked vases and ancient toasters. My mother had once loved food and cooking. Back then she had been very proud of her kitchen, but now it was in the worst state of all.

What I most hated throwing away were my mother's cookery books. The kitchen had been steeped in damp and mould for so long that nothing organic had stood a chance. The books had not been immune; their pages were billowing and mould crept up the spines. I thought about drying them out gently at home, but the peculiar smell of her house at the end, of spores and nicotine and not caring, would have stuck to them for ever. They went straight from the shelves into a black bin bag, even though each disposal hurt me.

My feelings were illogical and ridiculous. I already owned a copy of almost every single one: the original Elizabeth David paperbacks from the early 1960s, *The Penguin Book of Jams, Pickles and Chutneys*, the Delia Smiths and modern Mrs Beetons. It shouldn't have mattered to me that these battered old copies were going to the tip, but I minded very much indeed. Now I would never have my mother's own copies, a tangible reminder of the love of food and cookery that she'd handed down to me.

The worst one of all to get rid of was the Katie Stewart *Times Cookery Book*, and it was the only one I seriously considered rescuing. My mother, both of my grandmothers and my aunt had all owned a copy, while mine had been handed down when my grandmother Antoinette had died. The book was more than a family tradition, it was a birthright. They marked who belonged to our family as though they were identity cards. Or silver napkin rings.

We clutched them tight for good reason, because the book is a compendium of every recipe a sensible person might need, from Victoria sponge to roast duck, along with treats like the richest vanilla ice cream imaginable, which I'd been making since I was a student. I'd used the book to bake cakes with E, so I'd wanted to take my mother's copy to pass on to her one day. But I couldn't. Katie Stewart had to go into the oblivion of black plastic like all the other books. Nothing in her kitchen had been able to survive.

With the shelves and worktops cleared, the room looked even more derelict than before. Ed had boarded up the panel in the back door, but some of the kitchen cupboards were broken and open, while underneath the sink, the entire unit had been eaten away by a leaking pipe.

The room was beyond hope, but I nonetheless set out to make it as right as I could. I scraped black encrusted grease from the cooker and found the strongest bleach the supermarket could sell me to remove mould from the cupboard doors that remained. This was a labour with no purpose. Not a single part of this room would ever be saved. No one would be more likely to buy the house because I had scrubbed years of filth from the worktops and tiles. Even so, I carried on each week, returning with disposable wipes and stronger cleaners until I had done the best job I could. I owed this to my mother. She had not only loved her house; through the act of restoring it the building had become part of her. Just as my brother and I had laid out some of her best clothes to take to the funeral directors, even though no one would ever see her in her coffin,

I had to make sure that her house finished up in the best state I could manage before I handed it on, however futile this gesture might be.

On this visit, I had wiped the doors and worktops down one more time, then scrubbed the cooker to get the last remaining black streaks out of the crevices. The final job I needed to tackle was the sink. The water had been turned off for weeks now, so I couldn't wash it out, but I scooped all the black sludge into bin liners without looking at what it contained. Then I turned to the dish drainer, a simple wooden rack which I'd bought for her from IKEA many years ago. Its whole fabric was sodden, and on top was a heap of something brown and mucky which, when I looked closely, was running with tiny grey weevils. Then I realized what this was. I had found what I was looking for. This heaped seething mass was what had become of my mother's Pride.

The cutlery was the most painful thing I had to bring home with me. Days passed before I could face the job, and even then I could only work in small bursts. Each piece required careful attention. I rubbed thick black tarnish from the plate, sanding and repolishing stains out of the bone knife handles until they looked as good as they would ever do. Their experiences had left scars: patches of brown on the bone, tiny marks on the forks and spoons where the silver had been dented or eaten away by tarnish. Even so, they ended up more than good enough to keep.

The problem was, I couldn't begin to think of using them to eat, or even putting them into the drawer with my own set. The cutlery was no longer a sign of happy times. Instead, each piece had become laden with new meanings, too heavy to ignore. Like Lawrence's dagger, their elegant silver forms now memorialized a part of my mother's life, but one that I did not want to remember. How had it come to this? How had I, her daughter, allowed all the good things to fall away? Could I have done anything differently? All those feelings now resided in the metal and bone, and I couldn't help believing that they would live there for good.

Putting the cutlery in a shoebox, I hid it away in the attic.

Cleaning still left plenty of time spare for my distraction techniques. I had buried myself so thoroughly in hoarding research that I saw it wherever I went. If the studies were right, there were more hoarders in the population than there were Alzheimer's sufferers. At first I couldn't bring myself to believe this statistic, but gradually as I drove and walked around, I learned to recognize the signs – a press of cardboard boxes against a dirty window or a stack of plastic buckets and pots behind a gate – until I realized that hoarding really was all around me.

But the more I read, the more I began to wonder whether my mother really qualified as a diagnosable hoarder. The second criterion for Hoarding Disorder in the *DSM* refers to 'a perceived need to save the items and the distress associated with discarding them'. Watching the television programmes about hoarding, I could see the agonies that their subjects suffered when faced with throwing away just one or two items from their hoard. They winced and flinched, they shouted and stormed out, demanding that the filming be stopped at once. Or they went back into the skips and dumpsters each evening, trying to reclaim what they felt so desperately was theirs.

Had my mother lived to see the way in which Jim and Ed

had cleaned up her house, how between us we wiped and swept and scrubbed, cleared back the garden, peeled away the carpets, she would probably have become very depressed, but not in the same way a hoarder would. Instead, our labours would have demonstrated to her how easy it was to sort things out and how bad she was for not having done that herself before now. She would have understood that once again she was wrong. But would my mother have mourned the hoard, that litter of out-of-date newspapers, official mail, cardboard, old tights and dust?

If the hoard was essential to her, it was as a mass. She wouldn't have missed individual parts of it so long as the whole served to muffle the agonies represented by Alastair's napkin ring, the paperwork about the divorce or Carrie's album of cat pictures. She might have found the mess comforting too, in the way that it walled her off from a hostile outside world, just as those early Orkney settlers had been protected by their midden at Skara Brae. In this, my mother seemed different. Only when my reading took me into a very specific byway of hoarding behaviour did I begin to find people exactly like her.

On the fringes of hoarding case lore lurks a special situation, sometimes called Senile Squalor but most often known as Diogenes Syndrome. These labels are very subjective, with no *DSM* definition of what they might be describing. There's not even any agreement that this subset of people – usually elderly and refusing help even though they live in a hoarded mess – are different enough from hoarders to need their own name.

The only consensus is that, whatever might be going on with these patients, Diogenes Syndrome is the wrong name for it. The Greek philosopher Diogenes was best known for living in a barrel with no possessions at all, to demonstrate that happiness was not dependent on external sources but came from within. Diogenes sufferers, like hoarders, live up to their necks in stuff and don't particularly want anyone to take it away.

The difference, though, is that almost everything that surrounds these people is rubbish. Sometimes they set out to collect it, while others, like my mother, simply allow it to accumulate around them. Many abandon their personal dress and hygiene in the same way, but that's not always so; in some cases the person concerned comes out of the house dressed immaculately every day, even though they live in utter chaos.

My mother belonged to this latter group. The state of her house was even more shocking because she herself had given no sign of it. She turned up for visits and family gatherings clean and neatly dressed in the kind of smart clothing that was expected of a woman of her age and class: a couple of Jaeger jackets and jumpers, with the rest of the ensemble from Marks & Spencer. She arrived for her volunteer shifts at the Oxfam bookshop in exactly the same presentable state. The camel woollens and patent shoes made it impossible for anyone to imagine what lay behind her front door. Every single person, from the policeman onwards, had been horrified when they found out, but in the world of Diogenes this was entirely normal.

Each of the accounts I read told a familiar story. One very early article, written in 1957, gave a description that could have been written about what I found when I entered Rose Terrace after my mother had been taken to hospital:

The room in such cases is the epitome of neglect. Dust lies thick everywhere and cobwebs abound. The windows are barely translucent and the curtains are in shreds. Rubbish, odds and ends and remains of food are found everywhere. The bed is often broken and the sheets, if there are any, are dark grey.

I still find some parts of my mother's house very hard to think about, and one of those is her bed. Somehow my mother had been managing to keep herself clean, even though the bath didn't work properly and all she had was a sink with no hot water. She even managed to keep her clothes in good order without a working washing machine. But there was no way she could have hand-washed the sheets of her double bed. When I came into her house, the duvet was pulled back, revealing a great patch of greasy grey where she had lain for I didn't want to know how long. I smoothed the cover back over because I couldn't bear to look at it.

A later piece of research told me that Diogenes sufferers don't do well in hospital. You might think that having been rescued from the mess and the rotting food, they'd be rejuvenated. The opposite happens: they die far more quickly and more frequently than any other kind of elderly patient. One study reported that a third died within a few days of admission. My mother, once again, had been entirely typical. Knowing this helped. At the time, I had taken her decision to die so abruptly and before I got there as being another part of her awkwardness, aimed at me personally. Now I understood that it was just what people like her do.

More disconcertingly, these papers didn't only describe my mother's actions but also her personality. Diogenes sufferers are, it seems, very much a type. Although very bright, they are also aloof, detached and suspicious. And that's the polite version. Another description is of a 'domineering, quarrelsome and independent individual with gradually developing rejection of the community'. Stubborn is another word which comes up a lot. The syndrome, it seems, is a pre-existing set of traits which hardens into gross personal neglect and isolation. Or, in my favourite description of all, 'something that creeps up on slightly odd people over a long period of time'. All of these work as descriptions of my mother.

My mother's awkwardness and belligerence weren't weapons that she ever aimed at me. Had I done something to upset her, she would simply withdraw and not phone me for a while; most likely she would be drinking too. Other people, though, could make her very angry indeed. Each time, my mother was always certain she was in the right and mistreated: the council had behaved terribly, the manager of the Oxfam shop had no people skills. I could often hear a different story seeping through the gaps, one in which my mother was a difficult, argumentative old lady who simultaneously dismissed any help she was offered while at the same time raged against these people who were supposed to be on her side, because they would not rescue her.

Doctors were the worst offenders. Before my mother gave up entirely, she had been to her GP to ask for help to stop drinking. They referred her to specialist support services, but nothing the nurses and occupational therapists did was ever right. The antidepressants always made her worse, the doctors never listened to her and the whole process was hopeless. The common factor was always that my mother deeply resented people who had authority over her. Her real fury, never named or acknowledged, was with her father, who had disappeared, abandoning her to a vague and emotionally absent mother, ruled over by a snobbish, manipulative grandmother. Doctors are a kind of parental figure whom we trust to make it all better in the end, so it's perhaps inevitable that they, most of all, were the triggers for her upset.

I only really heard the full force of her anger once, just a couple of months before she died. Anne's funeral, over on her small island in the West Indies, had been arranged too quickly. That's what my mother told me when she phoned up. 'I can only get a flight twice a week.' She spat out the words one by one. 'They must have known I wouldn't be able to go.'

This was an entirely impotent fit of temper. As far as I know, my mother didn't even have a current passport, but I didn't dare point that out; in this mood she would have slammed the phone down on me straight away. I didn't know if she even believed she was really going to go or not, but she still felt slighted. This wasn't just because Anne had, for one last time, not thought of her; I'm sure she also still deeply minded not having attended her own mother's funeral in Bequia all those years before.

I'd never heard her be so openly angry in my presence before. I know that old people can become more fractious, but most likely my mother had carried the kernel of this with her all along, as her reference from teacher-training college, written more than sixty years ago, shows. After a couple of paragraphs about her academic and teaching ability, it goes on to describe her character with a forthrightness unexpected in such a bland bureaucratic format:

> Miss Gilmour was in many ways an able student and could have contributed more generously to the life of the community. She had strong opinions but did not find it easy to see the best in other people. As she becomes more tolerant and as her sympathies widen she should have much to give to a school.

Aloof, stubborn, quarrelsome. My mother had been like this all her life. What changed was how much she was able to keep these emotions in check. Perhaps she did become more circumspect in time, as the reference suggested she might, but then old age or the insidious damage inflicted by all that whisky loosened her inhibitions all over again. However it happened, the result was the same: my mother was a perfect example of Diogenes. Her strangeness hardened into dogma over time.

There's another important aspect of Diogenes that more recent research is very keen to stress. These people are not mad. On the contrary, they are entirely sane. Being obstinate and dirty and aloof does not constitute a mental disorder. Like my mother doing her *Telegraph* crosswords in the hospital, these people are entirely in control of their lives with, more often than not, no other mental issues which would require attention. The only problem is the way they have chosen to live.

The psychiatrists and social workers who deal with Diogenes cases now don't see it as their job to send people off to hospital or even to clean up their homes. People like my mother have the right to make unwise decisions, and all the professionals can do is let them live as safely as possible in a way that doesn't impinge on the wider community. In any case, given their propensity to die when they get there, hospital clearly isn't a good place for them to be. Many old people fear dependence, but these obstinate, proud but damaged people would rather die than rely on others to survive.

It seems I did the right thing in giving up my attempts to get Rose Terrace cleared up and my mother transformed back into a conventional member of society, even if I reached this place entirely by accident. By speaking to her every week and listening to what she had to say, I was supporting her in the best way possible. My research on hoarding had already taught me that curing my mother was an impossible hope; what I learned from the Diogenes specialists was that it wasn't down to me to make the choice anyway. My mother had the right to live exactly as she wanted, and all I could and should have done was be there.

Relief flooded through me as though I had cleaned the windows of my own soul. I went back through the papers again, hoping for more and more enlightenment. One thing that struck me very strongly was that, in contrast to what I read about hoarding, real people inhabited even the driest of these academic papers. Their personalities, however cantankerous and unconventional, punched through the text, almost in defiance of the measured and scientific prose. With this came a sense that the psychologists and doctors, time and again, couldn't help admiring their subjects. Although no one would wish their living conditions on an enemy, nonetheless it seemed impossible not to envy, just a bit, their freedom from the concerns of convention, other people's opinions or propriety. But I wasn't able to think of my mother with approval. However much I knew that I could not have changed her, I still felt shame at the state in which she had ended up.

I also discovered that there may be a real and definable cause for Diogenes. The syndrome correlates, very strongly, with problems in the frontal lobe of the brain. This area is associated with executive function and decision making, but also, when damaged, with loss of inhibitions and an indifference to social pressures such as embarrassment and normality. Damage to the frontal lobe can happen for a whole raft of reasons. Most often the cause is a particular kind of dementia which attacks this region of the brain, but it can happen as the result of a head wound or a stroke. Or it can be caused by a long-term dependence on alcohol.

While I didn't like what was being described, this, nonetheless, was my mother. Finally, I had a map for a territory where until now I had been marooned with only clues. My mother was not mad, and more than that it hadn't been up to me to change her – the professionals agreed it would have been wrong of me to try. I was off the hook at last.

mrs beeton: *bookish*

Mrs Beeton's Everyday Cookery and Housekeeping Book

London, 1870s

Published by Ward, Lock and Co.

Purchased late 1980s

E ACH TRIP TO Worcester saw me returning with a full boot of salvage, so now the remains of Rose Terrace were piling up in my own house. The boxes and crates had been dumped in our spare room. Stacked in one corner against the battered plasterwork and dirty lino, my mother's possessions must have thought that they'd arrived in a place not much different from their old home.

When we bought our house, more than two years before my mother died, it was old and filthy, with crumbling plaster, black mould on the walls and a year's worth of junk mail piled up in the hall. The windows were boarded up and light switches hung by their wires from the wall. The work I had been doing on my mother's house was nothing new; the last two years had been made up of clearing, restoring and renovating.

This upstairs room where I stacked her stuff was the last bastion of the old disorder. When our house had been two flats, this was a kitchen, but now it was empty and unused, its battered walls waiting for the plasterer to come in. We had no urgent need for the space, and my attention had been elsewhere, so over six months or more it had turned into a dumping ground for old rugs, boxes of decorating equipment and spare bits of furniture, along with the mop and a step-ladder. It had become a warehouse, or what my mother used to call a 'glory hole' – a space of deliberate chaos. Hers used to be a cupboard under the stairs whose contents often spread to a folding table which sat outside the door. Maybe this was where the hoarding had begun, gradually growing and expanding until it outgrew the space she had permitted it, spreading like rising dough throughout the house from the ground floor up. Once she'd let the mess in, maybe it had developed its own agency. From then on, she had had no choice.

The advantage of maintaining a small patch of disorder in my own house was that the last remnants of my mother's life could join the motley selection and become invisible. Once they were stowed, I wouldn't have to think about them if I didn't want to. The temporary mess acted as my own hoard, where I could hide the difficult things that had returned with me rather than be forced to listen to what they wanted to say. I was sick of things and their endless meanings.

Despite this, I found myself digging into the boxes a few days later. E was doing a project on the Edwardians, and we'd started to think about all the objects from that era we might have in the house. I'd shown her the art nouveau vase I'd inherited from Antoinette which had, most likely, been one of Carrie Jenkins' wedding presents. Then I'd remembered the cookery books.

For all my determination not to be like my mother in any way, there had always been a few interests that connected us and which I would admit to sharing. At various points in the past, these had included auctions and italic writing, but for many years a substantial part of our relationship had been formed out of vintage cookery books. When she first moved into Rose Terrace, the miscellaneous copies of Mrs Beeton and Eliza Acton had already begun to gather on her shelves, and new ones would appear each time I visited.

Considering that every one of these cooks had died long before my mother was born, she had surprisingly strong opinions on them.

'Mrs Beeton might have been popular, but she wasn't a very good cook.'

My mother stands at the kitchen worktop, chopping onions for our supper, which, as usual, she has started rather later than she meant. 'Eliza Acton was much better.' The knife comes down on the wooden board for emphasis.

The kitchen is small, so I am standing at the door where I can keep out of the way while still being able to talk to her. I am definitely not allowed to help. Radio 4 is murmuring in the background, as it always did.

The onions go into the pan. 'Mrs Beeton copied some of her recipes, you know.'

I did know, because we'd had this conversation before, so I nod again and let my mother talk, watching the steam condense on the kitchen windows.

'You could cook from Eliza Acton even now.'

My mother's relationship with these writers was like that of quarrelsome neighbours: while she might have disapproved, it was impossible for her to walk away. I don't know precisely what Isabella Beeton had done to incur my mother's disapproval, but the conversation always went this way. Her other heroines were Elizabeth David, who had rescued my mother from the beige hell of institutional food in the early 1960s, and Delia Smith, both also fans of Acton, but perhaps that wasn't a coincidence.

These most prized books had survived by being shelved not in the mouldering kitchen but in the relatively dry safety of the study upstairs. There weren't many, no more than a dozen or so stiff-bound volumes. As I picked my way through their leather and hessian spines in the box, they struck me as being not only a miraculous survival but a collection of sadness. My mother had loved cooking and once upon a time had been part of a family and provided food for them every day, just as Mrs Beeton, Florence Jack and all her other authors imagined. The books were instruction manuals for a life that she no longer lived, one with a household and children. That chance to cook and be useful was yet one more thing that had slipped through her fingers.

My mother didn't stop cooking when she was first on her own. One of the pieces of paper I found in her office was a list, apparently written in an attempt to become more organized. On it, my mother was setting out what she planned to accomplish each day and then recording what she'd actually managed to achieve. This dates from before her partner Patrick died in 1988, because she's written at the top of Saturday: 'am. Patrick here – nothing gets done!'

For the rest of the day she seems to have kept herself very busy, and almost entirely in the kitchen. She's in the thick of preparations for Christmas, which means making the pastry for mince pies, stripping a chicken for terrine, then boiling the bones for stock, as well as preparing all the meat for a galantine. On Sunday, she assembles and bakes sixty mince pies, makes the chicken terrine and beef galantine, cooks a tongue and then finally sits down with the papers.

My mother isn't cooking for me and my brother. We never spent Christmas with her, not until much later in her life. Now I feel guilty and ashamed I let that happen, but at the time I never even questioned why this was. My father, once again, had imposed his will on everyone, and my mother, even after many years of separation, never dared to fight. Instead, she spent the day with her mother and sister, as though she were a Victorian maiden aunt. The difference was that my mother cooked up an entire banquet to bring with her.

Gradually, though, my mother lost interest in cooking, just as she had given up on cleaning. Not even the smallest act of looking after herself seemed worthwhile any more. This made the fork which I'd found in the opened can of baked beans doubly sad. My mother had abandoned herself many times over, until every single thing she loved had gone.

Alongside my mother's Victorian collections, squeezed down one side of the box was a book which I'd chucked in with the others, just in case. Covered in grubby brown paper, the exercise book had yellowed pages and bent corners, and as I pulled it out I wondered why I'd bothered saving it. But when I opened it up, I remembered. The front page read, in blue ink with underlining: *Carrie Rickatson – High Class Recipes*.

What my mother must have seen in the title, with its inherent one-upmanship, was her grandmother's snobbery. Carrie was learning to cook not in a Paris finishing school but in Sheffield, where the instruction included the fantastic Franco-Northern hybrid 'Petit Gateaux à l'Ethel'.

Growing up, I couldn't help having a sneaking admiration for Carrie, despite everything that the rest of the family said about her being mean and overbearing. She seemed to be the only complete person in my mother's family. All the men were dead or disappeared, while both my mother and grandmother were only half there, vague and translucent. I had opinions, ideas and demands, far too many of them; I was so full of life that it made me clumsy and awkward, battling the world. My great-grandmother might have been a complete witch, but she was the only one of them who seemed remotely to resemble me. I wish I'd asked my mother more about her, while at the same time knowing that I would have learned nothing new. The answers would have been, as they always were, a repetition of the same few stories that my mother could bear to tell.

One of her ways of coping with the terribleness of her past had been to fossilize it into repeated myths. Whenever I think of her, she is always sitting at her dining table smoking a cigarette, and what she's doing is telling one of those stories. I was such a difficult child; my brother and I didn't let her sleep for years and my father was no help at all but men didn't do that then; Great Granny was hateful and her cats weren't much better. She had hidden away huge chunks of her past and herself to survive in such a painful world. No wonder she seemed so transparent, not fully present. And no wonder too that I ended up scrabbling through a mound of odds and ends, hoping to finally perceive her after her death. It's possible that she existed more in these things than she ever dared to do in life.

I could only ever get around these defences when circumstance threw up a memory that surprised her. We once went to visit the Worcester Museum of Rural Life, which wasn't much more than a couple of barns containing tools and accoutrements that had been collected from people's farms and kitchens. Nonetheless, an old wooden butter churn sparked a light in my mother's eyes.

'I used to use one like that when we went round to Great Granny's.'

'Really?' This was an unexpected picture. Great Granny had always been presented to me as more of a lady with pretensions than a ruddy-cheeked farming housewife.

'Yes, she used to send us into the kitchen to churn the butter.'

That made more sense: children were not for coddling; much better that they did something practical, preferably elsewhere.

My mother leaned back on the scrubbed kitchen table which was one of the exhibits. 'She used to have two house cows, a Jersey and a Guernsey. And when they were in calf, the farmer would send another one over to replace them. So there was always milk. And butter.'

A courtesy cow. I imagined this black and white Friesian interloper peering through the iron railings of Oldbury Grange, watching my great-grandmother trying to keep up the lifestyle of a country lady through the forty years of her widowhood as the world changed around her. I wondered when the cows finally went, and she surrendered to the convenience of the milkman.

My family had a habit of slating my great-grandmother's snobbery, when this vice wasn't hers alone. None of them was immune, least of all my mother. Very soon after the divorce, she took my brother and me down to London, and the only part of this trip that I remember was getting our hair cut at Harrods. Only eight at the time, my memories consist of a series of pictures: my brother, dark-haired against a Harrods-green wall; a toy train that each of us got to sit in while we waited, its body painted the same colour with gold edging; the tea we had in a pink café afterwards. This was meant as a treat and it must have felt like one, because it's one of the few memories I have of this miserable period. I'm sure, though, that it was a bittersweet interlude for my mother. This was the life she had been destined to lead, but now it was out of her reach. All she could do was go on short trips to visit what might have been.

Now that Rose Terrace was almost emptied, I could finally lift my head and see beyond its four walls again. What I found was my mother's story echoing around me in strange and surprising places. Most of all this was through one of her own persistent passions: books. Rereading Alan Bennett's *The Lady in the Van*, I took his story in with new joy. Miss Shepherd, I realized, was the most accurate description of someone with Diogenes Syndrome that I had found. She hoarded old newspapers in her car and worse – urine, nappies and faeces – but it wasn't the practicalities that I recognized so much as her character, which embodied every trait in the professional literature. Bright, stubborn and contrary, she spent much of her life set apart from the rest of society, while at the same time being entirely sane. Apart from the fact that she lived in a van on someone else's drive and used plastic bags instead of a toilet. People had been telling me from the start that my situation could have been worse. Alan Bennett demonstrated that this was true.

It wasn't only Miss Shepherd that I was pleased to encounter in the book. In her pull–push relationship with Bennett himself, where she was sometimes delighted to see him, sometimes retreating from him and at moments inchoately furious, I could see parts of those last years with my mother. Most resonantly, after his accidental lodger died, Bennett chose to sift through the fifteen years of accumulated rubbish that Miss Shepherd had left behind. While he was trying to make sure that nothing of value was discarded, at the same time he was also looking for clues as to who this woman had been and why she ended up living as she did. I was so pleased to at last meet a fellow traveller on this road.

Miss Shepherd isn't the only Diogenes sufferer to be found in books. In Gogol's *Dead Souls*, Plyushkin is a wealthy land-owner who cannot bear to throw away anything he finds, collecting old shoe soles, rags, iron nails and potsherds, so in Russia they speak of 'Plyushkin Symptom' rather than Diogenes. In this country it's sometimes suggested that the syndrome might be better named after Miss Havisham from *Great Expectations*, but I'm not convinced. While she is de-scribed as being faded and withered, living in seclusion in an uncleaned house full of dust and mould, the windows barred, Miss Havisham doesn't collect rubbish, nor, in trying to mani-pulate the world through Estella, has she withdrawn from it entirely.

While she is using things as a defence against people, I'm not sure that Miss Havisham is even a hoarder, never mind the literary embodiment of Diogenes. She reminds me much more of Queen Victoria, keeping Prince Albert's bedroom intact for years after his death, instructing the servants to put out warm water for him each morning even though she knew her husband would never use it to shave. For both these women, objects are not a substitute for people. Instead, they have become a kind of theatrical prop, used to sustain a ver-sion of events that simply isn't true.

In any case, Miss Havisham's transformation happens overnight, and this isn't how hoarding begins, with a sudden seizure. Even though hoarders often talk about death or aban-donment as a trigger, that doesn't mean that the hoard and the mess suddenly arose like a kraken out of a lake. The loss simply marks the moment where the hoarder lost the will to fight any longer. Stuff comes in like a slow tide over the years, sometimes ebbing and flowing as people clear up and then relapse, until the pressure becomes too much and they let the mess flow over them and fill up the house. Miss Havisham is a baroque and fascinating character, but she can't be held up as a representative of hoarding, let alone Diogenes.

Dickens did write another book, however, which is filled to the brim with references to the subject. Krook, in *Bleak House*, collects old legal papers as well as rags and bones, animal skins and glass bottles. A rag-and-bone man would normally sell them on, but the shopkeeper hates to part with anything once it has become his. Krook himself admits he won't have any 'sweeping, nor scouring, nor cleaning, nor repairing going on about me'. Tellingly, Krook is an alcoholic; gin being the only stuff he loves more than the contents of his shop. Today, he'd very likely get a diagnosis of Diogenes, if not Hoarding Disorder. All that differentiates him from modern sufferers is the varieties of street finds available for him to collect.

He's not the only hoarder in the book, either. Miss Flite, with her stacked cages of birds in the room above him, would nowadays be seen as hoarding animals, while the middle-class Jellyby household is also a vast accumulation of disorderly objects:

> . . . such wonderful things came tumbling out of the closets when they were opened—bits of mouldy pie, sour bottles, Mrs Jellyby's caps, letters, tea, forks, odd boots and shoes of children, firewood, wafers, saucepan-lids, damp sugar in odds and ends of paper bags, foot-stools, blacklead brushes, bread, Mrs Jellyby's bonnets, books with butter sticking to the binding, guttered candle-ends put out by being turned upside down

in broken candlesticks, nut-shells, heads and tails of shrimps, dinner-mats, gloves, coffee-grounds, umbrellas . . .

In classic hoarder fashion, Mr Jellyby offers to help clean up, but when faced with the chaotic miscellany of what tumbles out from the cupboards, he becomes paralysed with indecision.

Dickens wasn't the only Victorian who recognized the phenomenon. Sherlock Holmes was well on the way to becoming a hoarder, as Conan Doyle revealed in his story 'The Musgrave Ritual'. In this he describes how Holmes keeps his cigars in the coal-scuttle and tobacco in the toe-end of a slipper, while relics of past cases turn up in the butter-dish, much to Dr Watson's discomfort. But as for so many hoarders, it's paper that's the biggest problem.

> He had a horror of destroying documents, especially those which were connected with his past cases, and yet it was only once in every year or two that he would muster energy to docket and arrange them . . . Thus month after month his papers accumulated, until every corner of the room was stacked with bundles of manuscript which were on no account to be burned, and which could not be put away save by their owner.

What makes Sherlock Holmes exceptional, however, is that his hoarding is justified, a state of affairs that perhaps can only ever exist in fiction.

Hoarders refuse to throw things away often because they perceive usefulness and importance in objects that others would consider to be trash. Holmes prides himself on seeing the significance in tiny details that others would miss, but for him this is not a character flaw, rather his modus operandi and the secret of his success. The plot of 'The Musgrave

Ritual' turns on an obscure and ancient manuscript which only Holmes is able to decipher fully, allowing him to unravel the crime. The message is that the oldest and least obvious thing may have a crucial significance.

The mess and disorder in Holmes's rooms is psychologically plausible, because he does think like a hoarder. What sets him apart, however, is that he is right. What the rest of us see as an irrelevant scrap may in fact contain the solution. Best indeed not to throw a single one away.

Hoarders not only appeared in the fiction of the time, they exerted a fascination for the Victorians in real life as well. Like today, journalists reported hoarding stories with an excitable mixture of repulsion and glee. When two elderly sisters from Gosport in Hampshire were badly burned because their dresses caught fire but neighbours couldn't reach them because the house was stuffed with rubbish, papers across the country covered the story.

> The place could not have been cleaned since it has been in the occupation of the women, a period of nearly twenty years, and the filthy state of the bed and bed-clothing fully bears out this conclusion. Upon one of the women was found a bag containing a quantity of silver coin, and it is alleged that when the women paid their rent the coin was so begrimed with filth and dirt that their landlord was compelled to cleanse it immediately upon its receipt.

Both women died, and the newspapers reported on how four wagonloads of miscellaneous items were cleared from their rooms, including a ton and a half of coal, which had been covered over with rubbish. Every detail of this story would make good copy for a journalist today, the only difference being the length of the dresses which set off the disaster in the first place.

In real life, just as in literature, hoarding was not confined to the poor. When Sir Thomas Phillips died in 1872, he had amassed the largest and most important collection of books and manuscripts in private hands. This wasn't an orderly collection – he wrote that he was 'buying printed books because I wish to have ONE COPY OF EVERY BOOK IN THE WORLD' and was unable to throw away anything with writing on it. The state of his house was notorious. When the then Keeper of Manuscripts at the British Museum came to inspect Sir Thomas's holdings at his Gloucestershire house in 1854, he reported:

> The house looks more miserable and dilapidated every time I visit it, and there is not a room now that is not crowded with large boxes full of MSS . . . I asked him why he did not clear away the piles of paper &c. from the floor, so as to allow a path to be kept, but he only laughed.

The smell was apparently unbearable. My mother's study was a relief in comparison, and her collection of books only slight.

Phillips was notoriously querulous, opinionated and self-centred, alienating everyone around him and quarrelling with any authority that crossed his path. I can't help feeling that he would have made a great addition to the literature about Diogenes. His strangeness hardened into dogma long before he got old.

Although we would now identify these people as hoarders, that's not how Dickens, Conan Doyle or their fellow Victorians would have understood them. Then, hoarding was what you did with money rather than stuff, so to be a hoarder was the same as being a miser. In their world it's Scrooge who is the hoarder; Sherlock Holmes, who refuses payment for his services and can't always manage to pay the rent, is not.

Back then, however, there was much more overlap between the two, not least because amassing money did necessarily mean accumulating a physical hoard. The two Gosport sisters had a stack of money in amongst their collection of worthless remnants, but more extreme misers had to deal with huge volumes of coins. In popular reports they keep their stashes in pots and pans, under mattresses and, most often, up chimneys. These hoards are metal; they cannot decay or be eaten away by fire.

The original meaning of 'hoarding' goes back to Middle English, where the word describes both treasure and the place where it is hidden, and is why dragons guard hoards of treasure and archaeologists excavate hoards of coins. Back then a hoard was a source of security and safety in times of danger, imperishable metal heaped against an uncertain future, just as it was for the Victorians who secreted coins about their houses.

What's surprising, given how ubiquitous the word has become, is that its meaning shifted only recently to mean those who keep stuff. When I worked on *The Life Laundry* in 2002, we never used it. The mess we found was not hoarding, and the people we worked with were not hoarders. Instead, the team simply went into people's houses to help them clear out the clutter. Nothing was named, never mind pathologized or diagnosed.

While the Victorians might not have used our word for it, they were very able to describe the situation. Dickens and his fellow journalists were interested in hoarders in the same way that our television channels are today, and for the same reasons. Hoarding was the appropriate form of madness for a world that was suffering from a sudden profusion of stuff and becoming anxious that it might, if left unchecked, overwhelm them entirely.

The Industrial Revolution not only produced ships, looms and steam boilers, it also released an unprecedented quantity of cheap consumer goods into people's homes. Until this point, any thing that a person owned tended to be very expensive indeed, even if it were made of the most basic materials. Before the machine age, a single new shirt would be worth the extraordinary sum of £3,500 in today's money, the high cost coming from all the growing, carding, weaving, spinning and sewing needed to produce it. No wonder that even the most basic item of clothing was kept or passed on until it was worn through, then recycled into children's clothes, underwear, cloths and eventually rags. Very few people could own more than the barest essentials, so every object, whether a wooden chair or a piece of bed linen, was treasured as befitted its value.

The corollary was that little remained to be hoarded. Most of what was thrown out would have rotted, while the rest would have been recycled or mended or burned. Whole trades like rag-pickers, marine store proprietors and rag-and-bone men were based on the reuse of what we would now consider to be rubbish. Becoming a hoarder in pre-industrial England would have been very hard work indeed.

Mechanization turned that world on its head. Using machines and cheaper materials such as papier mâché, thin brass or gutta-percha allowed things to be produced at a far lower cost. Many more people could furnish their home with ornaments as well as domestic necessities. Stamped, moulded or printed with copper plates, almost every product could also be decorated as busily as the consumer liked at almost no extra cost because those trailing tendrils or bursting fruits were no longer the work of a skilled craftsman on his hourly wage. More was cheap and also very definitely better. My mother's black teapot is the exemplar of this in black clay: the edges curved and scalloped, the handle crowned with a flourish, every surface patterned and then writhing with flowers. In their excitement at the possibilities of the machine, nothing could ever be too much. As the British led the Industrial Revolution, so they were pioneers of stuff as well. The Great Exhibition was the harbinger of this brand-new age, piling a hundred thousand different objects, from threshing machinery to ornate caskets filled with man-made pearls, into one translucent space. The exhibition's greatest purpose was to heap up the vast quantity of goods that had been compelled into existence by industry.

As stuff started to swarm, so did rubbish. Now there were objects ephemeral enough to be discarded rather than repaired, and so waste became a problem. Dickens worries away at dirt and rubbish in many of his books, whether that's the filth of the slums, the garbage heaps and Golden Dustman of *Our Mutual Friend*, the mud that Jo sweeps from the road in *Bleak House* or the contents of Krook's shop. He has understood that there is so much more refuse than ever before.

Despite the rising tide of debris, most ordinary people were delighted by the new profusion of affordable things which surrounded them. Foreign visitors to mid-Victorian England were amazed by the quantity of portable goods that people's homes contained. These things also came to be seen as morally improving. Despite biblical warnings about camels passing through a needle's eye, the meaning of possessions was reinterpreted. The uncluttered asceticism of early monks and saints was no longer seen as the earthly route to salvation; instead, a well-decorated room became the means of uplifting its occupants. The precise mechanism by which this might happen was left unclear; what was certain, however, was that bad design led, inevitably, to damnation. Should the head of the house permit imitations such as fake marbling, or a hearth poker twisted into the form of a snake into his house, this could only be the start of a slippery slope of accepting lies in other parts of his life. Bad taste was only a step or two away from taking a mistress; in its presence, ruin was inevitable.

If the right furnishing was morally improving, then clearly the more a person owned, the more virtuous they would become. The mid-Victorian home was cluttered in a way that we would find psychically uncomfortable. Every room was stuffed with a jumble of assorted and unmatched furniture which left almost no floor space free. One upper-class music room of the 1870s contained a piano, a set of extending dining tables, six further tables, eleven chairs, three music stands, four ottomans, two footstools and a prie-dieu. Literally on top of these would stand a smaller skyline of lamps, statues, crocheted flowers and glass domes, plants, embroideries and other ornaments, while the fireplace would have been draped, fringed and swagged, then topped by an overmantel with shelves to hold even more bric-a-brac, edged by pictures two or three deep on the walls around. However spacious the room, the effect must have been suffocating.

At heart, the Victorians were hoarders. They found these brand-new mass-productions irresistible and collected them in their homes until they were almost barricaded in by their own possessions. The accumulated stuff made them feel safe, warm and secure. Home was their haven, and no one believed that too much stuff was a sign of mental illness or that clearing out the clutter could make a person morally superior.

As the century turned, these feelings began to change. By the 1880s, some people were starting to find the profusion of objects and the intensity of their decoration alarming. The Arts and Crafts Movement tackled the problem by trying to restore the values of a time before machines. William Morris preached that a person should possess only those objects they believed to be either beautiful or useful, but he also believed that the most virtuous objects were hand-produced by craftsmen. His attempts at turning back the clocks failed to work; people liked their new cheap stuff however it was made, and even Morris's own designs ended up being mass-produced in factories.

The battle against clutter had to be waged by other means, and the next assault came after the First World War, in the form of the Modern Movement. While the Victorians had invented the idea that interior design had a moral dimension, it was modernists who decided that righteousness came in the form of less rather than more. The German architect Bruno Taut declared war on the pointless piles of doilies, trinkets and pictures which currently occupied people's living spaces. These were to be replaced with emptiness and built-in storage. If the modern housewife did not have to dust so much, she could spend time becoming a better person.

These new aesthetics weren't only meant to result in more efficient lives but also in improved people. Le Corbusier, his tongue only slightly in his cheek, suggested that a coat of whitewash would lead to inner as well as outer cleanliness, while Adolf Loos declared that ornament was crime, condemning it as degenerate and backward. Victorian morals had been turned on their head. No longer did a righteous life depend on choosing the correct kind of household furniture. This new world view decreed that goodness could only be achieved by throwing as much as possible away. The right kind of homeowner would get rid of unnecessary bric-a-brac and decoration, leaving only wide open spaces of white, in which they could live their life on a higher, more efficient plane.

These moral imperatives still underlie our reaction to stuff to this day, even if we never consider why they have come about. Great heaped piles of things repel us; hoarding is the mark of moral degeneracy. This minimalism doesn't mean that any of its practitioners are free from the thrall of stuff. On the contrary, it's the flip side of the same obsession, in the same way that anorexics are just as aware of the importance of food as fat people. They just flee from its powers instead of embracing them.

When my mother's problems were at their worst, as well as watching hours of hoarding programmes on television, I also read Marie Kondo's *The Life-Changing Magic of Tidying*, in pursuit of the same kind of vicarious pleasure. My own house was quite organized, but if I couldn't persuade my mother to reform, the next best thing was nonetheless to clean myself up all over again.

When I cleared out Rose Terrace, I found myself thinking about Kondo once more. The high priestess of pared-down simplicity, she advocates living with the barest minimum of stuff, keeping only things which in her words 'spark joy' and throwing the rest away. Her goal is order and calm. Despite this, she has a great deal in common with hoarders, and so with my mother.

Just like a hoarder, she admits to preferring things to people. She imbues things with life, believing that possessions have their own personalities, along with feelings that are worthy of respect. This comes through most powerfully in her dealings with socks, which she worries about as though they were pets or children, or at the very least co-workers. She believes that they hate being balled up and would prefer to spend what she thinks of as their holiday time in our drawers relaxed and stretched out. When putting her socks away, she thanks them for the work they have done in supporting her feet, and she wants us all to perform this ritual when we throw our old socks away.

In her beliefs about things, Kondo is the anti-hoarder, her obsessional minimalism the negative print of their mess and excess. Hoarders seek to represent the unhappy chaos of their minds in the disorder of their homes, but Marie Kondo reverses the chain of cause and effect. By sorting out her possessions into perfect order, she hopes that, in turn, her whole existence will become more bearable. She offers her readers the promise of modernism all over again: that an emptier house will cause its occupier to lead a better life.

Kondo's book is a total expression of the philosophy which still prevails in our culture. Her attitude may have sprung from a Japanese aesthetic, but its message has found a ready audience in the West, shaped as we are by the principles of the Modern Movement. Things still have moral purpose, but only in very small numbers. Space and light will do us good.

These modernist truisms are now the backbones of the way we live. Le Corbusier and his friends have won the battle. Absence is better than clutter; throwing stuff away is a positive act. Marie Kondo and William Morris skip hand in hand together, exhorting us to own only what we need. Less is not only better, it is morally improving. All of which means that hoarders are degenerates who need to be reformed.

Contrary as ever, my mother began her adult life as a modernist but ended up becoming a Victorian. During the 1960s, when I was a child and my mother was setting up home in Edgehill House, modernism was at the peak of its influence in Britain. The country was booming, and young people wanted to look forward to the future with sleek, sparse furniture set out in acres of open space. They believed that society after the war was becoming different and better, so its interiors needed to reflect that altered state.

My mother was no exception, channelling the minimal taste of the 1960s into her new home. The sofa had a black metal skeleton and thin turquoise cushions; our sideboard was long and low, made from glowing teak. My memories of Edgehill House are of the spaces between things. The sitting room held only four pieces of furniture: the sofa, my father's special armchair, which my brother and I were only permitted to sit in when ill, a standard lamp and a coffee table. Later, these were joined by a television set, but even that still left open fields of prickly brown carpet between them.

In this, my mother was following fashion, but her own optimism resonated with that of the times. She'd escaped her family unhappiness and was free; the sparse rooms in which she lived reflected that new life.

In the books and scientific papers the orthodox view of hoarding is that it starts early in life, gradually increasing as years go by, which is why most problem hoarders, like my mother, tend to be elderly. But given how little was in Edgehill

House back then, I can't say that my mother started to become a hoarder from an early age. The studies which prove that hoarding starts in childhood are retrospective, asking sufferers about how they behaved twenty or thirty years ago. This inevitably makes the results fallible. It's easy to view the past through the lens of what has happened subsequently. Any previous attachment to objects becomes the prelude to full-blown hoarding. The results are a bit like writing a biography; if the subject has become a famous artist, their childhood sketchbook carries a significance it would not have done had they become an actor or a nuclear scientist.

What these accounts inevitably leave out are the people who are messy and accumulate stuff but never progress into full-blown hoarding. People who love objects, collect too much, find personalities in everyday things but who can still walk around their houses with ease. People like me, in other words. Were I to have become a hoarder, the progress would have seemed inevitable. If I didn't, though, I would never trouble the literature. No one would ever notice that I had all the characteristics which should have made me a hoarder and yet had escaped the disorder because, somehow, I was still able to throw things away.

Furthermore, when the clutter first arrived in my mother's house, this was also because she was in tune with the times. When she bought Rose Terrace, in 1981, its Georgian neatness had become newly fashionable, and with this came a desire for furniture and furnishings to match. The past was no longer being jettisoned by the modernists; it had come back in vogue.

My mother papered walls and painted shutters and panelled doors; she found a grand marble fireplace which was being thrown out by the council and installed it in the sitting room. Along with what she inherited from Carrie Jenkins, she acquired more old wood and iron bedsteads. Her biggest investment was a neat Georgian table and chairs in dark mahogany, with curved backs and ball-and-claw feet, for her small dining room.

The sense of reclaimed heritage would have been visible even to the postman who delivered a parcel. My mother had kept the original, shallow-panelled front door, painting it a deep gloss red. She'd also kept the tiny Victorian letterbox, engraved with swirls of brass flowers but entirely impractical because it was too small for anything more than a postcard, so the postman had to ring the doorbell quite often. When she opened the door, he would have seen the wide hall which she'd papered in a grey Regency stripe, with a matched set of eighteenth-century prints of Worcester in black frames hanging from the picture rail each side. My mother had collected these views of her home city, from the cathedral and city gates to a river scene, one by one and had them all framed as a set. Overhead hung a brass gasolier with its original engraved bowl of glass, converted for electricity. To one side was a small Georgian rosewood table, for the phone, and as a resting place for car keys and her handbag, while at the end stood Carrie Jenkins' chiffonier, monumental as a grave with its dark carved wood. The only modern furnishing was the deep-red carpet.

The shift in her tastes was extreme, but then my mother's own situation was very different too. Her share of the modern furniture from Edgehill House had somehow disappeared since the divorce, and she didn't seem to want to replace it. No longer looking forward to the future, there was no bright and different life of her own to be made. She had sunk back into the embrace of her earliest family history, bringing this into her home in the form of furniture. Not only the chiffon-ier in the hall but the chests of drawers and beds in the top rooms were antiques, all the legacy of Carrie Jenkins. From this moment on, long before she began hoarding, my mother's attention had shifted. She had turned back towards the past.

Along with this new aesthetic came not only the old cook-ery books but, in places, an almost Victorian level of clutter. On a round table in the corner of her sitting room, my mother displayed the ornaments she'd collected over the years. Some, like the carved elephants and balsawood chicken on a pillar, were souvenirs from her own travels; the teapot came in on a whim. But here also lived a vase from my great-grandmother's house along with Antoinette's big wooden penguin. All of this was the matter that modernism wanted to tidy away. Even before she became a hoarder, my mother, with her collections, her dust and her sentimental attachment to stuff, had become a problem which society needed to tidy up for her own moral good.

no/thing: *object removed*

Object Removed

O N MY LAST couple of visits, I had been working alone in the house with only the radio to fill up the empty space. I had wiped walls and woodwork and cleaned the kitchen one more time, slowly removing the evidence. Driving up the motorway each time, I could see that spring was starting to rise in the hedges and trees. We needed to get the house sold while the light streamed into each empty room and before the rain seeped into the roof again next winter.

I wasn't sure I was ready to let go of Rose Terrace, not yet. A part of me would have preferred to carry on with this work for ever, coming up to Worcester week after week to scrape away another layer of nicotine and dust. There would always be something more to clean, and I hadn't yet finished tidying up the past.

At the same time, I knew that I couldn't hold on to my mother's house for ever, nor could I restore it. As the veteran of one big house renovation, I'd thought about taking the work on, and my husband and I had discussed it seriously, more than once. This would have been the ultimate reparation, but Worcester was now a foreign territory for me. I didn't know any helpful builders or electricians, nor even anyone to recommend them to me. In any case, supervising the work from nearly a hundred miles away would have been impossible. Even I might get sick of the motorway.

I went through these arguments over and over again in my

head, always coming to the same unwelcome conclusion. I had no choice: the house would have to be sold in the state it was now, and this meant I could no longer keep other people out.

When I returned to Rose Terrace that next week it was not to slow, solitary work but an unremitting procession of visitors. Three estate agents were booked to come and look at the house at intervals throughout the day. Also arriving in the morning would be the auctioneers, ready to take whatever furniture and goods they might deem worth their while.

These were all people whose lives were spent appraising, valuing, judging. I had laboured for weeks, but I was sure they would be able to see through my attempts at a cover-up. The house was still a mess; I couldn't hide the facts of its decay. Even a cursory look would reveal that something unfortunate had happened here. I'd explained as little as I could get away with over the phone, but, like the social workers and nurses, like Jim and Ed, the agents and auctioneers had all understood after only a few sentences. My mother's house held nothing they hadn't seen many times before.

The morning passed in a whirl of people coming in and out, of decisions about what to keep and what might go. Only a few of the solid wooden pieces were of any interest to the valuer, most of the soft furnishings being too damp and cigarette-infused, but I knew this already. All I did was say yes or no; there was no time to think about what was happening, let alone get upset about it. In the middle of all the shifting and labelling, the first estate agent arrived, the pristine sheen of his suit standing out like a starling amongst sparrows. Jim, Ed and I were all dressed in fleeces, old jeans and dust, and his clean fabric coming across the threshold made me uncomfortable.

For the last two months my mother's house had been like a separate kingdom, making its own laws and with its own taboos about dirt and cleanliness, but now the conventional world that surrounded it was invading. Pretending that I was too busy to help, I let each estate agent pick their way past the chairs and boxes and go upstairs on their own. I didn't want to see them looking. I had to remember to tell each one not to go too far into the rooms on the top floor. Ed had fixed a piece of hardboard over the hole where the policeman had put his foot through, but none of the floorboards could really be trusted. Cleaning alone couldn't fix everything.

At lunchtime, I left Jim and Ed loading up the van with what the auctioneers had turned down. They had promised me that whatever possible would go to the charity shop, but we all knew that this wouldn't amount to very much. Almost everything, however precious it had once been to my mother, was only fit for the tip.

I had one more estate agent booked for later that afternoon, but that still left enough time to head into Worcester for a fresh cup of coffee and the use of a functioning toilet. My walk had become a reassuring ritual every time I visited the house, taking me past the red-brick terraces then through the park where, during the Civil War, the Royalists had built ramparts in their last stand, only to be slaughtered at the city gates when they tried to flee. My mother had a habit of living on battlegrounds.

From here, I had a choice. When I'd walked into town with my mother, we'd always gone straight ahead, through the pedestrian precinct which lay beyond the Giffard Hotel on the roundabout. With its panoramic wall of smoked-glass windows and monogrammed doors, this had always looked

enticingly glamorous when I was a child. I imagined it full
of women in sparkling evening dresses and men who dressed
like James Bond. Now faded, it had become a Travelodge, and
I'd learned to turn right before then, into a much older road
which my mother never used. The first block had been rebuilt
into a modern multiplex and car park, but down the far end
straggled a whole row of ancient houses, now shops, but still
with leaning timber frames and warped doorways.

I had been shocked to discover anything unknown in the
city. I had come and gone from Worcester throughout my life,
and thought I knew every part of it. Well before my mother
had moved back, we'd visited regularly, because it was where
all three of my grandparents still lived. I'd played in its parks,
bought bread from its bakers, wondered at the way its milk-
men delivered their milk in square plastic bags instead of
bottles. I'd never thought that the city held anything undis-
covered, especially so close to my mother's house.

At the far end of Friar Street stood the most intriguing survival of all: a long black and white half-timbered building with
high gables, its first floor jettied out over the street. The only
entrance had been sealed up by a tall wooden gate, as though
some Tudor merchant's family were still in residence, preserving their privacy against the bustling city without. When I got
close, a small wooden board at the doorway told me that this
was Greyfriars, a National Trust property.

I'd been walking past the house ever since my first visit to
Worcester, and I'd still never managed to see inside. At first it
was closed for the winter, then it only opened twice a week and
I came on the wrong day, then I got the right day but arrived
too early and didn't have time to return. Today, I was determined to enter. I needed to take one positive memory from all

these visits to Worcester, to counterbalance all the mourning and mess and misery. Today might be my last chance, and finally the gate was open to me.

I stepped into a bright courtyard, but the days were still short and cold, and the plants stood stiff and dead against the walls, so I didn't linger. Through a small doorway to the right, curving wooden stairs took me up into the house itself. As soon as I came into the first room, I felt comfortable, even at home. Greyfriars was no stately mansion. Instead, I'd walked into what felt like a private sitting room, with wing armchairs arranged around the fire, a side table placed by each for books and cups of tea, along with a screen to keep the draughts out. Deep-red carpets and dark panelling were set against white emulsion paint and 1960s light fittings; rich old woods contrasted with the nylon of net curtains.

My mother would have liked it here. She would have appreciated not only the history but also the sense of calm and the invitation to sit by the fire.

The only other people present were a pair of volunteer attendants, the distilled essence of the National Trust. A lady in a tartan skirt and pastel blouse bustled in and out, making arrangements, while a tall elderly man sat in a chair by the window. Seeing me lingering, he came over and began to talk about the house, how it had once been prosperous and smart but was eventually divided up and used as shops. By the nineteenth century, Greyfriars had become the worst slum in the city, its back rooms filled with greengrocers' waste, its structures so rotten that part of the timber framing collapsed into the street. Only in the 1950s, with rain pouring through the roof and demolition planned, was the building rescued. Its saviours were a brother and sister, the Matley Moores, who rebuilt its structure then filled it with furniture and fittings that befitted its Tudor glory. The house was not so much a survival as an imagined museum, or perhaps even a film set.

As I wandered around the room, touching the smooth wood of a chair arm, admiring the tiny stitches of an embroidery, I felt warmth held in the colours of the faded hearthrug and tapestries, the swirling patterns of the china over the fireplace. The air seemed to be filled with the personalities of the couple who had restored it. I imagined the Matley Moores looking like Granny and Grandpa, my father's parents: him balding with a trim moustache and a sleeveless tank top over his shirt, her kindly and small, keeping an eye on everything. Worcester people.

More than anything, the house was a memorial to the act of restoration. Once Greyfriars had been ruined and now it had been reclaimed; rooms had once been open to the sky above but now fires flickered in its grates. I could only see it as the mirror image of what had happened to Rose Terrace, which had gone from home to ruin. Today, the rain seeped in through that roof instead. The contrast disheartened me; I wished that I could restore Rose Terrace, with its soft bricks and elegant windows, and maintain that as a shrine to my mother in the same way.

The inappropriate tone of my mobile cut into my thoughts. The last estate agent was just passing by Rose Terrace after another viewing. His voice was in a rush; would I mind if he came over now? I did mind, but told him that Jim and Ed would let him in the door, and I would be back as soon as I could manage.

When I walked away from Greyfriars, I knew that I would probably never return. The city no longer belonged to me.

Despite having been rooted here all her life, my mother had departed Worcester leaving no trace and no reason for me to return. What upset me most was that when the house was sold, she would have no memorial here of any kind.

My brother and I had been talking about this on and off, never reaching any conclusion. In truth, it was only me who wanted there to be something permanent. We could have had a plaque put up in the gardens of the crematorium, on what was called a Wall of Remembrance, but it would only stay up for twenty-five years, and who would go to look at it? He didn't feel the need, and I hate visiting graves, so there didn't seem to be much purpose. A temporary sheet of brass wasn't going to prevent her being forgotten, not if no one ever went to see it. All it would do was bring one more unhappy object into the story of my mother's life.

Greyfriars hung on my conscience, and I walked back to the house despondent. My mother's memorial should have been Rose Terrace, restored, but I hadn't been able to make that happen. As someone who cared about stuff so much and used it to think with, it seemed important that she should have had something solid as a marker in the world, to prove that she had once lived.

By the end of the afternoon, the house had been emptied. Jim and Ed had given the last help they could offer and disappeared into the cool afternoon. Suddenly, Rose Terrace had altered. I felt as though the papers and boxes, the damp carpets and dusty wood had been sucking up all the atmosphere and at last the house could breathe again. Or perhaps the change lay in me, and now I finally dared to let its atmosphere fill my lungs.

The afternoon sun was lowering yellow through the trees and I needed to get home, but instead I headed up the stairs to make sure that nothing had been left behind. The house was almost beautiful again. Jim and Ed's last act had been to strip out the carpets. Each room now showed the dark-stained Victorian floorboards, with a square of pale wood in the centre where the rug would have gone, a reminder of people who had lived in these rooms long before my mother arrived. Despite my scrubbing, the wallpaper and woodwork were deeply yellowed, like paper left out in the sun. Even so, a sense of peace had returned, and I could shut the door behind me without worrying about what lay behind it.

I drove home, eyes tired in the grey dusk light, the car heavy with stuff. The finality of the furniture being removed had proved too much for me, and I'd taken far more than I had intended. Two big cardboard boxes of china and knick-knacks filled the boot. The auctioneers would have lumped these together in their sale for ten pounds, which didn't seem right or fair. Squeezed into the back seat was the mahogany table from the sitting room, which had once displayed all the ornaments. I wasn't sure I wanted to keep this or where it would go in our house, but I felt I owed it to my mother to hold on to one piece of furniture, at least for now. In yet another box, wedged into the footwell, the engravings from her hallway rattled their black frames together. I'd put these to one side when Jim and Ed had been clearing, because people like this sort of local interest and so they would go well at auction. Or so I had thought. The auctioneer flicked through the box with one jaded look and told me that the yellowed paper was ruined. The prints were worthless. His indifference had infuriated me, so I was determined to prove him wrong. If I had learned one thing from the last few weeks, it was how much things could be cleaned.

Had I not salvaged these last few unruly pieces, everything that my mother had owned would have been dispersed for ever, and I could not bear for that to happen, not yet. I'd hurried the process along, and now so much of what she'd left behind had been discarded, when I should have been trying harder to remember her. Or at least not clearing away her presence so quickly.

In bed that evening I cried properly for the first time in weeks. My mother had been dead for nearly two months, but with the house entirely empty I felt her absence for the first time. She had never been truly present when she was alive, but now she was no longer anywhere on earth, and I understood that she would never return.

The next day I washed all the ornaments then rewrapped them in their newspaper. Cleaning wipes made easy work of the tar and dust on the framed prints too, but even being right couldn't cheer me up. I found it impossible to decide which objects might mean something to me and which should go, because that would mean choosing the parts of my mother I was going to remember and which I was going to leave behind. How could I do that when I still wasn't entirely sure who she had been in the first place? Nothing remained to clean; no more of my mother was left to restore and repair. Grief crept up on me, filling the empty space.

After a couple of days of this aimlessness, I found myself at home on a quiet afternoon, sitting on the floor with my grandmother's photograph albums. This time, instead of looking through the pictures, I started at the back, where my grandmother had preserved all the newspaper announcements of family events. Each yellowing scrap of tiny print had been cut out and stuck on to the black paper of the book, a roll call of the family history.

The earliest cutting was older than my grandmother herself, being a report on my great-grandmother's wedding in 1910, from which I discovered that the Friends Meeting House in Scarborough was 'tastefully decorated'. My grandmother's own birth announcement was in there too: a first child for Carrie Jenkins and her new husband Harold in Rotherham.

Most of the cuttings, though, must have been stuck there by my grandmother herself. Her engagement and wedding merited four separate notices, in the *Morning Post*, the Quaker newspaper *The Friend*, Berrow's *Worcester Journal* and the *Derbyshire Times*. The last, almost as snobbish as Carrie Jenkins herself, enjoys pointing out that the groom, my grandfather

Antoinette and Allan on their wedding day in 1934, at Oldbury Grange. Carrie looks pleased.

Allan Gilmour, was a nephew of the then home secretary. Following quickly are birth announcements in the *Telegraph* for Anne and my mother, one in the *Glasgow Herald* for Alastair, then, in the tiniest scrap of all from an unnamed paper, the notice of his death. Funeral private. No flowers. My aunt and uncle were born. Then, once the surviving children had grown up, come the engagements. Finally, after all the weddings, is the death of Carrie Jenkins née Rickatson at the age of ninety-two, peacefully in a nursing home.

These two black pages contain the start and end of my grandmother's family, yet the stock phrases of the newsprint revealed nothing of all the happiness and miseries that had taken place in between.

I'd read all this before, many times, but now what struck me was how many clues these clippings contained. When he married, my grandfather Allan was described as not only the nephew of the home secretary but also the son of Major Angus Gilmour of Eaglesham and Finglesham, pleasingly distinctive words for searches.

Within half an hour, I had two family histories of the Gilmours, who turned out to have been significant enough for other people to have written about them. Spurred on by this early success, I kept going. The research filled my days to the point of obsession until I found myself with a densely packed family tree, contacts with new cousins in Canada and South Africa, and a deep dent in the sofa where I had sat for hours at a time without even a cup of coffee. With my mother's house cleared, I needed a new focus, and the family tree filled that gap very well.

As the days passed into weeks and its branches grew older and wider, I realized that there was another, more profound reason for all this work. With my mother's death, I had become an orphan or, if I were too old for that, at least a person without parents. No longer was there anyone to whom I belonged. By conjuring up a whole legion of family members from the shadows, I made myself a little bit less alone.

In the process I was also unearthing the truth behind some of the family stories which my mother had told. It turned out that there had once been a great family house, with a lot of money too. Back in the 1840s, my Gilmour forebears had made a fortune importing timber, mainly from Canada into Glasgow, where the firm of Pollock, Gilmour and Co. owned one of the largest private fleets in the world.

The mistake they made was to give up working and live like gentlemen. Even their great wealth could not sustain a lifestyle of shooting, socializing and marrying off their daughters into the aristocracy. Within sixty years, the money was all gone. My grandfather Allan had grown up surrounded by all the trappings of wealth, but the appearance had been a sham. At the time his own father, Angus, had inherited in 1917, the estate was already so encumbered with debts and entails that there had been no choice but to sell. Allan only lived there because it had taken until 1930 to make this happen. Antoinette married into a family that had the money to buy Oakbank House, but no more.

What they had lost was Eaglesham House. In 1849, with the family money at its peak, an earlier Allan Gilmour had bought the estate of Eaglesham from the Earls of Eglinton. His successor, another Allan, built the neo-Baronial mansion of Eaglesham House, employing Victorian Scotland's leading architect, David Bryce, a man who built banks and public schools as well as sprawling residences for the new upper

I will only ever know Eaglesham House from postcards because it burned down in 1954, while being used as a hay store.

classes. Here at last I'd found the lost stately home of which the whole family had dreamed and for which my mother and I had pined. We had never known its pleasures, yet somehow it had still enchanted us down the generations, enticing us with dreams of the garden walks and morning rooms, the staff indoors and out, day and night nurseries, a life of elegance and leisure to which we should have been born.

That was the fantasy. The reality was very different. Eaglesham was not a creation of grace and taste, rather it sprang solidly from the great engine of Victorian trade. The house was a monument to the expansiveness of the Victorian imagination and possibly also P. G. Wodehouse's aphorism that few of that era were to be trusted within reach of a trowel and a pile of bricks. Its exterior faces were an eclectic mixture of Scottish castle turrets by the dozen, crow-step gables and Elizabethan doorways; the facade sprouted coats of arms, mullions, corbels and balustrades.

As catalogued for sale in 1930, the interior fittings were no less profuse. Even after years of wear and alteration, and when the family had already taken all the pieces they wanted to keep, the house was still rammed to the brim with furniture and fixtures.

Every downstairs room contained a menagerie of settees and chairs, oak and stuff-over, circle back and mahogany. There were turn-over card tables and pianos, parrot stands and mantelpiece mirrors, violins, telescopic fire screens and billiard sets. The dining room had cabinets full of crystal and china; the bedrooms were stacked with bedsteads and feather mattresses. The entrance halls alone contained 179 dead stuffed birds in glass cases. In its rooms lived the Victorian love of more, unrestrained by any breath of modernism. Eaglesham was the true ancestor of Rose Terrace, only the difference was that in its endless vast rooms the excess of stuff was a decorative choice rather than the result of a series of disasters.

Perhaps my mother accumulated so much stuff partly to restore the family fortunes. Rose Terrace was the result of tide after tide of histories. My mother's own tastes had followed fashion in their journey from modernist to historic, while at the same time she was remembering her own childhood in a Victorian house. Yet with the layers of clutter and old furniture in Rose Terrace, she'd also delved much further back into the collective memory of her ancestors. In filling her own house with bric-a-brac, ornaments and miscellaneous oddments, one of the things that my mother was doing was recreating the world of the Gilmours at the height of their power and splendour, in their grand house rammed with furnishings and celebrating the joy of too much stuff.

*

I didn't only discover a house in my searches. Unexpected family likenesses also appeared. My mother's family, in particular, seemed to make a habit of divorce and separation, which I could trace back up the generations like a recessive chin or a Roman nose.

I'd known for a long time that my grandparents Allan and Antoinette's divorce must have been very uncommon when it happened just after the Second World War. Even when my parents split up in the 1970s, that made our family unusual, freakish even. I was the only person I knew in the world – or at least in my school class and family, which pretty much was my world – whose parents were no longer together. So I kept it as a secret, tight to myself. At school, I pretended nothing had happened. The only person who knew was my best friend.

How much more shameful it must have been for my grandmother and mother in 1947. I suspect they coped by doing exactly what I did and saying nothing at all. Plenty of men had disappeared in the war, one way or another, so it might be that their situation was easier than I imagined. If they just stayed silent, people would assume that the missing husband had been bombed or shot or drowned at sea, and so would respect their loss in the very British way of never mentioning it. In fact Allan was still alive and in Scotland, but no one needed to know that particular truth.

I'd always assumed that the death of their firstborn son was reason enough for Allan and Antoinette to split up, but what the archives revealed was that this had not been the beginning. Divorce ran through the family like a geological flaw. Allan's own parents, Angus and Ethel, had divorced in 1920, after only ten years of marriage, the alleged cause being Angus's adultery with a nurse and 'intimacy' with other servants.

This divorce didn't spring from a clear blue sky either. Marital unhappiness flickered in and out like a flame in Angus's family: his sister divorced in Australia in 1916, his grandmother died at the other end of Britain from her husband, in Sussex, where she had lived with her daughter for some years. Ethel's family, though, had problems so intense that they could be made out even through the impersonal bureaucracy of censuses and records. In the 1880s, she and her parents are living a comfortable middle-class existence in Chelsea; her father, William, is a company secretary, which gives them enough money to rent an entire house, plenty of space for his four children. Ethel has a twin brother, John, as well as a younger brother and sister, all born within three years of each other.

Within ten years, the family is broken and scattered. In 1891 Ethel and her sister Dorothy are being looked after by a childless aunt and uncle in Staines, and her younger brother, Bertie, is at a Brighton boarding school, leaving her father, William, on his own in lodgings in Chelsea. Her mother is nowhere to be found.

What's happened in between is that Ethel's twin, John, has died, aged four, of meningitis. Once again, the death of a young child has blown a family apart.

When Alastair died and Allan's own marriage broke up after the end of the next war, he must have felt as though he was condemned to repeat the miseries of the past. I was starting to feel as though this was the fate of the whole family. Our history seemed to be an endless set of variations on the same mournful themes. Couples were unhappy and separated, parents disappeared from their children's lives, and homes were lost. And each time, it seemed, the cause of this was a dead child.

Our ancestors had not left us great houses nor fortunes. They had tilled fields of misery, and that was our inheritance. Time wasn't linear; it did not bring progress or change. Instead, it repeated endlessly, forcing us to live the same story in each generation. Sadness never had a beginning but had been handed down in an unbroken chain from parent to child each time, like a piece of heirloom furniture that everyone hates but no one can bring themselves to throw away. My mother, born into this recurring history, never had a hope of happiness from the start.

The dead children were as frequent as the divorces. I'd always known about them, but my research now gave me names and dates, often for the first time. Ethel's tiny brother, John, Alastair, and of course my own sister, Fiona. The searches had, inevitably, led me to the registration of her death. Just as she had been a dot on the timeline my mother had made, she also only existed in the records for one brief day in September 1964. Her age at death a sad zero. This was the first proof I'd ever found of her existence. Until this point, all I had heard were a small handful of stories.

For many years I'd never even known I had once had a sister. I remember very clearly the day I found out. My brother and I were visiting Granny and Grandpa, my father's parents, for tea. My grandfather called us into the dining room, where he had a family tree laid out on the dark wood table. This was soon after the divorce, so I would have been nine or ten, just old enough to understand what all those lines and names represented. At first I wasn't surprised to see a third person set out next to me and my brother, assuming it was my new stepbrother. But when I looked properly, the name wasn't his.

Instead, I found another girl, Fiona. My grandfather must surely have explained, but what remained with me was the image of those three names branching out from my parents when I thought we were only two, and the creeping shock that my family history wasn't the one I thought I knew.

It's surprising that my grandfather, of all people, decided we should be told. Brought up at the very end of the Victorian era, he wasn't an open or demonstrative man. Perhaps he did not want my sister to be forgotten, so felt the need to pass his memory of her on to us.

Like the divorce, I kept this secret to myself for a long time. My father never spoke of his first daughter, and I never dared ask, while it took my mother many years to break her own silence. Only when I had become an adult, and we sat at the dining table with our glasses of wine, did she start to speak about Fiona.

As she did with every difficult part of her life, she'd parcelled up the experience into a single story that was all she could bear to repeat. She never said anything to me about the birth, or how she had felt at the time, or how she had dealt with the pain, the loss, the anxiety of becoming pregnant again with me. The only thing she would ever tell me was how, afterwards, people she knew would cross the road rather than speak to her, because she had been pregnant but now there was no baby. Her grief was so terrible that no one dared see its face.

The wound remained with her for the rest of her life. In her late sixties she let it slip to me once that she had called Sands, the stillbirth charity, to talk to their volunteers. She never told me what she said to them, and I never dared ask. Even so, I can guess at her pain, at least a bit. Although I only have one child, I've been pregnant five times. The other four were miscarriages, each one coming with its own ration of upset and distress. My sorrows were tiny compared to the death of Fiona, but these missing children have never left my side either.

How much worse must it have been for my mother, carrying her baby and her future for nine long months, believing the birth to be the beginning, not the end. I never told her what had happened to me, but then I always hid anything difficult from her for fear of her breaking. I looked after her far more than she ever looked after me.

Fiona's birth and death had been one of the sad events which had most defined my mother's life, but I found little trace of it in Rose Terrace after she died. Hoarding cascades from losses, so I could easily imagine my mother holding on to every single scrap which told her that her daughter had once, however briefly, breathed air on this earth. Yet however hard I looked, Fiona's birth had left no relics. Perhaps my father had forced her to throw any remembrances away. That was always his way of coping with bad things, by pretending they had never taken place. My mother may not have had much choice about what she was allowed to keep.

Nowadays, a child who died at birth would be treated so very differently. Fiona would have been acknowledged as a person who had lived and whose memory should be clasped close; the hospital would have made sure, through all the chaos and bewilderment of death, that there were photographs, memory boxes, footprints of tiny hands and feet to last for ever. My sister would have been allowed a grave. But could my mother have borne the weight of these memories, fastened tight on to things? Would she have lost the keepsakes or hidden them away in the darkest recesses of a cupboard as well?

To find my sister, I needed to read between the lines. She existed only in absences and gaps. One tiny slip of paper, dated October 1964, confirmed that my mother was eligible for a Home Confinement Grant (£6). Maternity Grant (£16) is crossed out neatly in the bureaucrat's blue ink. After all, there had been no baby and so they saw no need. How my mother must have cried when this cold form arrived in the post.

This was the only record in all the paper that my mother had kept. I'd never know what my father thought or felt, nor whether it was her death that had broken their marriage apart. I'd never know what kind of person Fiona would have been had she lived, or how my life would have been different as a little sister. Or whether I would have been born at all. I had no choice but to consign all those thoughts to the past. Everyone who might have answered them is now dead.

Other questions were not so easy to dismiss. What did Fiona die of, and was it linked to why I had miscarried so many times? Had my mother miscarried too? When I looked at her timeline again, more than three years passed between her marriage and Fiona's birth, then another two years before I was born. It's possible that all those long gaps arose from choice, but I couldn't help wondering.

When I was pregnant with E, my mother told me that Fiona had been born with severe spina bifida. The condition is hereditary, so the midwives prescribed me extra doses of folic acid, and I worried until the first scan told me I was carrying a healthy child. A few years later, when my mother was again telling her story about how people had crossed the road to avoid her, she told me that Fiona had died from being born with her organs outside her body. I was too shocked to ask why the facts had changed, unable to believe that she would gift my pregnancy, already fraught after one miscarriage, with an extra layer of uncertainty.

I was too old now for another baby, but what about E, who might one day want her own children? If she had a mother and grandmother who miscarried time and again, whose unborn children died because of some genetic flaw, then the great stack of sorrow could be handed down one more time.

I was desperate to separate myself out from this misery and return to the ordinary world. Why should I have to live my life wraithed in the ghosts of dead children as my mother had done? The problem was, parts of this history seemed to be encoded in my genes, and I would have to live with the consequences for ever.

❊ *15* ❊

plastic bag: *the art of hoarding*

Disposable shopping bag

England, before October 2015

Plastic

Manufactured by Tesco PLC

Provenance unknown

WITHOUT THE SATISFACTION of clearing out Rose Terrace, I was rudderless and adrift. All I had left were my mother's own griefs, which still lived in the world like the vibration of a bell long after it had been struck.

My dreams were of sorting through bones, trying to discover which ones were human, but the work was too hard. The meaning didn't need too much interrogation. An archaeologist can never recover a whole person, with their quirks and personality. My search was failing in exactly the same way. I would only ever be able to find a skeleton, not my mother.

My brother and I put Rose Terrace on the market. Odd flashes of emotion ballooned in the emptiness while we waited for it to sell. One evening I suddenly became possessed with a hatred of my glasses. They were too big and too round, the frames too thick and red. I detested them because they made me look like my mother.

On a family day out, I had a fit of temper in the street outside a shop that sold pointless gifts and knick-knacks. Everyone was doing what they wanted and being looked after apart from me. No one cared about me and this wasn't fair. This was a small child's temper tantrum, full of foot-stamping and rage, left over from a past in which I really did believe that no one had looked out for me at all.

I'd never dared be angry with my parents as a child, and even into my adult life. The fear was always that my father might leave or my mother might break entirely. Now they had both gone and there was nothing left to break, no one remaining to abandon me. A whole lifetime of buried fury was waiting to get out, like magma finally breaking through the weak spots in my crust.

Understanding the mechanics of what was happening didn't help; geology textbooks are no use at all if you need to hold back torrents of lava. I raved at inanimate household objects, cried over imagined slights and sometimes at nothing at all. With the fury came relief. I was feeling at last, even grieving; not for the person who had died, but for the family life I never had. I was mourning the fact that my childhood unhappiness would never now be redeemed by my mother's love.

Despite this, I could never manage to aim my anger at her. I tried, repeatedly, to write out how she had failed me in the hope of exorcizing the upset from my system, but after two or three lines my feelings always petered out into sympathy. It seemed heartless to persist when my mother in turn had been damaged so badly, given her own hard load of lovelessness to bear. Just as always happened, I was going to have to look after myself.

While the descriptions of Diogenes did make some sense of the way my mother's life had ended up, I still found them frustrating. In blaming her actions on damage to an important part of her brain, I was performing the trick that I hated so much when used by psychiatrists. I was looking for a mechanistic, organic explanation rather than seeing her problems as the very human result of a complex personal story. Most of all, though, if her hoarding and chaos were so simply caused by those years of whisky and vodka chipping away at her ability to choose and decide, then why was I still so like her?

There was still a vast gulf between us though. My house remained uncluttered, and I could throw things away without feeling pain. I couldn't even get that bit right. I was a failed daughter; now I had failed to be a hoarder too.

Except that this wasn't completely true. Other means of hoarding exist as well, ones which don't make quite such a mess. Psychologists are now identifying digital hoarding as a growing problem in people who can't delete a single email they've ever received, or who spend every waking hour ordering and sorting their digital photo archive. They do this for the same complex reasons as others hoard tangible objects: from the fear of throwing an important document away by accident, or just in case the information it contains might come in handy some day. I am like these hoarders only in analogue. What I hoard is words on the page: ninety A5 notebooks, my diaries for the last thirty years.

They contain an unedited stream of consciousness, with no explanations or footnotes for the reader, or indeed any external reference points at all. They will be no use to my descendants nor as a historical record. That doesn't matter to me. I never set out to write them for anyone else, or with the expectation that they will ever be read again. Like any good hoarder, all I require is the reassurance of knowing they exist.

What I am hoarding is experience. When my parents separated, I didn't lose many physical things, apart from Edgehill House, but what did disappear was the first eight years of my childhood. My mother was absent, and my father refused to speak about that time. As the only remaining witness to my old life, I needed to cling on as tightly as I could to those times. Like any other hoarder, what I fear most is loss, but what I am scared of losing are my own memories. The diaries are reassurance in physical form: the events of my life were not only real but now can never be lost.

This fear of forgetting is very common in hoarders. Sometimes it can cause an attachment to very specific objects. These souvenirs from the past magically hold the essence of an event. If they are thrown away, the hoarder fears that the memories themselves will disappear entirely. For others, the objects are not so emotionally charged; instead, they keep odd pieces of paper, junk mail, notes of phone numbers and contacts just in case they might ever need the information, but their physical form is essential.

Unlike my mother, I managed to take the bad things that happened to me and turn them into traits I could use in the world: energy, academic achievement and independence. So it was with hoarding too. Instead of cluttering up my house with old bits of paper, discarded clothes and broken household goods, I chose to hoard in a way that not only doesn't take up much space but can even be seen as a positive choice. Diary writing, apparently, sparks creativity, acts as therapy, calms the writer down and generally turns them into an all-round better person.

The articles about journaling, as it has been rechristened, seem to imply that there are no downsides at all, but in my view I don't think this is always true. For example, Alexander Thynn, Marquess of Bath, has spent almost thirty years writing his autobiography, which now runs to six million words. He has accumulated experience on an incredible scale. At that length, his writings must contain almost every incident in his life so far, recorded in close to real time.

It must also have taken a very long while to write. One of the definitions of hoarding is that it causes impairment to ordinary life, and although getting six million words down on the page is an impressive achievement, it may well have stopped Lord Bath from doing other things over those thirty years – including, perhaps, communicating with people around him.

In a recent documentary about Longleat it was easy to spot the clutter building up in Lord Bath's office. A journalist who interviewed him recorded that the miscellaneous items on his desk included the cast of a hand in plaster, a soft-porn magazine, sweets, a loose Brazil nut, a chessboard and a small piece of blue cheese – and that was only the top layer.

Lord Bath had a difficult childhood, with a disapproving father and an absent mother. In an all too familiar pattern, his oldest brother died aged just one and his parents later divorced. Growing up in the treasure house of Longleat, it would understandably be easy to learn to love the house and the glittering treasures it contained, instead of these unreliable people. In any case, this allegiance is the aim of every aristocratic upbringing. The house and its irreplaceable contents are the prize with which the heir is entrusted, and it is his duty to preserve them for future generations. Things, in short, are often more important than people.

Being British, how we think about hoarding very much depends on social class. Should someone live in social housing, then hoarding is a problem for the landlords, the neighbours, the fire service and plenty of other people besides. My mother owned her house and was clearly middle class, so I found it almost impossible to convince anyone in any kind of authority that there was an issue. Even though Rose Terrace was so derelict as to be legally uninhabitable, my mother's status meant that she had a right to live as she wanted. When someone is as patrician as Lord Bath, no one would suggest that any part of his lifestyle is unusual. More than that, he's celebrated as an endearing eccentric, one part of this country's great heritage of oddness.

The practicalities are different for the super-rich. If you live in a house with 130 rooms and a thousand acres surrounding, it's easy to hold on to unimaginable quantities of possessions. If you don't clear up and can't decide what to throw away, there will still be a housekeeper to get rid of mouldy food and keep the mice at bay. When the money from your estates alone will sustain you, it's possible to spend as many hours as you wish in writing down the events of your life. No one is going to stop your benefits or suggest you get out a bit more.

For the most stratospheric of celebrities it's possible not only to be indulged but to turn the stuff you collect into money, or art, or even both. That's what Andy Warhol managed to do.

It's now generally accepted that Warhol was a hoarder. When he died in 1987, his New York townhouse was crammed to the brim with stuff. Some of it – biscuit barrels, art deco furniture, jewellery and Native American art – could be justified as collections, although their constituent parts were stacked deep throughout the house rather than being on display. Warhol also bought omnivorously, taking in anything which took his fancy, from Miss Piggy memorabilia to space toys, satin slippers and 1950s china, but never discarded anything, until only the kitchen and one bedroom of his six-storey townhouse was usable. The posthumous auction of his collections exceeded all its estimates. Warhol was an artist and a celebrity, so his possessions were doubly filled with magic and power, and the collectors swarmed around every single object. If they couldn't afford his art, they wanted a piece of him any way they could.

Like Lord Bath, Warhol was obsessed with memory, but instead of writing things down he used a tape recorder to keep hold of his thoughts and experiences, sometimes referring to it as 'his wife'. For more than ten years he took it everywhere with him; by the time of his death there were more than ten thousand hours of tapes, as well as over sixty-six thousand photographs. Like many other hoarders, Warhol had no faith in his own memory.

Warhol's memory hoarding and his physical hoarding came together in his Time Capsules. These cardboard boxes originally held junk from his desk as a temporary measure when Warhol's Factory moved buildings, but some never got re-opened again. Many people have a box or two in the attic of stuff from an earlier life which never gets looked at, ending up travelling from house to house with them, but Warhol turned these accidental keepsakes into a way of life. More than that, he used the Time Capsules to solve his hoarder's hatred of throwing any thing, however trivial, away. Each month, he would start a new box, filling it with the detritus that accumulated on his desk, from stamps and letters to used batteries, uneaten birthday cake and forks taken from Concorde. At the end of the month, the box would be sealed, dated and sent off to storage. Warhol considered selling them for $4,000 a piece in some kind of bizarre art lucky-dip, which might have won you either an original Warhol drawing or a used condom, or quite possibly both. Like a hoarder, he never got round to it.

Now, all 612 of Warhol's Time Capsules are considered to be one serial artwork. The Warhol Foundation in Pittsburgh spent six years slowly cataloguing their contents. Each new box was opened with the same reverence that would be accorded to the relics of a medieval saint; every item recorded, numbered, listed and conserved. Curators wore protective gloves, while some of the later boxes were opened as a form of performance art, in front of an audience and live-streamed on the internet. Some of what is found repays this treatment: there are letters and photographs, drawings and pictures not only by Warhol but also other artists such as Cy Twombly. But these are mixed in with souvenirs, a pair of Dirk Bogarde's shoes, Christmas wrapping paper, old sandwiches and dead ants. One box even yielded up an ancient mummified foot. All artists perform magic, but Warhol became the first alchemist of hoarding, transmuting the base matter of paper, cardboard boxes and junk that makes up every hoard into gold, or at least art.

Like Lawrence's dagger, the boxes were Warhol's way of solidifying moments that otherwise would not have lasted. This intention makes sense in the context of his whole output. Warhol made his name through focusing in on subjects, like soup cans or supermarket packaging, which were usually considered too banal and trivial to be noticed by fine art, so it's hardly surprising that his Time Capsules don't commemorate an important event but instead memorialize the inconsequential nature of everyday life.

At the same time, Warhol ended up crammed into a small corner of his vast house, with rotting food on the counters. He was a hoarder at least as much as he was an artist, and the Time Capsules may be artworks but they simultaneously exist as part of his hoard. He claimed that his conscience never let him throw anything away, even if he didn't want to own it. Like other hoarders, he and his stuff were one.

Warhol is representative of many artists in his fascination with stuff. Pop art, he said, was about liking things. That's one way of looking at hoarding too. Hoarders don't only hate throwing things away; many of them also love what they hold on to, being hypersensitive to the infinite possibilities of things. Some hoarders, often men, see the potential in what others would regard as trash. A broken broom or a defunct lawnmower could be repaired, a derelict car part put together with another and then some more until it worked. Discarding anything would be to give up on its humming mass of possibility, so they rescue whatever they can find in skips and roadside dumps, always hopeful even when the repairs never take place. Others, who are more likely to be women, stockpile fabric and yarn, each purchase alive with the project it might become, but all too often piling up unused. Or they might be unusually aware of the physical presence of objects, appreciating seemingly ordinary items like a tin can or foil wrapper, and finding a beauty that the rest of us fail to see.

There is a kind of joy in these perceptions, as though hoarders have been blessed with a thinner skin, leaving them, like artists, more attuned to the vast range of stuff that surrounds us all. Or for hoarders, the universe contains an extra dimension, and the rest of us inhabit a flat and insubstantial space occupied by inert matter. No wonder hoarders want to hold on so tightly to these extraordinary things.

I don't know whether my mother loved the appearance of the stuff she hoarded, but I found it hard to see beauty in the things she left behind – in the plastic bags, fridges, old bottles and copies of the *Daily Telegraph*. She had cared very deeply about the way that things looked, so why had it not disturbed her to live in such chaos?

One Saturday morning, E and I found ourselves part of a small crowd staring at a young tree in the sunshine. Dozens of plastic bags, red, blue and white, had been tied to its spindly branches like accidental bunting, but what we were looking at definitely wasn't litter. We were in an art gallery, so this had to be art. I was old and jaded enough to know that this is part of the game, but E too had been coming here for long enough to be clear in her beliefs as well. Everything can be art if the artist wants it to be, she said with confidence. Even a plastic bag.

She hadn't always been so certain about conceptual art. When this smart art gallery first opened near us, their shop was selling copies of Martin Creed's Work No. 88, a crumpled piece of A4 paper in a neat box. E couldn't quite believe people would pay a hundred pounds for something they could easily make themselves. Time and experience, however, had converted her. This was useful, because we had returned to see an entire exhibition of Creed's work. He was the artist who had tied these plastic bags to the sapling in the courtyard, or at least commanded that it should be done.

'Famous artists can ask for whatever they want,' said our guide, cheerfully in charge of explaining Martin Creed to a gaggle of under tens and their attendant parents.

As the plastic bags rustled in the breeze, I couldn't help but think about hoarding, because to me they had become one of the signifiers of a hoard. Before the 5p charge was introduced, the bags were ubiquitous, arriving unbidden almost every day, filling up drawers and being thrown away without a thought. The only exception to this was hoarders, always profoundly aware of the potential in objects. Plastic bags are useful in a house full of things, because there is stuff that needs storing and keeping together. Plastic bags are free storage, and they keep arriving. One of the reasons that hoards tend to look much the same is because, whatever the hoarder loves most, the chances are that it's all stored in plastic bags. Martin Creed, like Andy Warhol, enjoys playing around with the idea that common things might be art. That's why the plastic bags were here, but I was starting to see other meanings in them too.

Our guide looked around at her audience. 'Another thing about Martin Creed is that he hates making decisions.' At this point I almost snorted with laughter. Even before coming to the exhibition, I'd wondered whether its content might feel all too close to home.

The thought had arisen when I'd read an article in the paper, in which one of the highlighted quotes was Creed saying that he never threw anything away. The exhibition poster was a photograph of Creed sitting in his crowded Barbican apartment. Stacked all around him were papers, boxes, guitars – filling the shelves, the sofa, the floor around him. Plastic bags too. His flat was nothing like as bad as Rose Terrace, of course, but could still potentially hit a 4 on the clutter scale.

Each room of the exhibition held something that I would have thrown out of my mother's house without a thought. In the first space, in amongst the paintings and sculptures, a desiccated bouquet sat on a plinth. Creed had been given it four years ago, and it had remained in his flat, gathering dust, ever since. Piled in the corner of the next room was another stack of stuff. Paper carrier bags sat on taped-up boxes, while another heap of plastic bags had been stuffed under a chair, a desk lamp balanced precariously on top, their arrangements recreated exactly from their original home in Creed's kitchen. The tour came to a halt in front of this, allowing both children and adults a moment of contemplation.

'So who thinks this is art?'

E had her hand up straight away, but I was no longer so certain. The exhibition was beginning to make me feel uncomfortable. This came to a head in the final gallery, where a small, secure museum case held not a piece of metalwork or a fragile sculpture but a pile of Creed's own hair clippings: grey curls heaped up like a dead animal. Only the most intense hoarders hold on to their bodily waste, but Creed was not only holding on to his cut-off hair but had put this into a gallery to make the rest of us admire what he had done. A person or a museum might even pay money for his detritus. This was a commercial art gallery, after all, and everything was for sale.

Creed was expertly playing the game of fine art, teasing us, along with the gallery, the critics and the purchasers, about what might or might not have value. However I do it, the screwed-up piece of paper in my dustbin is rubbish and will never be art. The one created by Martin Creed, sold in a numbered box, very definitely is. Hoarding in my mother's house was a problem; here in the gallery it had become art.

The provocation was deliberate, but at the same time, as we processed through the galleries to the end, I couldn't shake my disquiet. His exhibition was taunting me, deadpan. 'Isn't it funny that I keep this stuff?' Only I couldn't take the joke. I found myself furious that Creed was trying to make us accept the unacceptable, at the same time performing that old hoarder trick of diversion, forcing us to look in detail at all the assembled junk in his house rather than addressing the problem. I couldn't bear that any of this should happen. Because of what my mother had done, I would not allow that there might be any good in being a hoarder.

None of these emotions was embedded in the work; they came entirely from the inside of my own head. Martin Creed had understood that I might feel this too. Back at home, I read anything I could lay my hands on about the exhibition, trying to understand what I had felt. 'Art is just things in the world,' says Creed. 'It's people who have the feelings and the reactions.' I'd brought my own upset into the plain white gallery space. The problem wasn't of his making at all.

He's right, of course. While the pictures may show his living room to be rammed with boxes and bags and stuff, it doesn't look dirty or as though the structure is bending under the strain like it would with a true hoarder. Perhaps some people can live like this without hurting anyone or having a problem. Creed is not a recluse, far from it; he's going out into the world performing music as well as creating art. It's just that sometimes he brings his things with him.

I found myself thinking about the exhibition a lot over the next few days, two ideas in particular rolling around in my head. One was that my fury at the art was misplaced. My anger should have been directed at my mother, but this was still something I found hard to do. Even though she was dead and unassailable, I was still too afraid that my emotions would break her.

The other was whether I could have approached her hoarding differently. What would happen if I looked at her hoard in the way that Martin Creed might, as an arrangement of objects in space? While I had examined some of the individual items my mother had collected very closely, I had refused to acknowledge the hoard as a totality. Instead, I threw it away with my eyes averted. Now I felt ashamed; I should have tried harder to look at what was in front of my eyes.

This failure to look isn't mine alone; it's true of almost every person who deals with hoarding and hoarders. We walk around the hoard, we hate it, we see the quantity of stuff as a problem rather than examining its contents. More than anything else we want the hoard to be gone, as quickly as possible. The one thing we never do is engage with it.

This elision is part of what the hoard wants. Objects meld together in its great mass until it's difficult to distinguish one from another, to see what is underneath the heap, to find valuables in amongst the papers. The hoard is paradoxical: it fills our vision but at the same time does not want us to look.

One of the reasons Martin Creed's exhibition made me so uncomfortable was because it forced me to face the substances which constitute a hoard. In the gallery I had been compelled to examine old plastic bags and cardboard boxes, dried-out flowers and hair clippings as closely as I would an oil painting or marble statue.

What would happen if I attended to the material my mother had amassed with the same care? On one hand this was an absurd idea, mainly because there was nothing left. Aided by Jim and Ed, I'd thrown her entire construction in the bin, but I'd done this because I believed that the great big pile of stuff that my mother had left behind was a side effect, an accident caused by her unhappiness. Maybe I'd been seeing this the wrong way about. What if the hoard itself had contained the answers that I'd been seeking all along?

I had found meaning in some of the singular objects my mother had left behind, so surely the hoard itself could have spoken in a thousand tongues. There was so much more in its wholeness; its mass could have been an encyclopaedia of my mother if only I had thought to examine it, treat it as though it were a work of art.

The problem was, I had no idea how I might be able to interpret what it meant. All I could do was bear careful witness to the things of which it was composed, from the papers upstairs in the study to the ancient spices and damp cookery books in the kitchen, the open can of beans, the heaps of unopened post, even if, as with Martin Creed's installations, I could not yet bring myself to admire them.

My mother wasn't an artist; the mess was framed not by a pristine white gallery but a leaking, ramshackle house. Nonetheless, her intent was clear. The dark vortex of sadness and worthlessness that lived inside her had been set out in the form of newspapers, plastic bags and rubbish. What my mother created also functioned like a medal; it made her losses and suffering into something empirical, visible and concrete. But the hoard had advantages over a medal because it could not be put into a drawer and forgotten about, even if I had no idea what it was trying to tell me.

I woke up a few mornings later with a new idea. Even if I might never understand her whole house and hoard, what did make complete sense to me was my mother's study. So much of what I'd found had come out of that room, as though the space had been an installation representing the contents of her head.

I should have seen the mess and the chaos not so much as a problem to be cleared away but as a message. The whole room was a disorder of ideas in which old papers and new, photographs and notes mingled exactly as the family past and her own history swirled around in my mother's memory. The papers also stood for more than the information they contained; their sheer mass mattered as well, representing the great weight of loss.

Shards of her personality could be found in here as well. Her love for the house, all her different roles from councillor and daughter to mother and teacher were represented in the papers. The white IKEA shelves showed that my brother and I could be supportive, while the rows of novels they contained represented one constant in her life: however bad her depression, my mother could always read and take pleasure from it. At the very end of her life, when the house was falling apart around her, she still turned up for her shift to sort stock at the Oxfam shop every week. The books endured to the very end.

I'd found the photo albums, with all their hidden histories, on these shelves, along with the very best of her old cookbooks. The cupboard in the corner had held three of her hoovers. Even the photographs she took of nothing, the wide unpeopled landscapes and distant animals, now make sense as part of her whole creation, representing a world in which she was never truly present. The more I stared at the study in my mind, the more I could see it as a complete picture of my mother. At the same time, it had also contained things like the Palestine Police Veterans badge that I would never understand. However hard I looked at this room, I would never truly know who my mother had been.

Even so, the study represented her well. Damp and disorder had stolen into the corners of the space, above and below all was chaos, but somehow my mother had remained intact despite a life that would have ruined many people for good. I could see her not only in the room but also in the view out of the tall window: past the lime tree over the road, down past the sweep of Victorian villas with their red-tiled roofs, towards the needle-thin spires and modernist telephone exchanges of the city. Here I found her continuing love for Worcester, her home city.

When I'd stood on tiptoe in my mother's study in winter, squinting out past the leafless branches, I could also glimpse the topmost finials of the cathedral towers. My mother's spirit had endured, right up until the end.

briefcase: *going under*

BRIEFCASE WITH HARD FRAME, CONTAINING SEVENTY-SEVEN ITEMS OF PAPERWORK

Date and origin unknown

Tan leather with metal fitments

Found in study at Rose Terrace

I NEEDED TO go back to the museum I had made in the leather briefcase, that random collection of odds and ends that I had pulled from the chaos of my mother's house. After all the work I had done on the family history, I knew these papers would give me facts, even answers, yet I found myself swerving away from the task each time. There was always a new branch of the family tree to follow, some domestic chore to be done. Eventually, I ran out of excuses.

Rather than spread the papers out on a table, in front of T, I took my cup of coffee to the corner where I'd stowed the briefcase. I had my laptop next to me, my plan to create an inventory, as though I were keeping a proper museum, forcing me to concentrate and finish the job.

A lot of the documents were official records like my mother's GCE certificates, along with results from college and vaccination records. I discovered that she'd won three life-saving awards while at Sibford School, each one more advanced than the last. The only person they couldn't teach her to rescue was herself.

Other documents were more revealing. I'd already noticed how many papers my mother had kept from the divorce and the sale of Edgehill House. These showed me the shape of a time which I had refused to remember. I numbered my list in the order I found the items. No. 73 is a letter about the divorce hearing from March 1975, while No. 13 is some notes from October that same year about the sale of Edgehill House and

313

the distribution of the proceeds. We'd only stayed there for six months with my stepmother in the end.

Like any museum, my archive was not a neutral assemblage of items. Every collection has an ideology behind it, and mine was no different. Some things I had kept not because they preserved a part of my mother's life but because they told a story I wanted to believe. One of these was a clipping of E pictured in the newspaper, proud in her bright-red uniform at starting school. I had cut that out and sent it to my mother in the post, and I wanted to believe that my mother treasured it. Or is it that I need E, if she ever finds this box and looks through it, to see that her grandmother cared? The reality is that I will never know whether my mother meant to keep it or simply never got around to throwing it away.

I suspect that she never adored her granddaughter in the way that I wanted her to. In the box was the picture of E that I'd rescued out of the chaos of the ground floor early on in the clearing, battered and crumpled with the marks of muddy footprints on the back. I had kept it because I couldn't bear to dispose of a picture of my own daughter, whatever state it was in. Looking at it again, I understood what my mother's problem with it had been. E as a toddler, with her neat blonde bob, is a direct copy of me at the same age, taking my mother back to a time that she never wanted to think about again.

Other items now gave me more subtle clues. One was a black and white photocopy of an old snapshot, with a brief note from Mags clipped to it. Not long before my mother's death, her sister had phoned me up about this.

'I'm a bit worried about Pat. I sent a picture of her and Anne in the post, and she hasn't said anything to me about it. She's not answering her phone either.'

With Anne having died so recently, Mags was doing her best to keep lines of communication open, not wanting to lose her last remaining sister. I said I'd have a try at speaking to her about it, although I never did. All too soon, I found the picture when I was clearing up the house, and put it to one side because it seemed a shame to throw my aunt's thoughtfulness away. When the picture came out of the briefcase and I examined it properly, I could see that Anne had her arm round my mother in a clumsy two-year-old kind of way, looking all too much as though she wanted to strangle her baby sister. I was pretty sure this was what my mother would have seen in it too. Anne, overbearing, yet again. No wonder she didn't want to answer Mags's calls.

Even apparently dull documents like accounts and trust statements revealed odd nuggets of information, like the names of cousins or old addresses. I started to wish I had kept more. All the things I'd thought had no purpose – financial papers, illegible notes, photographs of nothing in particular – had gone in the bin. I'd only kept things that clearly told me a story, unable to bear the thought of bag after bag of musty, cigarette-smelling paper cluttering up my own home. I hadn't even wanted to share a car with it.

Most of what had been stuffed in the drawers or scattered across the floor was at best boring and mostly worthless. But I couldn't help feeling that I might have missed one essential piece of paper which, now that I knew so much more about my mother and her family, could have provided me with the vital clue. I should have been like Sherlock Holmes and kept everything.

These regrets were hoarder thoughts.

'If only I hadn't thrown that away.'

'It might have come in useful.'

'I just can't tell what's important or not.'

These phrases ran round in my head as I sifted through the papers, digging out pictures of people I could now have a stab at recognizing, legal letters in which the divorce solicitor is definitely flirting with my mother, certificates to show that she had been vaccinated against smallpox: her colourful timeline again. Among them were three copies of her funeral service. I'd buried these deep in the same way that my mother would have chosen to lose a difficult piece of paper in the chaos of her study.

More certificates from other schools, more legal letters. Then I found the notes. I hadn't read these before. Two sheets of lined A4, the edges browned, my mother's handwriting in pencil setting out all the losses and sadness she had endured, this time in list form. I was making a numbered tally of her things; she had prefigured this by making a list of her own life. There was an odd prologue, written as though to be performed to an audience. Or was it addressing me?

A brief résumé of my life too might help you understand, I am only marking the main events. Some of the experiences that happen on my journey to 'find me' may well stretch your credulity but I must relate what happened.

I couldn't help wondering what she thought the surprises might be, because there was nothing on the list that was new to me. But I would never know what they might have been, because, typically, she'd never finished it.

What my mother had created was a register of all the unhappiness, starting at number one with her very dominant older sister, then going through Alastair's death, her father's bankruptcy, the polio and the boarding schools. Even though I knew every one of these stories now, the total of them still wrenched my heart. My mother's greatest talent was for survival. Not many people could have endured so many losses and kept going.

Then number nine.

Birth daughter two. Didn't sleep much – hell as a small child.

Sitting on the carpet, I read the words and took them in, knowing they were bad but not feeling their impact. Then I carried on with my work, listing the final contents of the museum box: newspaper cuttings about her time on Worcester City Council, a leather frame containing a pretty picture of my mother as a teenager and an ancient letter from a school parent asking her to make sure a child in her class was eating lunch. That done, I got on with the rest of the day.

Only much later did I feel the punch of what she had written. A sense of futility crept up on me unobserved until, by evening, I was convinced that I was a hollow waste of everyone's time. I was not beloved of her. I had been hell. These were the lessons she had passed on to me. If I was so awful that even my own mother could not love me, how could I expect anyone else to?

Sleep healed nothing, and I felt worse when I woke. But overnight my mind had blocked out the cause. Had what I seen been a note or a typed letter? Who had it been written for? I could picture every other paper in the box except this. My old childhood trick of making memories disappear had returned. Amnesia was far better than feeling the pain.

This time I was a grown-up, so I went back to the briefcase, facing up to what my brain had tried to erase. Her pencil words offered me a scrap of consolation. Number thirteen on the list, after my brother's illnesses, her broken nights and the divorce, was guilt about abandoning us. Even so, I couldn't help thinking that this was more about her own feelings than concern for her children. She had never really bothered about me.

It wasn't enough to make me feel any better. What I'd found spelled out in my mother's writing was what I'd never wanted to admit to myself. I would never get any consolation from my mother, however hard I looked.

Unbearably furious, I headed to the kitchen in search of food. This wasn't anything new: I've eaten to make myself feel better all my life. I ricocheted from cupboard to fridge and back again: peanut butter, a handful of crisps. Nothing worked, not even the crisps. These usually did the trick, because they were the first food I'd ever used to make myself feel better. Before my parents separated, my mother would pick my brother and me up from school each day and, very occasionally, we'd get a packet of crisps as a treat. At least that was how it worked until the unreal interlude during which we had been told about the divorce but it hadn't happened yet. Then my mother would still collect us, but every single day we'd get crisps. These were all her unspoken fears and love transmuted into a pack of salty treats, and I ate up every crumb.

My mother's love had always been tangled up with food, as one of the rare things that she was good at and enthusiastic about. When she cooked for me and my brother, I knew she loved us, even if it was almost the only means I had of telling. She too knew the connection. The single story she told about her time at boarding school was the way, in the rationed years after the war, they had made rice pudding. Dried milk on the bottom of the dish was covered in a layer of rice, then another of sugar. Water was poured over this, and it was baked in the oven. But no one ever bothered to stir it.

'It was revolting,' she would tell me. 'And I've never been able to eat a milk pudding since.'

Then she'd laugh, making light of her troubles, but really her disgust was all tangled up with being sent away from home and the knowledge that no one cared. Of course she didn't want to taste that again.

I scoured the kitchen, unsatisfied. What I was doing had a name: comfort eating. I'd known that for most of my life, but for the first time the words sang with meaning. My mother had not looked after me. Food gave me the security and succour that should have come from her.

In the six months since she died I hadn't only been searching for the person my mother had been. What I'd wanted to find in the chaos she left behind her was a sign that she had actually loved me, that she had cared as a mother should. Instead, what I'd found was a truth that at heart I had always known. I had never been her beloved child. When I needed her most, she thought I was hell. The only love I found came in the form of sugar and crisps.

With that thought, something shifted in my head. If I really wanted to console myself, it didn't have to be in crumbs. I would make a whole glorious pudding instead. The recipe would of course come from Katie Stewart's book, that bible for my entire maternal line, but I would be doing far more than cooking a rhubarb crumble. This would be rewriting history in the form of food.

I'd always assumed that my out-of-control eating was another way of avoiding becoming my mother. She was slim, so I needed to be fat. Being thin meant being attractive – and look where that got her. Much safer to be undesirable and in control of my own destiny. That's how I had thought the logic ran. But as I measured out flour, butter and brown sugar, I realized that my eating didn't separate me from her at all. Instead, we were the same. Just as she kept paper, junk and old hoovers around her to make a fortress of her home, I ate to defend myself. My extra weight wasn't so much a castle as portable armour, but the aim was identical: to keep other people away. Fat is, after all, a different kind of rubbish, as unacceptable in our culture as old newspaper and plastic bags. Neither of us felt we were worth other people's concern.

Hoards are in part a sign that their creators feel bad and worthless, a person apart, and my fat also laid out the facts in solid form, telling the world that I was not right and needed to be avoided. How could I be a worthwhile human being when not even my own mother was able to love me? Hoards and fat are both ways of screaming that something is very wrong without having to explain what the matter is.

My love of food could sometimes come close to hoarding too. I have a tendency to stockpile and store far more than I really need. I'm aware that I do this, and mostly it's under control. There are two exceptions: I still always keep far more butter and olive oil than we might ever need. I can justify this, because these two fats are the foundation of every meal – how could I make toast or fry an onion without them? Even so, my stocks are ludicrous. I need to be certain that we will never go without. Fat is as closely packed with meaning and comfort for me as my mother's house was for her. With bottles of oil in the larder and butter stacked deep in the fridge, I am consoling myself, performing magic, keeping myself safe. Just like a hoarder does with things.

E, T and I shared the crumble for supper. Not only would I never get any salvation from my mother now, her words had shown me that it had never been available. I wasn't going to harm myself with comfort eating. Instead, I would cook up an approximation of love from the family book and give it to people who did care about me. This had to be better than eating peanut butter and crisps on my own.

The crumble served only as a temporary cure. I woke up the next morning still awash with emotion. A huge part was sadness; who wouldn't be upset to find rejection written down like that? But my hurt shaded into a darkness and worthlessness that would not leave.

This low bore down on me, draining all my energy. I couldn't cope with decisions; any talking was too much. At the same time, I felt a huge release in letting go, allowing myself to tumble into the abyss. Nothing mattered any more. We all die in the end, so why worry about anything? I gave up, happy to free-fall into oblivion. Until now I'd always fought against this sadness, because I feared becoming like my mother. If she had been depressed, I did not dare to be. Now that she was dead, I could experiment with inertia at last.

This must have been how my mother felt in her lowest times. Why else would she have filled her house with rubbish, let rain come through the roof, lost her bed under a spreading tide of books? Allowing myself to become like her, at last, felt oddly like freedom. No longer was I held by a straightjacket of my own making, the constant, vigilant effort to be different. We were the same, and at last I could give up trying. My tight bonds had been sprung.

I started to think again about the museum in the briefcase, not about its contents but about what was missing. For a hoarder, my mother had thrown a lot of things away. I had replied to all her letters as a teenager, then later from university too, but I only ever found a single one of these in the entire mound of paper. It seemed that these were far less precious to her than the house, or at very least far more frightening. For the first time ever I hated my mother. Why had I tried so hard to save her?

My feelings boiled inside until I thought they would pull me under for good. All my reading and writing and researching was an attempt to fix things the only way I knew: using my brain. If I could understand hoarding and hoarders, put napkin rings and squat black teapots in their rightful place, tell my mother's life so that the story made sense to other people, then, I believed, I might survive. I had made a raft for myself from history and anthropology, material culture and, God save us, thing theory. Underneath this churned a sea of emotions I could not name but which pushed me to and fro in the dark. Now these forces were threatening to overturn the raft altogether, and I didn't know why I'd bothered building it in the first place. I should have known that I would always go overboard in the end.

For three days I sat in bed distracting myself with books and the internet, only occasionally daring to survey the landscape of my mind. Gradually, I started to understand that one crucial difference set me apart from my mother. I had hope. Past experience had taught me that, if I waited long enough, I would be able to haul myself out of these feelings, or at least push on through them. My mother had ended up mired for ever, unable to escape the prison of her own worthlessness. It had been her depression which kept me from knowing her. I refused to let the same disaster happen twice.

*

When I eventually resurfaced and attempted to go through the motions of ordinary life as though they mattered, a thin brown envelope was sitting on my desk. I knew it would contain the death certificate for Annie Runcieman Woods, my mother's great-grandmother. The death of her small son, which sent Annie spiralling away into unhappiness and even madness, separating her from her family, seemed to be the place where our family's misery had begun.

The thin slip of paper told me that while Annie had died of pneumonia, the subsidiary causes were drink and exposure.

Of course. I hadn't expected to find anything else.

Only she'd died at an address, 29 Chadwick Street, and I didn't understand how anyone could die of exposure inside. I wanted to dismiss Annie's death as something that had happened far away from me in time and space, taking place in a world of horse transport and long skirts, at the heart of dense Victorian streets with intense poverty rubbing up against the lives of the richest. At the same time, there was a closeness that was almost unbearable.

This small yellow paper was an ephemeral record, but also a monument to a living suffering person who was fragile and broken by life, estranged from her children and dependent on drink. Someone who must have been a lot like my mother, in other words. When I looked a bit more closely at where Annie had died, it turned out that alcohol wasn't the only thing they had in common. Both had also lived in total squalor.

Annie had died at the heart of the most notorious slum in London, the Devil's Acre. London held worse living conditions, but the Devil's Acre was infamous because it sat at the heart of Westminster, under the noses of those who ruled Britain. When the reformer Charles Booth mapped London,

Chadwick Street was lined with black. This meant a street of the lowest class. Vicious. Semi-criminal. On Booth's visit in 1899, his notes are damning. 'Houses: black and grimy; open doors, dirty children and bad-faced women.' Inspector Cousins, who accompanied him, thought that thieving and prostitution were the chief occupations.

Our family had a personal connection to Dickens' concern with rubbish and filth. Most of the slums in his books, from Tom-all-Alone's in *Great Expectations* to Folly Ditch in *Oliver Twist*, have their origins in the Devil's Acre, which Dickens had come to know well when he had been working as a parliamentary reporter. Annie Woods lived in a place almost unchanged from his earlier depictions:

> Rooms so small, so filthy, so confined, that the air would seem too tainted even for the dirt and squalor which they shelter . . . dirt-besmeared walls and decaying foundations; every repulsive lineament of poverty, every loathsome indication of filth, rot and garbage; all these ornament the banks of Folly Ditch.

The year before Annie died there, the census recorded almost seventy people crowded into the single building at 29 Chadwick Street. These were wastepaper dealers, charwomen and labourers: the bottom of the Victorian heap. Nothing had changed in the seventy years since Dickens had first visited.

While Annie lived in this overcrowded tenement, her daughter Ethel had been leading an entirely different life. As an adult, she had returned to live at home with her father, only a mile and a half away but worlds apart. William had been mayor of Chelsea three years in a row, and they had been living on a street which Booth paints a comfortable, middle-class red. They would never have visited a place like Chadwick Street, not unless they had come to bring charity.

Two years before her mother died, Ethel had married Angus Gilmour in the smart church of St Luke's in Chelsea. A year after that, she'd given birth to her first son, my grandfather Allan, in faraway Scotland. Did Annie even know she had become a grandmother? Perhaps she had been as disturbed by it as my mother had been.

Annie's fate in the dark squalor of Victorian London was the prefiguring of my mother's. Chance alone had prevented another version of my mother's life in which she had drunk a bit more one night and fallen but then not managed to get to the telephone. She could so easily have died in her own squalid home and, four generations on, the story would hardly have changed at all.

It took several weeks before I dared return to the briefcase, but eventually the storm within me ran its course and I knew I had to go back and see what else it contained. After all, there are an infinite number of ways of writing a life; I knew, because that museum held a whole sheaf of my mother's various attempts.

I pulled out all the stories I could lay my hands on. As well as the unhappy list, there was also her multicoloured factual timeline and the record of her two days of Christmas cooking that she had written down when Patrick was still alive. I also found a tatty and yellowed version of her CV from the early 1980s, taking her from teacher to being at home to a string of estate agent and insurance jobs. The only thing she managed to stick at for more than a year and a half was her eight years of being a housewife. That's probably why, at the top of the page, she mentions that she is divorced, with two children living in Denmark. My brother and I are the only two solid accomplishments that she could point to. Even then, we were a long way away.

She also wasn't the only person to have told her story. In the papers I had found two people examining my mother and reporting on their results. One is an occupational psychologist, assessing her in 1974. My mother had returned to teaching but wasn't happy. The prose is boiler-plate and deliberately impersonal: my mother likes books, she wants more intellectually stimulating work, she has no aptitude for science. But it also contains glimpses of another life, in which she's been on the board of a charity and organizing local childcare, all when I was too young to remember her doing anything but cleaning out yoghurt pots and making breakfast.

A less optimistic version of my mother's life was contained in a letter from an NHS psychiatrist. She has been referred to him for her depression and drinking after Patrick's death. He has conducted a long interview with her and is recounting his findings back to her GP, a letter which, in turn, has been copied to my mother. The result is a hall of mirrors, with my mother's story reflected in the consultant's opinion and the dry prose of a medical referral, but even so what strikes me is that this doctor understands my mother. Even from one meeting he can see that her state is due to a long history of losses, and that these, not the drink, are the core of her problems. What she needs is psychotherapy, not detox.

More heartbreakingly, the psychiatrist can see my mother with sympathy. She describes herself as 'a lively, sociable person who although insecure, is also courageous'. He doesn't disagree, perceiving her as being well presented and an excellent historian. My mother obviously wanted to tell him about the tragedies in her life, and he finds himself aware of a great sadness, 'which is understandable'. She is 'intelligent, psychological and likeable'.

I found this enormously sad because it was the first time, in any of the pieces of paper, in any of the time I had spent clearing her house, that I had discovered a single person being nice about my mother. At best the hoarding literature had turned her into an objectified set of neural impulses rather than a person; at worst the television programmes condemned her as a freak. Despite her despair and tragedies, her drinking and her chaos, this man still managed to see the good in her. In calling her courageous, what he had said was true. Even through the drink and the hoarding, my mother still got up, arrived for her shifts at the Oxfam shop, she dressed, looked after herself, even phoned me up most weeks. The one thing my mother never did was give in.

What made this letter even more upsetting is that she never took the chance that it offered. The letter said that my mother was enthusiastic about finding a private therapist and that it would help her. At that point, it might have saved her from what happened next. But she never did. Instead, she chose to carry on wrestling with the past on her own, right up until the end.

Last of all I dared to go back to the handwritten litany of woe. Now I could see that this was just one point of view. In it she is performing for her intended audience – whoever they may have been – the shocking scale of the awful things that had happened to her. Moments of happiness had no part in the narrative she was putting together. Her hurtful words were never meant to be the whole truth about our relationship.

More than that, this piece of paper didn't have to be the final judgement either. This small leather box held lots of different versions of my mother, and I didn't have to choose the worst scenario, the one that damned me to misery.

The thought helped me, but only a bit. Underneath the rhythms of ordinary life, my low mood still persisted. Gradually, over the next few days, a realization crept over me like a mist. I had found my mother, but not where I had been seeking her. I could never truly get close to her from the possessions she had left behind, nor the myriad versions of her story on paper. Instead, she had come to me in the form of her sadness, which now lived on inside me. Hers was the voice that whispered in my ear telling me that there was no point in doing anything, and hers were the feelings that tugged at my being. These feelings were my mother, still present in the world.

I'd spent my life fighting this, trying to be as little like her as I could manage, but the time had come to accept what she had handed down. With this realization came the glimmerings of a new peace. Now that I had finally found my mother, it might at last be time to move on.

bracelet: *an end*

THICK CUFF-STYLE BRACELET

England, 2016

Silver, made from recycled metal

Designed and manufactured by
Eleanor Christine Jewellery

Commissioned work

Time trickled on. I got out of bed and got on with life. My mother's things settled into their new perches in our house. I hardly noticed the red glass bird on my bookshelves, while my grandmother's wooden penguin now sat in pride of place on the windowsill by the stairs, looking so at home that I couldn't imagine letting it go. Many things had been passed on, but my mother's sitting-room table and the pictures from her hall were billeted in the attic, the boxes of books still sat in the spare room. I still wasn't ready to find everything a final home, and in so doing declare my mother irrevocably gone.

This stasis extended to the outside world as well. For several long months, as spring erupted into summer, my mother's house didn't sell. The experience fell into a cycle. Several people would come to view, then one, or sometimes two, would make an offer. My brother and I would accept one. Then the buyers would get a survey and pull out. Rose Terrace was too ruined to sell. The limbo state of mourning, it seemed, could go on for a long time. Perhaps her things would stay in my loft for ever, and I would never fully manage to lay my mother to rest.

Summer passed over and the holidays ended. With E back at school, I had too much time on my hands in which to think, so I got involved with the local appeal to help refugees in Calais.

Within a week, I found myself responsible for a mountain of donations that arrived almost overnight, dumped into a warren of rooms once home to social workers. The two largest were almost filled by an unsorted jumble of tents, foods, tarpaulins, torches, sleeping bags and boots, but also clothes of every kind, an entire vanload of toiletries donated by a local company, raffia table mats, vases and a tube of haemorrhoid cream, half used. For more than a month I arranged sorting systems, created size charts and labelling rules, volunteer rotas and logistics. We started out with chaos and, dozens of helpers and five weeks later, ended up with total order. Anything that could be used in Calais had been packed into camper vans and buses and sent over; winter clothes for women and children were on their way to Syria; summer clothes that couldn't be used anywhere were sold and the money went to buy more food. Toiletries were organized into individual care packs, boots and clothes labelled and boxed by size. Blankets and fleeces were checked, counted and folded, sleeping bags squashed into giant sacks. Old towels and blankets went to a pet home; macramé hangings, pen tidies and inexplicable donations to the charity shop. Only a few odd shoes and the grubbiest of duvets went to the tip. Every single thing was used as best it could be, each one ending up in the right place.

As I worked, happy to be useful again, I believed that I was using my television production experience. Logistics was second nature to me, and I loved the chance of using that part of my brain for the first time in a few years. Only well after I finished did I realize that my satisfaction sprang from other, more profound sources. In my sorting and organizing I had been vanquishing my mother's hoard all over again. If anything, the work had been bigger and stranger. The disorder and the sheer quantity had been greater than anything my mother had left behind, and the building, with its maze of adapted rooms, strange wood-lined Victorian safes and long, dirty, institutional corridors, a dream-like reinvention of her home. Only this time there had been a proper ending. Every single thing that had come through the doors had been examined with care and then found its rightful destination. I'd had my second chance, and this time I had done my mother proud.

Nonetheless, some things still resisted sorting. In a cupboard sat Alastair's napkin ring and my mother's christening tankard, and even through closed doors I could not forget their presence. I'd polished away their tarnish, but this had only made the battered state of the tankard even more noticeable, and T said that it looked as though my mother had taken out her resentments and troubles on its surface. From then on the dents and nicks seemed to contain all her abandonments and disappointments. I didn't want to keep this any more than I wanted Alastair's napkin ring but at the same time I couldn't let it go. Discarding the cup would mean that my mother's misery had counted for nothing.

Gradually, a decision began to form within me. I would take these two terrifying pieces of silver and turn them into something new. I wanted to make an heirloom that I would treasure, rather than keep two things that had become so imbued with other people's unhappiness that I couldn't bear to have them on display. My friend Ellie was a jeweller, and I decided that she could turn them into a bangle for me. With all that weight of silver, she could make something big and chunky which I could enjoy and then, in time, hand down to E. An inheritance to be proud of.

The idea seemed faultless, but the practicalities turned out to be more difficult than I had imagined. Ellie needed the pieces melted down and then drawn into thick wire for her to work with. The problem was that I couldn't find anyone who would refine the silver and promise to give me the same stuff in return; the metal simply isn't valuable enough to make that worthwhile. I was back to being stuck, landed with exactly what my mother had left me, whether I wanted it or not. There was no way of changing what had been handed down.

Until I had another idea. Maybe we wouldn't need the silver smelting. The tankard, after all, was already round. When I got it out again, I saw what I was hoping for. Its base was exactly the right diameter for my wrist. I took it and the napkin ring down to Ellie's studio to see what she thought.

She held the tankard up in the light, looking at it from one angle then another, running her long fingers over the detailing at its base.

'Maybe,' she said after a minute or two. Now she admired the scalloping around the edges of the napkin ring. Perhaps, she wondered, this too could be kept, worked into the design. Then she stopped. 'Do you want to keep the engravings?'

'Christ, no,' I said, far too quickly. Here I was again, up against other people's expectations about families, about what you might want to keep, what needs to be remembered.

Ellie looked surprised, but I hadn't told her very much about what had happened after my mother had died. I hadn't spoken to anyone but T about that, never mind the stories that had led to it. I told her the story of Alastair's short life and long mourning. Ellie nodded, clever enough not to say anything more.

After more looking, and measuring my wrist with another bangle, she decided that the project was on. Not only did she like the idea, it was also something she felt technically able to do. I walked away leaving the silver sitting on the shelves above Ellie's workbench. This was probably the last time I would see the tankard. It might be the last moment that Alastair's napkin ring existed at all. I knew that it was the right thing to do, but even so I couldn't help feeling guilty. I was, after all, getting rid of something that mattered a great deal.

After six months of waiting and disappointments, Rose Terrace was finally sold to a developer who would strip it down to a shell and then restore it. Having had so many false hopes, all I could feel was relief. I was starting to believe that the house would weigh me down for ever. The sale, too, was the last act I would ever perform on my mother's behalf. Once the contracts had been signed and the money distributed, her estate would be wound up. My brother and I could get on with our own lives now, without needing to worry about hers.

I went back down the hill to Ellie's to get my bracelet fitted. Once she started to apply the decoration, the silver couldn't be bent any more, so she needed to be sure that it was the right shape for my wrist before she began. This was never going to be a delicate piece of jewellery, I knew that, but still the solidity of the piece she'd created surprised me. She'd taken a curve of the christening mug and bent it into an oval, making a wide cuff, as heavy and present as a prehistoric torc.

Ellie showed me how to slip it on to my wrist, around the thinnest part so that it wouldn't get stressed. On, it felt huge and weighty, like armour. I knew that the result would be amazing and trusted Ellie completely, but I was also frightened by what she had made. Was I brave and flamboyant enough to wear it? I had always been too much for my mother, so she'd left me constantly wary of being too much for everyone else in the world as well.

When I looked down at the weight of it, I could still see what the metal once had been. My mother's name, Patricia Gilmour, was still cut into the face of the silver in looping italic, but it would soon disappear, covered over by the scrolled face of Alastair's napkin ring. This was Ellie's clever compromise. She hadn't taken off any of the engraving. Instead, the two names would be turned inward, facing each other. Present, but invisible. This was how I wanted to keep my memories from now on.

As I went out, Ellie told me that she had been so nervous about cutting into the mug that she kept putting it off in case she made a mistake. Straight away I told her that I wouldn't have minded if she had, and this was true. The moment I had handed over the silverware to her, the pieces had been transformed. No longer were they my problem. In giving them away I had broken the charm that made them so potent. I only wish that my mother had been able to do the same.

As the summer shaded into autumn, my mood began to shift. Instead of angry depression, a softer melancholy crept up on me. I didn't mind the emotion; in fact, I almost welcomed it in, because it was new. I'd spent the long months since her death haunted by my mother's feelings: her grief, misery and darkness. But this gentle unhappiness was entirely my own.

After a few sombre days, I understood why it had arrived. We were heading for the end of October, and my mother's birthday was only a few days away. For most of my adult life I had found it almost impossible to remember the date, in some kind of unconscious revenge for the innumerable times she'd forgotten mine. Eventually, an app remembered on my behalf, so for the last few years of her life I had got a present and card to her on time, regardless of what had happened in the past. Now, when it was far too late, my mind was contrarily determined to mark the date. I was missing her. At last, this was mourning.

The world around me was moving on too. For the first time in months I looked online for my mother's house because I wanted to find out what date it had been built. But when the search page appeared, I felt a sharp electric shock of surprise because at the top was a new picture of Rose Terrace, one I'd never seen before. The developer had already done it up, and the property was now back on Rightmove, at a much higher price of course. I flicked through to find a bright white kitchen and bathroom, carpets on the floors and a green lawn in the back garden. The pictures brought up a strange sensation in me, as though I was having an out-of-body experience or a dream. I knew what they represented, but could not believe in it.

The house had been restored, which was what I wanted from the beginning. The chaos and the hoard had been banished for ever. What this metamorphosis also meant was that another part of my mother had disappeared. The house no longer belonged to her, nor was it even the place that I had rescued from the mess she left behind. Nothing of her remained in Rose Terrace at all, and so another of the thin threads connecting her to the world had been snipped.

I was tying up other loose ends as well. On a work trip to London, I carved out an extra couple of hours and headed to Westminster, to see if there was more to know about what happened to Annie Woods. The streets of her day have almost entirely disappeared. I walked round every place she was recorded as living in, and found only blocks of flats and offices. In Chadwick Street, where she had died, her lodging had been replaced by the headquarters of Channel 4. As a freelance producer, I was regularly summoned there for meetings, briefings and interviews. The dirt and grime of Annie's life had been replaced by braced steel, exposed pipes and shimmering panels of glass. In all my visits there, I'd never considered what had come before, never mind that it had anything to do with me.

The squalor of the past was so dreadful that it had been almost entirely erased. The only old buildings I could find were pubs, and one solitary house which survived on Chadwick Street. Against the 1960s red brick that surrounded it, the house looked tiny. I could not think how so many people had crammed into houses like these.

This walk wasn't my main purpose. Annie Woods' death certificate reported that there had been a post-mortem, and I'd been told that these were often reported in the local paper, which relished the sensation.

After only ten minutes in the library, I had found exactly what I was looking for. 'A LONELY DEATH' reported the paper: 'CHADWICK STREET WOMAN'S END'.

Reassuringly, despite the headline, Annie hadn't entirely been abandoned. Her husband, William Fountain Woods, had been paying Annie an allowance for the last twenty-five years of what the paper called their estrangement. Others looked after her too. The evening before she died, Annie had been found at the bottom of the stairs by Mr and Mrs Cullen, who also lodged in the house. They'd taken her back up to her room, leaving her comfortable on the floor with her head on a pillow. When she wasn't heard the next morning, they went up and found her lying in the same position, dead.

What the paper also confirms is that Annie was, above all, a drinker. Dr Archer, who conducted the post-mortem, concluded that her pneumonia was brought on by neglect and her life of continual drinking. Mrs Cullen had gone up to check that next morning because Annie always went out to get a drink in the early morning, so when she hadn't been seen or heard by nine o'clock, her neighbour began to worry.

Other questions would never be answered. Why had the death of a child broken Annie Woods so completely, when all too many women of her generation suffered the same experience and, however deep the pain, stumbled on? What did her children think and how did they bear the pain of not having a mother? Most of all, how had this drinking and misery been passed down for four generations unchanged?

The cuff was now finished. When she emailed to tell me this, Ellie also warned me that it hadn't quite turned out as she'd expected. I wasn't surprised. Nothing important could be controlled entirely, least of all something which had once belonged to my mother.

Before showing me, Ellie explained that she hadn't been able to work the surface to a shine in the way that we'd first talked about. The lifetime of dents and nicks inflicted on my mother's tankard would have required polishing half its thickness away. So she'd given it a smart brushed finish instead. She thought it looked more modern, but really she was waiting to see my reaction.

When she opened the box, the light no longer reflected off the silver plate and the scrolls of its decoration; instead, it only shimmered. I liked the change. These were the shapes of Alastair's napkin ring, burnished and bent into something entirely new.

Picking it up, I held the solid weight in my hand. 'That's

fine,' I said. Its presence almost discomfited me, but then I
looked up and saw that Ellie was waiting for my reaction to all
her work. 'In fact it's great. I love it.'

Ellie looked relieved. She had created this strange and
wonderful object for me, not having done anything like this
before, and of course she was worried that she might not have
got it right, that I might not have liked what she had made.
There had been no going back, after all.

I slipped the cuff on to my wrist sideways, as she had shown
me. It wasn't what I had expected, but that pleased me. Once
again, the objects had taken charge. They had instructed us
what they wanted to become, and Ellie had simply done their
bidding. I had thought that the past could be wiped clean,
that all the marks and dents and scratches could be polished
out of existence, but of course that could never be true. All
Ellie could do was work with what had already happened and
transmute that into something different. But not new. It's not
possible to erase the past.

Over the next few weeks, I tried wearing the cuff, but it
was so much wider and weightier than anything else I owned
that I felt as though I was bringing a second person with me. I
couldn't tell whether the metal had become armour, or maybe
a magical amulet. Or a protective wristband for a Neolithic
archer with a hefty bow.

Its presence hung on the end of my arm as I walked, drove
and typed. This was what the weight of history and inheritance felt like, and I wasn't sure I should be heaving so much
of it around with me everywhere I went. The reworking of
metal hadn't altered my memories and associations as completely as I had hoped.

*

Sitting at my desk, I realized that I'd made my coffee in E's otter mug by mistake. She'd probably be outraged at my presumption, because this is her special thing, not mine.

At the same time, T pointed out, better that it gets used rather than sitting in the cupboard. Because everyone knows E likes otters, she's continually being given mugs with them on, along with a cushion, two towels, three T-shirts and countless plush cuddly ones too. She has so many that I lose track of the names, and their cousins ambush us at tourist attractions, stacked in plaintive heaps, yearning to be taken home. My mother, despite still being distant with E as she grew up, sent her an otter egg cup for Christmas, just before she died. E adores it and remembers Grandma every time it is used. Her animal totem forged a connection between them in the end, although every time I make a boiled egg I can't help looking at the china otter askance, wondering whether my mother deserved the affection E gave her.

E also has mugs with Dr Who and Moomins and DNA on them, as well as glasses with flamingos, owls and yet more otters. This is the way we all live now, amongst an endless parade of inessential possessions which spill out of the cupboards, too many for one small girl to drink from even were she to use a different one every day.

As a child, I had one single mug of my own. Hand thrown, it was glazed in a 1970s orange earth-tone and, most excitingly, had my name handwritten on the side in black. I can remember the visit to the local pottery where it was made, the clay spinning on the wheel and rising up in ridges, each the size of a finger. Most of all I remember the painfully long wait between the making and the finished mug arriving.

My brother had one too, glazed in a dull blue, but his broke.

By the time my stepmother arrived, my mug had a chip on the rim, so she wanted to throw it away. Distraught, I refused to let it go. I might even have rescued it from the bin. I knew, even if no one else wanted to remember, that my parents had once been together, and I was determined to hold on fiercely to any surviving fragments from that time, however damaged. This is how hoarding is forged, in the white heat of resentment and pain, one giant shout of refusal in the face of other losses which cannot be undone.

I've kept the mug to this day. It's now part of the displays on my bookcase, alongside my mother's black teapot, the red glass bird and a set of clay otters made by E. The rim still has its chip, but it has survived all this time. I've held on to many things, maybe too many, and I am still hyper-aware of every single object that comes into my life, but at the same time I can still find the floor in my rooms, the house isn't stacked with newspaper and post, and none of the ceilings have come through, so I am not the same person as my mother. Not yet, anyway.

I kept the mug because these prizes were so much harder-won when I was a child. My mug was rare, singular, special. I only had one, and so it meant everything. E's stuff stacks up in the kitchen, accumulating almost without her noticing. The result is that her things don't collect meaning in the same way. Her owl glass was a gift from a friend who then moved away, but when the transfers faded, leaving the owls whitened and dull, E was quite content to get rid of it. This gives me hope that she might be exempt from the family history. For her, things can be just things, nothing more. Maybe one day she'll keep the bracelet that Ellie made in her drawer as a memory of me, and that will be it. That's how I'd like her future to be, and I really hope it can happen.

Notes

62 no one wanted to know, never mind take responsibility:
There are almost no statutory ways of dealing with hoarding:
Almost the only recourse available is Section 47 of the National
Assistance Act (1948), which allows local authorities to
intervene if a person is:

- suffering from grave chronic disease, or
- aged and infirm
- physically incapacitated
- living in insanitary conditions, and
- unable to devote to themselves, and are not
  receiving from others, proper care and attention,
  and
- his removal from home is necessary either in his
  own interests or for preventing injury to the health
  of, or serious nuisance to, other persons.

From Debbie Brown and Rekha Hegde, 'Diogenes Syndrome:
patients living with hoarding and squalor', *Progress in
Neurology and Psychiatry*, 19:5 (2015)

These powers are however rarely used, in the main because they
are not seen as being compliant with the Human Rights Act.
If a person like my mother has capacity, then they are allowed
in law to live as they choose. This attitude is in contrast with
America, where self-neglect is categorized as a kind of elder
abuse, with mandatory reporting.

**62 My mother seemed to think she occupied an entirely normal
house:** At the time I understood that this was something like

anorexia, a kind of dysmorphia in which she saw her house as she wanted it to be, not as it actually was. When I spoke to hoarding experts later on, they pointed out that on some level my mother probably was aware of the condition of the house but was refusing to face up to it, because of the implications this would have for her life and in particular her independence.

62 But because my mother was the owner and the occupant: Because of this gap in responsibilities, the Fire Service have ended up as one of the agencies that are most concerned about hoarders, and with good reason. A blaze in a house which contains a hoard can be much more dangerous for both fire crews and occupants alike. A fire is also more likely to start in the first place – with the hoard blocking access to plugs, extension leads often trail across piles of paper, and a small fire can smoulder in a corner without being detected. The Melbourne fire service in Australia calculated that fires in hoarded homes made up 0.25 per cent of all incidents but resulted in a quarter of all preventable fire deaths.

86 The most notorious example of this is homosexuality: Gary Greenberg, *The Book of Woe: The DSM and the Unmaking of Psychiatry* (New York, Plume Books, 2014), pp. 35–6.

88 The brainwaves of sufferers are recorded: Randy Frost, Gail Steketee and David F. Tolin, 'Comorbidity in Hoarding Disorder', *Depression and Anxiety*, 28:10 (2011); David F. Tolin et al., 'Neural Mechanisms of Decision Making in Hoarding Disorder', *Archives of General Psychiatry*, 69:8 (2012); S. K. An et al., 'To discard or not to discard: the neural basis of hoarding symptoms in obsessive-compulsive disorder', *Molecular Psychiatry*, 14:3 (2009).

89 The books and leaflets addressed at sufferers: Two good examples are: David F. Tolin, Randy O. Frost and Gail Steketee, *Buried in Treasures: Help for Compulsive Acquiring, Saving and Hoarding* (New York, Oxford University Press, 2013), and Robin Zasio, *The Hoarder in You: How to Live a Happier, Healthier, Uncluttered Life* (Emmaus, PA, Rodale, 2012).

89 The apogee of this approach: Sophie Holmes (ed.), 'A Psychological Perspective on Hoarding: DCP Good Practice Guidelines' (British Psychological Society, 2015).

90 **Even I would prefer to be a hoarder:** At the time I was raging, but outwith scientific discourse the truth is of course more nuanced. The researchers who first identified hoarding have, along with research papers, written a book full of case studies and sympathy: Randy O. Frost and Gail Steketee, *Stuff: Compulsive Hoarding and the Meaning of Things* (Boston, Houghton Mifflin, 2011).

90 **only 20 per cent of hoarders show a sustained and continued improvement:** General rates quoted in Catherine Ayers et al., 'Cognitive-behavioral therapy for geriatric compulsive hoarding', *Behaviour Research Therapy*, 49:10 (2011), p. 7, although the waters are murky here because it's hard to measure exact results and determine whether any improvement is lasting. That particular study followed twelve people; three were classified as 'treatment responders', but the report is forced to admit that their gains were not maintained six months later. A more recent review – Claire Thompson et al., 'A systematic review and quality assessment of psychological, pharmacological, and family-based interventions for hoarding disorder', *Asian Journal of Psychiatry*, 27 (June 2017) – found that most people after treatment 'remained in the clinical range', i.e. still had a high amount of clutter in their homes. Even 20 per cent of participants hoarding a bit less is a result, though, when the rate of return to hoarding after a forced clear-out can be as high as 97 per cent.

Even achieving these limited results is an immensely time-consuming business. One programme in Hackney reported a successful outcome for one client which involved working with her for 158 hours over 49 weeks, and even that only cleared some of the rooms (Making Room project, Hackney, PDF report).

91 **This wasn't eight weeks of by-the-book reframing:** Some of the case studies in *Stuff* (Frost and Steketee) do suggest that, during the treatment process, the hoarder is working through old trauma in an analytical way. See the description of Bernadette, p. 95. The Thompson study quoted above (Thompson, et al., 2017) also notes that other interventions, such as drugs and 'cognitive remediation', which

aims to improve cognition and executive functioning, have approximately the same improvement rates as CBT. Perhaps it is simply the attention and understanding which helps in the end.

91 Hoarders' homes are rated on a scale of one to nine: David F. Tolin, Randy O. Frost and Gail Steketee, 'A brief interview for assessing compulsive hoarding: The Hoarding Rating Scale-Interview', *Psychiatry Research*, 178:1 (2010). The original rating scale on the questionnaire was 1–8, but this has been eclipsed by the 1–9 used by the Clutter Image Rating Scale.

92 Rather than describing their mess: Frost and Steketee, *Stuff*, pp. 59–61.

92 Researcher after researcher reports how much more accurately: Randy O. Frost, Gail Steketee and David F. Tolin, 'Development and Validation of the Clutter Image Rating', *Journal of Psychopathology and Behavioural Assessment* (September 2008).

92 they tend to think visually rather than in words: This point is returned to several times by the pioneering researchers of hoarding, Randy Frost and Gail Steketee. See *Stuff*, pp. 66, 211. Frost in particular sees this as one of the defining characteristics of hoarders: 'People who hoard tend to live their lives visually and spatially instead of categorically like the rest of us do' (interview on NPR, 5 May 2010).

115 We have storage containers: The A&E network understood that this connection was a big part of the appeal of *Hoarders*. Their senior vice-president of programming said when the series was launched that 'There's just a core relatability that people feel for this subject . . . People look at this show and see themselves to a degree, or see people they know.' Quoted in Hsiao-Jane Anna Chen, 'Disorder: Rethinking Hoarding Inside and Outside Museums', Masters report (University of Texas, 2011), p. 36.

115 While we may not all be in danger of hoarding: A survey in America revealed that only 25 per cent of garages were usable for cars because they were so packed with household overflow – Jeanne A. Arnold, *Life at Home in the Twenty-First Century: 32 Families Open Their Doors* (Los Angeles, Cotsen Institute of Archaeology Press, 2012) – and Britain seems to be heading the same way. There is eight times the volume of commercial storage space available compared to fifteen years ago, while the UK accounts for almost half the European market in self-storage – renting four times more space than the French and ten times more than the Germans (report by Cushman and Wakefield for the UK Self Storage Association, 2017, https://www.ssauk.com/media/1888/ssaukannualsurvey2017.pdf).

131 the condition does run in families: Eighty-four per cent of hoarders report a history of hoarding in a close relative: Romina Lopez Gaston et al., 'Hoarding behaviour: building up the "R factor"', *Advances in Psychiatric Treatment*, 15:5 (2009).

132 The specialists argue: The conclusion is that it can be passed on, but the cause is probably half genetic and half environmental: Alessandra Iervolino et al., 'Prevalence and Heritability of Compulsive Hoarding: A Twin Study', *American Journal of Psychiatry*, 166:10 (2009); V. Z. Ivanov et al., 'Heritability of hoarding symptoms across adolescence and young adulthood: a longitudinal twin study', *PLoS ONE*, 12:6 (June 2017).

132 one root of hoarding may lie in either impulse-control disorders: T. L. Hartl et al., 'Relationships among compulsive hoarding, trauma and attention-deficit/hyperactivity disorder', *Behaviour Research Therapy*, 43:2 (2005); J. M. Park et al., 'ADHD and executive functioning deficits in OCD youths who hoard', *Journal of Psychiatric Research*, 82 (November 2016); L. E. Hacker et al., 'Hoarding in Children with ADHD', *Journal of Attention Disorder*, 20:7 (July 2016).

134 This might be part of ADHD: The diagnostic label for this is 'executive function disorder', which is one of the aspects of ADHD but can also exist separately.

161 The partner's dining room holds: Monasteries do the same, and in America coastguards and lighthouse keepers have messes, which also mean napkin rings.

175 in the form of a bird, the penguin: As a small child, I knew my grandmother as Grannie-with-the-bird, but this was nothing to do with penguins. Rather, it referred to a small grey parrot which she used to own. The parrot died before I could remember it, but the name stuck.

178 She does not dare to engage: Jessie Sholl, *Dirty Secret: A Daughter Comes Clean About Her Mother's Compulsive Hoarding* (New York, Gallery Books, 2010), pp. 69–70.

189 These axes were not made to chop down trees: J. A. Sheridan, 'Old friends, new friends, a long-lost friend and false friends: tales from project JADE', in Vin Davis and Mark Edmonds (eds.), *Stone Axe Studies III* (Oxford, Oxbow Books, 2015).

189–90 When they came to the end of their uses: Sheridan, 'Old friends, new friends', p.4.

190 One survivor, in the British Museum: This is on display in Room 51 of the museum: Sheridan, 'Old friends, new friends'.

190 meaning, not function, drove technological progress: Colin Renfrew, quoted in Mihaly Csikszentmihalyi, 'Why We Need Things', in Steven Lubar and W. David Kingery (eds.), *History from Things: Essays on Material Culture* (n.p., Smithsonian Institution, 1993), p. 24.

190 Sometimes it can be a survival technique: Colin Richards and Richard Jones, *The Development of Neolithic House Societies in Orkney* (Oxford, Windgather Press, 2016).

191 This idea bled into law: Walter Woodburn Hyde, 'The Prosecution and Punishment of Animals and Lifeless Things in the Middle Ages and Modern Times', *University of Pennsylvania Law Review*, 64:7 (1916), p. 726.

191 was meant to kick out magic, replacing it with science: The process was, inevitably, rather less clear-cut. Those who are trying to get rid of magic things often find it hard to escape from the belief even as they do so. During the Reformation, the iconoclasts who destroyed Catholic images frequently did so as though they were trying to 'kill' them – statues were beheaded and paintings of saints were left standing but with their eyes scratched out. Their destroyers could not treat these objects as though they were inert; the manner of their decommissioning reveals that they were still seen as having life or power. I can't help but see links between this and the way that the jade hand axes were disposed of.

191 Life had drained from the world of stuff: Frank Trentmann, *Empire of Things: How We Became a World of Consumers, from the Fifteenth Century to the Twenty-first* (London, Penguin, 2017), pp. 95–105; Peter Stallybrass, 'Marx's Coat', in Patricia Spyer (ed.) *Border Fetishisms: Material Objects in Unstable Spaces* (New York, Routledge, 1988). The idea that things are inert is so embedded in our culture that discussion of their potential for liveliness and action is rare, existing on the edges of a range of disciplines, including consumer behaviour research, anthropology, media studies and psychoanalysis. The idea tends to be glimpsed sidelong, mentioned only during the consideration of another topic.

192 For us, things are things: These ideas have been challenged by writers such as Bruno Latour – *We Have Never Been Modern* (Cambridge, MA, Harvard University Press, 1993) – and Jane Bennett – in her lecture 'Powers of the Hoard: Further Notes on Material Agency' – and the many other proponents of Thing Theory, but the generalization still holds for now.

192 The most extreme hoarders hold on to exactly these things: The first description of this is Sir James George Frazer, *The Golden Bough* (London, Macmillan, 1890), p. 45.

192 we are missing the words to describe what is happening: Jane Bennett ('Powers of the Hoard: Further Notes on Material Agency') points out this absence in the language, that it is not normal to think about objects as able to do things and yet we experience them in this way. Part of the problem is that the English language automatically assigns activity to subjects. As she puts it: 'writing about vital materiality [her words for the experience of active things] is made hard by grammar'.

192 These are fetish objects: 'Fetish object' is the anthropological term most often used to describe something that is believed to contain a power or a spirit. Even though this is the concept I am writing about, I have mostly steered clear of the phrase because the words, over the years, have accumulated a silt of additional and distracting meanings alongside. This comes most notably from Freudianism (standing for a sexual desire which has been displaced on to an object) and Marxism, where commodity fetishism is the social relations and monetary value which are contained within an object, but which possess no direct relation to its physical form or utility.

193 As we are no longer peasants or Neolithic hunters: Sasha Newell, 'The matter of the unfetish: Hoarding and the spirit of possessions', *Journal of Ethnographic Theory*, 4:3 (2014).

194 there already exists a designer sink plunger: And indeed it does exist. The editor of this book saw the possibility of a designer sink plunger as a challenge and discovered one with a blue cup and art deco-style acrylic handle for sale online. It costs hundreds of pounds and has hundreds of positive reviews.

194 become incorporated into our wider being: Russell Belk writes about the boundaries between ourselves and our possessions in 'Are We What We Own?', in April Lane Benson (ed.), *I Shop Therefore I Am* (Lanham, MD, Jason Aronson Inc., 2000) and 'Possessions and the Extended Self', *Journal of Consumer Research*, 15:2 (1988).

197 One report described a hoarder: Melanie McIntosh, 'This Full House', Dane County Hoarding Task Force Report 1999/2000, Dane County, Wisconsin. This quote is far from the only example in the document: '"Stuff" had spewed off the kitchen counters onto the floor. Stuff had oozed out of every room and even into the bathtub. The home was so full there was only a small path left to walk through the house. The stuff consisted mostly of furniture, clothing, old mail, empty pill bottles and containers ranging from Rubbermaid gallon containers (that were going to be used to put the stuff in someday, according to her) to small, previously used food containers.' The objects have taken control, leaving the hoarder herself powerless.

200 Lawrence's essence was so important: The robes and dagger were sold at Christie's in July 2015, and the decision to bar their export was widely reported in the months after this.

203 the dead have left a piece of their selves: The way in which modern society uses material objects to mourn the dead and redefine our relationships with them is discussed much more fully in Daniel Miller and Fiona Parrott, 'Loss and material culture in south London', *Journal of the Royal Anthropological Institute*, 15:3 (2009).

212 this brand meaning evaporates: There are of course exceptions to this, most notably Daniel Miller, whose professional work is devoted to exploring the meanings that consumers find in the things that surround them in their daily lives, from denim jeans to cans of fizzy drink. (See the Bibliography for a list of his publications.)

213 three years studying and then working in the Victoria and Albert Museum: My course was a two-year master's degree in History of Design and the Decorative Arts, a joint enterprise between the Royal College of Art and the museum itself. I then worked for a year organizing an exhibition about the ceramic designers Queensberry Hunt.

214 it's hard to see museums and hoards as being kin: Even so, the archivists writing online and I are far from the only people to have made the connection. See Chen, 'Disorder'; Leah Broaddus, 'From White Gloves to White Coats: A Call for Partnership Between Archivists and Hoarding Psychologists', *Archival Issues*, 32:1 (2010).

217 When I offered them some duplicates: Should you want to look at one of these, V&A object number C.136–1992 is one of my donations: an Empire Ware plate, the same pattern of wavy checks that my mother is looking at in the photograph on p. 120 and also, as the museum information reminds me, featured in my thesis.

218 an extremely capacious handbag: Anthony Burton, *Vision and Accident: The Story of the Victoria and Albert Museum* (London, V&A Publications, 1999).

220 The museum becomes a shrine: I owe this thought to Carol Duncan and Alan Wallach, 'The Universal Survey Museum', *Art History*, 3:4 (1980), which completely changed my thinking about how visitors interact with the contents of museums. The idea that they are temples of culture also explains why museums find deacquisitioning so difficult. As anthropologists know, once an object has been offered to the gods, it has to remain in the temple.

228 a fish kettle: My best friend bought me a fish kettle for my fortieth birthday. Five months later, I got married.

234 more hoarders in the population than there were Alzheimer's sufferers: Ashley Nordsletten et al., 'Epidemiology of hoarding disorder', *British Journal of Psychiatry*, 203:6 (2013). This estimates hoarding at 1.5 per cent of the total population, while other studies have produced rates of between 1.5 and 5 per cent. But even at the lowest rate, this exceeds the prevalence of Alzheimer's at 1.3 per cent (Alzheimer's Society).

235 most often known as Diogenes Syndrome: The main book on the subject is called *Severe Domestic Squalor* – by John Snowdon, Graeme Halliday and Sube Banerjee (Cambridge, Cambridge University Press, 2012) – which is yet another term for a syndrome which has quite clearly not yet been fully described, never mind understood.

235 Diogenes Syndrome is the wrong name for it: Gabriele Cipriani et al., 'Diogenes syndrome in patients suffering from dementia', *Dialogues in Clinical Neuroscience*, 14:4 (2012); E. Cybulska, 'Senile Squalor: Plyushkin's not Diogenes' Syndrome', *Psychiatric Bulletin*, 22:5 (1998).

236 'The room in such cases is the epitome of neglect': Snowdon, Halliday and Banerjee, *Severe Domestic Squalor* (Cambridge, Cambridge University Press), p. 16.

237 One study reported that a third died: Of twenty-one cases who were admitted to ordinary hospital, seven died within a matter of days. Duncan Macmillan and Patricia Shaw, 'Senile Breakdown in Standards of Personal and Environmental Cleanliness', *British Medical Journal* (October 1966).

237–8 'domineering, quarrelsome and independent individual': *Ibid.*

238 'something that creeps up on slightly odd people': This comes from an anonymous blog, The Masked AMHP (themaskedamhp.blogspot.co.uk), written by a health professional whose job entails mental health assessments in people's homes to determine whether intervention is required, a caseload which includes a number of cases of Diogenes.

238 People like my mother have the right: The Masked AMHP blog concludes, after much consideration, that generally these people are otherwise perfectly sane and so entitled to choose to live as they wish: 'They just have a behaviour which most people find baffling or personally unacceptable. And that is not sufficient to detain someone in hospital against their will.'

240 these obstinate, proud, but damaged people would rather die: One expert even considers that 'a reluctance or at least an unwillingness to accept treatment and services is so common to almost be seen as a defining feature of the syndrome'. This too made me feel a lot better. Christopher Ryan, in Snowdon, Halliday and Banerjee, *Severe Domestic Squalor*, p. 151.

253 in Russia they speak of 'Plyushkin Symptom': Randy Frost and Gail Steketee (eds.), *The Oxford Handbook of Hoarding and Acquiring* (New York, Oxford University Press, 2014), p. 10.

254 Krook himself admits: Charles Dickens, *Bleak House* (London, Macmillan, 1895), p. 48.

254 Miss Flite, with her stacked cages of birds: This discussion of Dickens' portrayal of misers and hoarders is very much indebted to an excellent thesis, Nicole Lobdell, 'The Hoarding Sense: Hoarding in Austen, Tennyson, Dickens and Nineteenth-Century Culture' (University of Georgia, 2014).

254 'such wonderful things came tumbling out of the closets': *Bleak House*, p. 390.

255 'He had a horror of destroying documents': Sir Arthur Conan Doyle, *The Adventure of the Dancing Man and other Sherlock Holmes Stories* (New York, Dover, 1997), p. 1.

256 'The place could not have been cleaned': *Hampshire Telegraph* 11 and 14 December 1867. In May of the same year, the newspaper also reports on a man in Rottingdean whose house contained over two hundred cats, as well as a fox, a goat and various other fowl. The house was filthy and the floor covered in excrement. Victorian prurience was little different to our own, so a search of the newspapers would surely uncover many more hoarding stories.

257 'The house looks more miserable and dilapidated': There is a much longer and very entertaining description of Sir Thomas and his ways in Werner Muensterberger, *Collecting: An Unruly Passion* (Princeton, Princeton University Press, 2014).

257 Phillips was notoriously querulous: As with my mother, Muensterberger traces this anger back to a primal fury at his family – in his case an illegitimate birth and a domineering father.

259 the extraordinary sum of £3,500 in today's money: The detailed calculations are made by the historian Eve Fisher in a much-quoted essay on the Sleuthsayers website (www. sleuthsayers.org/search?q=£3%2C500). There's some argument about the amounts of money she has assigned to the time needed to make the shirt, which she calculates at the minimum wage. Some critics argued that women's work is traditionally paid at less than that, but that inequality doesn't counter the fact that this is skilled labour, and so could well have been of more value.

261 a well-decorated room became the means of uplifting its occupants: This argument is put forward in much more detail in Deborah Cohen, *Household Gods: The British and Their Possessions* (New Haven, CT, Yale University Press, 2009).

261 One upper-class music room of the 1870s: This comes from an inventory of the music room in Tyntesfield House, Somerset, in James Miller, *Fertile Fortune: The Story of Tyntesfield* (National Trust Books, 2006). Tyntesfield is an interesting example of how we find it hard to face up to Victorian clutter. Although the house is acclaimed as a monument to high Victoriana, the restoration has stripped it back considerably; an 1888 photograph of the drawing room shows a wealth of fringing, marquetry, painting, padding and general fussiness which is no longer present in any of the restored rooms.

261 the effect must have been suffocating: What's particularly intriguing is that no one, as far as I can tell, has tried to ascertain when this excess of stuff arose, never mind why. So much design writing is still underpinned by the ideas of the Modern Movement that when clutter is discussed at all it is taken as a given, in need of reform. Almost the only person who noticed its arrival is Virginia Woolf in *Orlando*, who describes the change from a chill neoclassicism to a Victorian world dense with glass cases, artificial flowers, small dogs and china ornaments.

262 The German architect Bruno Taut: Trentmann, *Empire of Things*, p. 222.

263 The best kind of homeowner: Paul Overy, *Light, Air and Openness: Modern Architecture Between the Wars* (London, Thames & Hudson, 2008).

284 In filling her own house with bric-a-brac: The *Oxford English Dictionary* definition of bric-a-brac – 'Old curiosities of artistic character, knick-knacks, antiquarian odds-and-ends, such as old furniture, plate, china, fans, statuettes, and the like' – is a perfect description of the kind of clutter which accumulated in both Eaglesham and my mother's house.

285 Allan's own parents, Angus and Ethel, had divorced in 1920: The whole divorce trial was reported in the *Glasgow Herald*, 19 June 1920. In October of the same year, Ethel placed a notice in the same paper announcing: 'Mrs A. C. Gilmour, lately of Eaglesham, wishes in future to be known as Mrs E. F. Gilmour, and all correspondence addressed to her at 43 Oakley Street, SW3, will for the present be forwarded.' By this point, her husband had already remarried. Their two sons were nine and eight.

286 Her mother is nowhere to be found: I did eventually track down Annie in the 1891 records, lodging with a rector's family at Torksey in Lincolnshire, who don't seem to be any kind of relation. The 1901 census reveals what she was doing there. Annie has departed, but two other lodgers are still in residence and both are labelled 'imbecile'. The rector and his wife are running a private lunatic asylum and, as was common in those days, Annie has been sent there to dry out. A woman's role was so very much to be the angel in the house that any deviation from this, like drinking, could only be seen as madness.

286 the cause of this was a dead child: The dead children weren't confined to just the Gilmour side of the family either. Carrie Jenkins' only sibling, her brother Philip, died at fourteen. Losing her husband and son at relatively young ages must have jarred that original pain as well as being sorrows in their own right.

299 the miscellaneous clutter on his desk: *Observer* interview with the Marquess of Bath, 10 March 2002.

299 Lord Bath had a difficult childhood: Nesta Wyn Ellis, *The Marquess of Bath: Lord of Love* (London, Dynasty Press, 2010); Daphne Fielding, *Mercury Presides* (London, Eyre & Spottiswoode, 1954).

300 Warhol was a hoarder: Claudia Kalb, *Andy Warhol was a Hoarder: Inside the Minds of History's Great Personalities* (Washington, DC, National Geographic, 2016); Chen, 'Disorder'.

300 but never discarded anything: Suzie Frankfurt, a friend of Warhol's since the 1950s, remarked, 'as for trading or selling – never, never, never. He believed in holding on to everything, squirreling it all away.' Quoted in Jonathan Flatley, 'Like: Collecting and Collectivity', *October*, 132 (spring 2010), p. 80.

301 For more than ten years he took it everywhere with him: *Ibid*.

301 as a form of performance art: Shown at the ICA, 21 September 2013.

302 an ancient mummified foot: Christopher Schmidt, 'Warhol's Problem Project: The Time Capsules', *Postmodern Culture*, 26:1 (2015).

302 All artists perform magic: Warhol was very good at turning art into money, although he never did this with the Time Capsules. Nonetheless, the Time Capsules did manage to create money after his death when an anonymous art fan paid $30,000 to open the very last one.

302 he and his stuff were one: Warhol's art and hoarding crossed over at other moments as well. Invited to curate an exhibition at the Museum of Art at the Rhode Island School of Design in 1970 ('Raid the Icebox I'), he confounded the staff by putting whole categories of things on display, including the museum's entire shoe collection and fifty-seven umbrellas and parasols. He, too, didn't like choosing. In this he wasn't only blurring the boundaries between art and hoarding, he was also questioning the nature of what belongs in a museum. Daniel Robbins, the museum's director, wrote, 'There were exasperating moments when we felt that Andy Warhol was exhibiting "storage" rather than works of art.' The museum had intended that Warhol would be the first among many artists to create an exhibition from their archives; they never tried it again. From Chen, 'Disorder'.

302 Warhol is representative of many artists: There's a strong and underexplored relationship between artists and hoarding. Turner's studio was a tip, and he would not let other people in; Francis Bacon lived and worked in what, had he not been a genius, might have been called a hoard. The cliché of the artist's workplace is a chaotic and grubby mess; the Modern Movement very explicitly wanted to clean up the studio as well as the private house.

302 Pop art, he said: Flatley, 'Like'.

304 He was the artist who had tied these plastic bags: Work 2708. The exhibition was 'What You Find', at Hauser & Wirth in Somerset, May–September 2016.

304 he never threw anything away: 'Martin Creed: I keep hair. And I'm afraid of cheese', *Guardian*, 18 May 2016.

305 a photograph of Creed sitting in his crowded Barbican apartment: Martin Creed. Work 2683.

305 a desiccated bouquet sat on a plinth: Martin Creed. Work 2698.

305 Paper carrier bags sat on taped-up boxes: Martin Creed. Work 2710.

306 here in the gallery it had become art: Some of Creed's earlier work hints at hoarding in more sidelong ways. Work No. 200, *Half the air in a given space*, from 1998, consists of a room in which half the space has been taken up by white balloons, making it hard to enter or get around, and Creed has recreated this work in various galleries over several years.

306 'Art is just things in the world . . .': 'Martin Creed: People know what's fake and what's not', *Observer*, 18 July 2010.

308 treat it as though it were a work of art: It's not only Martin Creed and me who see the potential for a hoard to become art. Frost and Steketee describe a student hoarder who not only began to think of the mound of possessions in the middle of her room as an artwork but also persuaded her roommate that this was the case: *Stuff*, pp. 223–4.

324 'Houses: black and grimy . . .': Charles Booth, notebook BOOTH/B/360, p.248.

324 'Rooms so small, so filthy . . .': Dickens is not only describing what he has found in the Devil's Acre but also in another more watery slum near what is now Shad Thames; the dust and degradation are common to both.

339 Mrs Cullen had gone up to check that next morning: There are signs of a person, and a community as well. Annie Woods was apparently well known as 'The Duchess' or 'Tall Annie', a woman who stood out in the area. I can't help thinking of another tall upper-class Anne, my mother's sister, just as visible as a white woman in her adopted West Indies home.

Bibliography

hoarding

American Psychiatric Association, *Diagnostic and Statistical Manual of Mental Disorders*, 5th edn. (Arlington, VA, American Psychiatric Publishing, 2013)

An, S. K. et al., 'To discard or not to discard: the neural basis of hoarding symptoms in obsessive-compulsive disorder', *Molecular Psychiatry*, 14:3 (2009)

Ayers, Catherine et al., 'Cognitive-behavioral therapy for geriatric compulsive hoarding', *Behaviour Research Therapy*, 49:10 (2011)

Canale, Anthony, 'Hoarding Disorder: It's More Than Just an Obsession', *Journal of Financial Therapy*, 4:2 (2013)

Frank, Christopher, 'Approach to hoarding in family medicine: Beyond reality television', *Canadian Family Physician*, 58:10 (2012)

Frost, Randy O. and Gail Steketee, *Stuff: Compulsive Hoarding and the Meaning of Things* (Boston, Houghton Mifflin, 2011)

Frost, Randy O. and Gail Steketee (eds), *The Oxford Handbook of Hoarding and Acquiring* (New York, Oxford University Press, 2014)

Frost, Randy O., Gail Steketee and David F. Tolin, 'Development and Validation of the Clutter Image Rating', *Journal of Psychopathology and Behavioural Assessment* (September 2008)

Frost, Randy O., Gail Steketee and David F. Tolin, 'Comorbidity in Hoarding Disorder, *Depression and Anxiety*, 28:10 (2011)

Bibliography

Frost, Randy O. et al., 'Diagnosis and Assessment of Hoarding Disorder', *Annual Review of Clinical Psychology*, 8 (2012)

Gaston, Romina Lopez et al., 'Hoarding behaviour: building up the "R factor"', *Advances in Psychiatric Treatment*, 15:5 (2009)

Greenberg, Gary, *The Book of Woe: The DSM and the Unmaking of Psychiatry* (New York, Plume Books, 2014)

Grisham, Jessica et al., 'Formation of attachment to possessions in compulsive hoarding', *Journal of Anxiety Disorders*, 23:3 (2009)

Grisham, Jessica et al., 'Compulsive hoarding: current controversies and new directions', *Dialogues in Clinical Neuroscience*, 12:2 (2010)

Hacker, L. E. et al., 'Hoarding in Children with ADHD', *Journal of Attention Disorder*, 20:7 (July 2016)

Hartl, T. L. et al., 'Relationships among compulsive hoarding, trauma and attention-deficit/hyperactivity disorder', *Behaviour Research Therapy*, 43:2 (2005)

Herring, Scott, *The Hoarders: Material Deviance in Modern American Culture* (Chicago, University of Chicago Press, 2014)

Holmes, Sophie (ed.), 'A Psychological Perspective on Hoarding: DCP Good Practice Guidelines' (British Psychological Society, 2015)

Holroyd, Sarah and Howard Price, 'Hoarding and How to Approach it: Guidance for Environmental Health Officers' (Chartered Institute of Environmental Health, 2012)

Iervolino, Alessandra et al., 'Prevalence and Heritability of Compulsive Hoarding: A Twin Study', *American Journal of Psychiatry*, 166:10 (2009)

Ivanov, V. Z. et al., 'Heritability of hoarding symptoms across adolescence and young adulthood: a longitudinal twin study', *PLoS ONE*, 12:6 (June 2017)

Kondo, Marie, *The Life-Changing Magic of Tidying: A Simple, Effective Way to Banish Clutter Forever* (London, Vermilion, 2014)

McIntosh, Melanie, 'This Full House: Dane County Hoarding Task Force Report', 1999/2000

McPhillips, Marcus, 'Hoarding: Key considerations and examples of best practice', National Housing Federation:

Bibliography

http://s3-eu-west-1.amazonaws.com/pub.housing.org.uk/
Hoarding_briefing_-_August_2015.pdf

Mataix-Cols, David, 'Hoarding disorder: A new diagnosis for DSM-V?', *Depression and Anxiety*, 27:6 (2010)

Nordsletten, Ashley E., 'Finders keepers: the features differentiating hoarding disorder from normative collecting', *Comprehensive Psychiatry*, 53:4 (2012)

Nordsletten, Ashley et al., 'Epidemiology of hoarding disorder', *British Journal of Psychiatry*, 203:6 (2013)

Park, J. M. et al., 'ADHD and executive functioning deficits in OCD youths who hoard', *Journal of Psychiatric Research*, 82 (November 2016)

Paxton, Matt, *The Secret Lives of Hoarders: True Stories of Tackling Extreme Clutter* (New York, Perigee, 2011)

Sholl, Jessie, *Dirty Secret: A Daughter Comes Clean About Her Mother's Compulsive Hoarding* (New York, Gallery Books, 2010)

Sorensen, Ryan J., 'Hoarding Disorder (Compulsive Hoarding): A Comprehensive Literature Review and Professional Training to Prepare Clinicians to Treat Problematic Hoarding', Doctoral thesis (University of St Thomas, Minnesota, 2011)

Thompson, Claire et al., 'A systematic review and quality assessment of psychological, pharmacological, and family-based interventions for hoarding disorder', *Asian Journal of Psychiatry*, 27 (June 2017)

Tolin, David F. et al., 'Neural Mechanisms of Decision Making in Hoarding Disorder', *Archives of General Psychiatry*, 69:8 (2012)

Tolin, David F., Randy O. Frost and Gail Steketee, 'A brief interview for assessing compulsive hoarding: The Hoarding Rating Scale-Interview', *Psychiatry Research*, 178: 1 (2010)

Tolin, David F., Randy O. Frost and Gail Steketee, *Buried in Treasures: Help for Compulsive Acquiring, Saving and Hoarding* (New York, Oxford University Press, 2013)

Wallman, James, *Stuffocation: Living More with Less* (London, Penguin, 2014)

Winters, Renee M., *The Hoarding Impulse: Suffocation of the Soul* (New York, Routledge, 2015)

Yourgrau, Barry, *Mess: One Man's Struggle to Clean Up His House and His Act* (New York, W. W. Norton, 2016)

Zasio, Robin, *The Hoarder in You: How to Live a Happier, Healthier, Uncluttered Life* (Emmaus, PA, Rodale, 2012)

the life of things

Appadurai, Arjun (ed.), *The Social Life of Things: Commodities in Cultural Perspective* (New York, Cambridge University Press, 1988)

Arnold, Jeanne A., *Life at Home in the Twenty-First Century: 32 Families Open Their Doors* (Los Angeles, Cotsen Institute of Archaeology Press, 2012)

Belk, Russell, 'Possessions and the Extended Self', *Journal of Consumer Research*, 15:2 (1988)

Belk, Russell, 'Are We What We Own?', in April Lane Benson (ed.), *I Shop Therefore I Am* (Lanham, MD, Jason Aronson Inc., 2000)

Belk, Russell and Melanie Wallendorf, 'The sacred meanings of money', *Journal of Economic Psychology*, 11:1 (1990)

Bynum, Caroline Walker, *Christian Materiality: An Essay on Religion in Late Medieval Europe* (New York, Zone Books, 2015)

Connor, Steven, *Paraphernalia: The Curious Lives of Magical Things* (London, Profile, 2013)

Csikszentmihalyi, Mihaly, 'Why We Need Things', in Steven Lubar and W. David Kingery (eds), *History from Things: Essays on Material Culture* (n.p., Smithsonian Institution, 1993)

Csikszentmihalyi, Mihaly and Eugene Rochberg-Halton, *The Meaning of Things: Domestic Symbols and the Self* (Cambridge, Cambridge University Press, 1988)

Dant, Tim, 'Fetishism and the social value of objects', *Sociological Review*, 44:3 (1996)

Douglas, Mary, *Purity and Danger: An Analysis of Concepts of Pollution and Taboo* (New York, Routledge, 1988)

Douglas, Mary and Baron Isherwood, *The World of Goods: Towards an Anthropology of Consumption* (New York, Routledge, 1979)

Bibliography

Frazer, James George, *The Golden Bough* (London, Macmillan, 1995)

Hodder, Ian, *Entangled: An Archaeology of the Relationships between Humans and Things* (Malden, MA, Wiley-Blackwell, 2012)

Hodder, Ian, 'The Entanglements of Humans and Things: A Long-Term View', *New Literary History*, 45:1 (2014)

McCracken, Grant, 'Culture and Consumption: A Theoretical Account of the Structure and Movement of the Cultural Meaning of Consumer Goods', *Journal of Consumer Research*, 13:1 (1986)

Maycroft, Neil, 'Not moving things along: hoarding, clutter and other ambiguous matter', *Journal of Consumer Behaviour*, 8 (2009)

Miller, Daniel, *Material Culture and Mass Consumption* (Oxford, Blackwell, 1987)

Miller, Daniel, *The Comfort of Things* (Cambridge, Polity Press, 2009)

Miller, Daniel, *Stuff* (Cambridge, Polity Press, 2009)

Miller, Daniel, *Consumption and Its Consequences* (Cambridge, Polity Press, 2012)

Miller, Daniel and Fiona Parrott, 'Loss and material culture in South London', *Journal of the Royal Anthropological Institute*, 15:3 (2009)

Muensterberger, Werner, *Collecting: An Unruly Passion* (Princeton, Princeton University Press, 1994)

Newell, Sasha, 'The matter of the unfetish: Hoarding and the spirit of possessions', *Journal of Ethnographic Theory*, 4:3 (2014)

Richards, Colin and Richard Jones, *The Development of Neolithic House Societies in Orkney* (Oxford, Windgather Press, 2016)

Sheridan, J. A., 'Old friends, new friends, a long-lost friend and false friends: tales from project JADE', in Vin Davis and Mark Edmonds (eds), *Stone Axe Studies III* (Oxford, Oxbow Books, 2015)

Stallybrass, Peter, 'Marx's Coat', in Patricia Spyer (ed.), *Border Fetishisms: Material Objects in Unstable Spaces* (New York, Routledge, 1998)

Bibliography

Trentmann, Frank, *Empire of Things: How We Became a World of Consumers, from the Fifteenth Century to the Twenty-first* (London, Penguin, 2017)

Walker, Katharine, 'Axe-heads and identity: an investigation into the roles of imported axe-heads in identity formation in Neolithic Britain', Doctoral thesis (University of Southampton, 2015)

Woodburn Hyde, Walter, 'The Prosecution and Punishment of Animals and Lifeless Things in the Middle Ages and Modern Times', *University of Pennsylvania Law Review*, 64:7 (1916)

museums

Baker, Malcolm and Brenda Richardson, *A Grand Design: The Art of the Victoria and Albert Museum* (London, V&A, 1999)

Barringer, Tim, 'The South Kensington Museum and the colonial project', in Tim Barringer and Tom Flynn (eds), *Colonialism and the Object: Empire, Material Culture and the Museum* (New York, Routledge, 1998)

Broaddus, Leah, 'From White Gloves to White Coats: A Call for Partnership Between Archivists and Hoarding Psychologists', *Archival Issues*, 32:1 (2010)

Burton, Anthony, *Vision and Accident: The Story of the Victoria and Albert Museum* (London, V&A, 1999)

Chen, Hsiao-Jane Anna, 'Disorder: Rethinking Hoarding Inside and Outside Museums', Masters report (University of Texas, 2011)

Cocks, Anna Somers, *The Victoria and Albert Museum: The Making of the Collection* (Leicester, Windward, 1980)

Duncan, Carol and Alan Wallach, 'The Universal Survey Museum', *Art History*, 3:4 (1980)

Pearce, Susan M., *Museums, Objects and Collections: A Cultural Study* (Leicester, Leicester University Press, 1992)

Pearce, Susan M. (ed.), *Interpreting Objects and Collections* (Oxon, Routledge, 1994)

Pearce, Susan M., *Collecting in Contemporary Practice* (London, Sage, 1998)

diogenes and squalor

Amanullah, Shabbir, Sabu K. Oomman and Soumitra Shankar Datta, 'Diogenes Syndrome Revisited', *German Journal of Psychiatry* (2008)

Brae, Suzy, David Orr and Michael Preston-Shoot, 'Self-neglect and adult safeguarding: findings from research' (London, Social Care Institute for Excellence, September 2011)

Brown, Debbie and Rekha Hegde, 'Diogenes Syndrome: patients living with hoarding and squalor', *Progress in Neurology and Psychiatry*, 19:5 (2015)

Cipriani, Gabriele et al., 'Diogenes syndrome in patients suffering from dementia', *Dialogues in Clinical Neuroscience*, 14:4 (2012)

Cybulska, E., 'Senile Squalor: Plyushkin's not Diogenes' Syndrome', *Psychiatric Bulletin*, 28 (1998)

Lauder, W. et al., 'Self-neglect: the role of judgements and applied ethics', *Nursing Standard*, 19:18 (2005)

McDermott, Shannon, 'The Devil is in the Details: Self-Neglect in Australia', *Journal of Elder Abuse and Neglect*, 20:3 (2008)

Macmillan, Duncan and Patricia Shaw, 'Senile Breakdown in Standards of Personal and Environmental Cleanliness', *British Medical Journal* (October 1966)

Snowdon, John, Graeme Halliday and Sube Banerjee, *Severe Domestic Squalor* (Cambridge, Cambridge University Press, 2012)

art objects

Flatley, Jonathan, 'Like: Collecting and Collectivity', *October*, 132 (Spring 2010)

Gell, Alfred, *Art and Agency: An Anthropological Theory* (Oxford, Clarendon Press, 1988)

Kalb, Claudia, *Andy Warhol was a Hoarder: Inside the Minds of History's Great Personalities* (Washington, DC, National Geographic, 2016)

Layton, R. H., 'Art and Agency: A Reassessment', *Journal of the Royal Anthropological Institute*, 9:3 (2003)

Scherman, Tony, *Andy Warhol: The Art of Genius*, (London, JR Books, 2010)

Schmidt, Christopher, 'Warhol's Problem Project: The Time Capsules', *Postmodern Culture*, 26:1 (2015)

the history of too much

Auerbach, Jeffrey A., *The Great Exhibition of 1851: A Nation on Display* (New Haven, CT, Yale University Press, 1999)

Ayers, James, *The Shell Book of the Home in Britain: Decoration, Design and Construction of Vernacular Interiors 1500–1850* (London, Faber & Faber, 1981)

Calloway, Stephen, *Twentieth Century Decoration: The Domestic Interior from 1900 to the Present Day* (London, Weidenfeld & Nicholson, 1988)

Cohen, Deborah, *Household Gods: The British and their Possessions* (New Haven, CT, Yale University Press, 2009)

Conan Doyle, Sir Arthur, *The Adventure of the Dancing Man and other Sherlock Holmes Stories* (New York, Dover, 1997)

Dickens, Charles, *Bleak House* (London, Macmillan, 1895)

Dickens, Charles, *Great Expectations* (Ware, Wordsworth Editions, 1992)

Fisher, Eve, 'The $3,500 Shirt': www.sleuthsayers.org/search?q=£3%2C500

Gloag, John, *Victorian Comfort: A Social History of Design from 1830–1900* (London, Adam and Charles Black, 1961)

Leapman, Michael, *The World for a Shilling: How the Great Exhibition of 1851 Shaped a Nation* (London, Headline, 2001)

Lobdell, Nicole, 'The Hoarding Sense: Hoarding in Austen, Tennyson, Dickens and Nineteenth-Century Culture', Doctoral thesis (University of Georgia, 2014)

Merryweather, F. Somner, *Lives and Anecdotes of Misers* (London, Simpkin, Marshall and Co., 1850)

Miller, James, *Fertile Fortune: The Story of Tyntesfield* (n.p., National Trust Books, 2006)

Overy, Paul, *Light, Air and Openness: Modern Architecture Between the Wars* (London, Thames & Hudson, 2008)

Sitwell, Edith, *English Eccentrics: A Gallery of Weird and Wonderful Men and Women* (London, Penguin, 1971)

thing theory

Bennett, Jane, 'Powers of the Hoard: Further Notes on Material Agency'. Lecture, available online at https://archive.org/details/PowersOfTheHoardNotesOnMaterialAgency

Brown, Bill, 'Thing Theory', *Critical Inquiry*, 28:1 (2001)

Candlin, Fiona and Raiford Guins (eds), *The Object Reader* (London and New York, Routledge, 2009)

Latour, Bruno, *We Have Never Been Modern* (Cambridge, MA, Harvard University Press, 1993)

other things

Bowlby, John, *Loss: Sadness and Depression* (London, Penguin, 1981)

Ellis, Nesta Wyn, *The Marquess of Bath: Lord of Love* (London, Dynasty Press, 2010)

Fielding, Daphne, *Mercury Presides* (London, Eyre & Spottiswoode, 1954)

Acknowledgements

This book owes its existence to my wonderfully enthusiastic and positive agent, Judith Murray, who believed in it right from the start, while its clarity and coherence have been teased out by the steely but always cheerful editorial eye of Andrea Henry. Between them they have found narrative and logic in my frankly hoard-like heaps of memories and information. Everyone at Transworld has been behind the book from the beginning, but particular thanks are due to Katrina Whone for her editorial input, Phil Lord for design work and Hannah Bright for publicity, as well as Richard Shailer for the wonderful cover. Viv Mullett produced the evocative illustrations, while Ailsa Bathgate was an incisive copy-editor.

That these people had anything to work with in the first place is mostly down to Lindsay Clarke, who has spent too many years improving my lazy diction, incomprehensible sentences and linguistic tics, but who has also encouraged me when he felt I had material worth persevering with. I'm also very grateful to Alice Jolly and John Paul Flintoff for their belief in the book at a crucial point, as well as all the other members of my writing groups over the years.

I am very lucky to have one of the country's leading experts on hoarding just up the road, and Professor Paul Salkovskis at the University of Bath was very generous with his time and expertise. Any remaining errors are entirely my own.

This book could not have been completed without my local library service in Frome, which allows me to order an incredible range of material online, and I owe particular thanks to the librarians for persevering with obscure but essential inter-library loans. East Renfrewshire Local Studies Library also dug out much new information about Eaglesham House for me.

Many more people have put up with a great deal in the course of my writing this book, but I particularly want to thank Isobel Eaton and Sofie Kinsey for listening above and beyond the call of duty when I first thought of the idea and for pestering me to turn it into a proposal. Thank you also to Andrew Ziminski for both moral support and the author photograph.

Liz Farrelly gave me pointers towards new writings on material culture, while Michael Horsham reminded me of writers I had forgotten, but I owe particular gratitude to Paul Greenhalgh, Charles Saumurez Smith, Christopher Frayling, John Styles and the many other people who tried to teach me design history. I hope they aren't too appalled by what I have done with their time and thoughtfulness.

I'm very aware that what I have written is only one version of my mother's story and I am very fortunate that my family – most of all my brother and aunt – have supported my writing this book when they would, perhaps, have told very different tales of their own.

Most of all, though, I owe this book to T and E, who have had to live through its writing and also the events that

Acknowledgements

precipitated it, not only without complaining but always insisting that what I was doing was necessary. I could not have done it without them.

About the author

Susannah Walker writes and lectures about design. She studied English Literature at Cambridge, followed by Design History at the Royal College of Art and the Victoria and Albert Museum. After starting out as a writer and curator, she then became a television director and producer, working on art, architecture and lifestyle programmes.

She has now returned to writing and has published three books about design as well as running a website about post-war graphic design and posters.